OXFORD WORLD'S

SIX FRENCH POE
NINETEENTH CENTURY

ALPHONSE DE LAMARTINE (1790–1869) prepared his first volume, *Poetic Meditations* (*Méditations poétiques*, 1820), in the aftermath of an unhappy love affair; its tone of intense personal feeling permanently changed the course of French poetry. His later volumes included the outstanding *Poetic and Religious Harmonies* (*Harmonies poétiques et religieuses*, 1830). Lamartine also had a distinguished political career, including a spell as leader of the French government after the 1848 Revolution. VICTOR HUGO (1802–85) was the most flamboyant and prolific poet of his age; among his numerous volumes of poetry were *The Empire in the Pillory* (*Les Châtiments*, 1853), *Contemplations* (*Les Contemplations*, 1856), *The Legend of the Ages* (*La Légende des siècles*, 1859–83), and *God* (*Dieu*, posthumously, 1891). Novels such as *Notre-Dame de Paris* (1831) and *Les Misérables* (1862) were almost a sideline in his massive output. In the course of a debt-ridden existence, CHARLES BAUDELAIRE (1821–67) wrote the poems that eventually appeared in *The Flowers of Evil* (*Les Fleurs du mal*, 1857; revised and enlarged, after an obscenity conviction, in 1861). Among his other writings were prose poems, art criticism, and translations of works by Edgar Allan Poe. PAUL VERLAINE (1844–96) delighted readers with such volumes as *Fêtes galantes* (1869), *Songs Without Words* (*Romances sans paroles*, 1874), and *Wisdom* (*Sagesse*, 1880), despite a turbulent and scandalous private life and a long struggle with alcoholism. Nearly all the poems of ARTHUR RIMBAUD (1854–91) were written in his teens; afterwards he turned his back on literature and settled in what was then Abyssinia, working as a trader and gun-runner. At the same time, STÉPHANE MALLARMÉ (1842–98) was leading a quiet life as an English-teacher in various parts of France and writing carefully crafted, radically innovative poems that received little circulation at the time, though they were much admired by his friends, including Verlaine.

The English versions in this volume have been prepared by four translators. A. M. BLACKMORE, Lecturer in Education, Edith Cowan University, Perth, Western Australia, and E. H. BLACKMORE, formerly Lecturer in Psychiatry, University of Western Australia, have published literary criticism, translation studies, and work on grammatical awareness; their translations include ren-derings of poems and plays by various nineteenth-century French authors, including Victor Hugo and George Sand. JAMES MCGOWAN is Professor of English, Illinois Wesleyan University, Bloomington, Illinois. He is the trans-lator of the Oxford World's Classics bilingual edition of Charles Baudelaire, *The Flowers of Evil* (1993). MARTIN SORRELL is Reader in French and Trans-lation Studies at the University of Exeter. He is the translator of the Oxford World's Classics bilingual edition of Paul Verlaine, *Selected Poems* (1999).

OXFORD WORLD'S CLASSICS

*For almost 100 years Oxford World's Classics have brought
readers closer to the world's great literature. Now with over 700
titles—from the 4,000-year-old myths of Mesopotamia to the
twentieth century's greatest novels—the series makes available
lesser-known as well as celebrated writing.*

*The pocket-sized hardbacks of the early years contained
introductions by Virginia Woolf, T. S. Eliot, Graham Greene,
and other literary figures which enriched the experience of reading.
Today the series is recognized for its fine scholarship and
reliability in texts that span world literature, drama and poetry,
religion, philosophy and politics. Each edition includes perceptive
commentary and essential background information to meet the
changing needs of readers.*

OXFORD WORLD'S CLASSICS

Six French Poets of the Nineteenth Century

Lamartine · Hugo · Baudelaire
Verlaine · Rimbaud · Mallarmé

Edited with an Introduction and Notes by
E. H. AND A. M. BLACKMORE

OXFORD
UNIVERSITY PRESS

OXFORD
UNIVERSITY PRESS

Great Clarendon Street, Oxford OX2 6DP

Oxford University Press is a department of the University of Oxford.
It furthers the University's objective of excellence in research, scholarship,
and education by publishing worldwide in

Oxford New York

Athens Auckland Bangkok Bogotá Buenos Aires Calcutta
Cape Town Chennai Dar es Salaam Delhi Florence Hong Kong Istanbul
Karachi Kuala Lumpur Madrid Melbourne Mexico City Mumbai
Nairobi Paris São Paulo Singapore Taipei Tokyo Toronto Warsaw

with associated companies in Berlin Ibadan

Oxford is a registered trade mark of Oxford University Press
in the UK and in certain other countries

Published in the United States
by Oxford University Press Inc., New York

British Library Cataloguing in Publication Data

Data available

Library of Congress Cataloging in Publication Data

Data available

ISBN 0-19-283973-x

1 3 5 7 9 10 8 6 4 2

Typeset in Ehrhardt
by RefineCatch Limited, Bungay, Suffolk
Printed in Great Britain by
Cox and Wyman Ltd., Reading

CONTENTS

Introduction   xi

Note on the Text and Translation   xxxvii

Select Bibliography   xli

Chronology   xliv

ALPHONSE DE LAMARTINE
TRANSLATED BY E. H. AND A. M. BLACKMORE

From *Poetic Meditations* (*Méditations poétiques*)

Isolation   3
The Valley   7
The Lake   11
Autumn   15

From *Poetic and Religious Harmonics* (*Harmonies poétiques et religieuses*)

The West   17
The Infinite in the Skies   21

From *Further Poetic Meditations* (*Méditations poétiques inédites*)

The Lizard   33

VICTOR HUGO
TRANSLATED BY E. H. AND A. M. BLACKMORE

From *Orientalia* (*Les Orientales*)

The Djinns   37

From *The Empire in the Pillory* (*Les Châtiments*)

That Night   45
The Night of the Fourth: A Recollection   47
Set Him Apart!   51
'Sound, sound forever...'   55

From *Contemplations* (*Les Contemplations*)

'Tomorrow, when the meadows grow...'   57
At Villequier   57
Shepherds and Flocks   69
The Bridge   71
At the Window in the Dark   73

From *The Legend of the Ages* (*La Légende des siècles*)

Conscience   79
Boaz Asleep   83
The Inquisition: Momotombo's Reasons   89
After the Battle   93
The Trumpet of Judgement   95

From *The Art of Being a Grandfather* (*L'Art d'être grand-père*)

Open Windows   105
More About God (But With Some Reservations)   107
'Jeanne was holed up...'   111
The Broken Vase   113

From *The Threshold of the Abyss* (*Le Seuil du gouffre*)

'I could see, far above my head...'   115
Another Voice ['Well, first of all...']   127
Another Voice ['You think yourself, perhaps...']   137
After the Voices   139

CHARLES BAUDELAIRE
TRANSLATED BY JAMES MCGOWAN

From *The Flowers of Evil* (*Les Fleurs du mal*)

To the Reader   147
The Albatross   149
Correspondences   151
Head of Hair   151
Sed non satiata   155
'The way her silky garments...'   155
A Carcass   157

The Harmony of Evening   159
Invitation to the Voyage   161
Autumn Song   163
The Cracked Bell   165
Spleen [I]   167
Spleen [II]   169
Spleen [III]   169
Spleen [IV]   171
The Swan   173
The Seven Old Men   177
The Blind   179
A Voyage to Cythera   181
Voyaging   185

PAUL VERLAINE
TRANSLATED BY MARTIN SORRELL

From *Saturnian Poems* (*Poèmes saturniens*)

Autumn Song   197

From *Fun and Games* (*Fêtes galantes*)

On the Grass   199
Without Guile   199
Weird as Puppets   201
Colombine   201
Muted Tones   203
Exchange of Feelings   205

From *Songs Without Words* (*Romances sans paroles*)

'It's languor and ecstasy'   207
'Falling tears...'   209
'You see, we have to be forgiven...' 209
'The piano kissed...'   211
'Endless sameness...'   211
Brussels: Simple Frescos I   213
Brussels: Simple Frescos II   215
Malines   215
Green   217
Spleen   217

Streets I   219
Streets II   221
Beams   221

From *Wisdom* (*Sagesse*)

'Beauty of women...'   223
'The humble life...'   223
'Voice of Pride...'   225
'Hope like a wisp of straw...'   227
'Peaceful eyes my only wealth'   229
'The sky above the roof...'   229
'The sadness, the languor...'   231
'A cold wind...'   231
'Uneven rows...'   233

From *Once Upon a Time* (*Jadis et naguère*)

The Art of Poetry   235

From *Love* (*Amour*)

Parsifal   237

ARTHUR RIMBAUD
TRANSLATED BY MARTIN SORRELL

Asleep in the Valley   239
My Bohemia   239
Lice-Seekers   241
Cheated Heart   243
Drunken Boat   243
Vowels   251
Blackcurrant River   251
Lovely Morning Thought   253
'O seasons, o châteaux'   255

From *Illuminations*

After the Flood   255
Being Beauteous   257
Departure   259
Morning of Drunkenness   259
City   261

Dawn   261
Seascape   263
Promontory   263
Sales   265

From *A Season in Hell* (*Une Saison en enfer*)

Night in Hell   265
Morning   269
Farewell   271

STEPHANE MALLARMÉ

TRANSLATED BY E. H. AND A. M. BLACKMORE

From *Poems* (*Poésies*)

Toast   275
Sea Breeze   275
A Favn in the Afternoon   277
Saint   283
A Few Sonnets: 285
   'When the shade threatened with the fatal decree...'   285
   'This virginal long-living lovely day...'   285
   'The fine suicide fled victoriously...'   287
   'With her pure nails offering their onyx high...'   289
The Tomb of Edgar Allan Poe   289
The Tomb of Charles Baudelaire   291
Tomb ['The black rock, cross...']   291

Explanatory Notes   295

Index of Titles and First Lines   325

INTRODUCTION

In France, as in most other parts of Europe, the seventeenth and eighteenth centuries developed elaborate rules and conventions for the writing of poetry. Indeed, nowhere were the conventions more rigid and the rules more precise than in France, and nowhere, perhaps, was the poetry more impressive; no writer has ever produced fine verse within narrower and more restrictive limits than did the seventeenth-century dramatist Jean Racine.

Racine's verse, like all other French verse of the era, always rhymed; and his rhymes were invariably arranged according to complex and inflexible rules. The shape of his verse nearly always mirrored its grammatical structure: sense rarely spilled across line-boundaries, as it constantly does in Milton and the later Shakespeare. His language was drawn from a remarkably small stock of acceptably dignified, 'poetic' words (a bottlenose dolphin, we are sometimes told, may use a wider 'vocabulary' within a few months than Racine did in his whole career). His subject-matter was correspondingly limited.

Most of Racine's eighteenth-century successors seem to have felt that he had written not merely one kind of poetry, but the best possible kind. Even Voltaire, who delighted in unconventionalities and novelties of thought, kept within the established conventions when he was writing verse, and looked back at earlier, pre-Racinian poets with the assured superiority of an educated adult listening to the prattle of ignorant children. When, for instance, in his *Commentaries on Corneille* he turned the pages of Pierre Corneille's *Polyeucte* (1642), he felt that he was in the presence of a 'masterpiece' written by a 'great poet', yet scarcely anything in it quite satisfied him. One turn of phrase was 'bourgeois', another was 'too colloquial', a third was 'not pure French'; he objected to repetitions of the same phrase in close succession, and to touches of comedy in a work that is supposed to be tragic. He spoke of certain words or phrases as 'forbidden': 'forbidden in tragedy', 'forbidden in dignified writing', or even 'in writing of any kind'. Above all, he disliked half-lights and ambiguities. 'This is scarcely intelligible,' he complained at one point. 'If you want to know whether verses are bad, turn them into prose; if the prose is incorrect, so are the verses. . . . Verses should have the clarity and purity of the most correct prose, combined with the elegance, power, boldness and harmony of poetry.'

Because the rules for writing 'correct' poetry were so stringent and so firmly entrenched in France, reaction against them came later and proceeded more slowly than in England or Germany. But by 1820 various young poets were starting to venture beyond the conventions. There must have been many reasons for this, but perhaps the deepest was a feeling that nineteenth-century thoughts simply could not be expressed in eighteenth-century ways. The rules of Racine and Voltaire (so Hugo argued in his famous 'Reply to a Bill of Indictment') had been generated by the pre-Revolutionary upper class, and were helping to maintain the social and political codes of that class. Those rules did not allow poets to say plainly that a king was a 'pig' (*cochon*) or a woman a 'whore' (*catin*); how could a poet who wanted to say such things—who wanted, for instance, to speak out bluntly against the tyranny and prostitution that the Old Regime had tolerated—abide by that regime's literary code? Again, Voltaire had declared that 'the periphrasis "the enemy of the human race" is noble; the proper name ["the devil"] would be ridiculous'. But how could a Baudelaire—who saw nothing that was 'noble', and much that was 'ridiculous', in the corruption of humanity—avoid using the ignoble, ridiculous name? And why should he avoid using it even if he could?

Nineteenth-century French poets also had a new awareness of foreign literature, and a consciousness that writers in other places handled their medium differently. Lamartine looked to such English poets as Gray and Byron; Gérard de Nerval to Goethe and Heine in Germany; Hugo to the medieval Spanish *Song of the Cid*. In French literature itself new, non-Racinian models were discovered or rediscovered: Ronsard and Du Bellay from the Renaissance, André Chénier from the time of the Revolution.

So, in various ways and to various extents, the old conventions began to crumble. Lamartine retained essentially the vocabulary and prosody of his immediate predecessors, but ventured into new areas of subject-matter. Hugo 'dislocated' the old verse-forms, allowing words to run over from line to line for expressive purposes, and made extensive use of a new, often 'unpoetic' vocabulary. Rimbaud, in a few of his later poems, rejected rhyme altogether and produced some of the earliest free verse in French.

Nineteenth-century critics often turned the old rules on their heads, and supposed that poets were 'good' or 'bad' in proportion to their degree of *departure* from the conventions of Racine and Voltaire: thus Hugo was regarded as an improvement on Lamartine, Baudelaire on Hugo, Rimbaud or Mallarmé on Baudelaire. Literary Darwinism of this kind is seldom seen today; recent criticism is generally more willing to approach each of these writers on his own terms—to accept Poet X as Poet X, rather than as an early approximation to the perfection of the later poets Y and Z. That is the approach that will be adopted in the following pages.

Lamartine

Alphonse de Lamartine was born of aristocratic parents in 1790, and entered the service of the restored French monarchy in 1815. At the health resort of Aix-les-Bains in October 1816 he met and fell in love with Julie Charles, a young married woman dying of tuberculosis. They arranged to meet again at Aix the following August, but Lamartine waited there alone. By that time Julie was too ill to travel; she died a few months later. His first volume, *Poetic Meditations* (*Méditations poétiques*, 1820), which reflected those experiences (though not as simplistically as earlier critics used to think), was immediately successful, and some of its poems remain among the best-known in the language. Later in 1820 he married (to the dismay, we are told, of the *Meditations'* numerous female admirers) and began a diplomatic career with the French embassy at Naples. *New Poetic Meditations* (*Nouvelles méditations poétiques*) appeared in 1823, and *Poetic and Religious Harmonies* (*Harmonies poétiques et religieuses*)—to present-day critics almost without exception, his greatest volume—in 1830. He also worked at an immense philosophical poem of which only a few episodes were completed, among them the verse novel *Jocelyn* (1836) which became his best-selling volume of poetry. But by that time his interests had been diverted more and more into politics, in which he had a highly distinguished career; indeed, for some months after the Revolution of 1848 he was the effective leader of the French government. His later writings— mainly prose, though he continued to produce occasional impressive poems—were generated by a Scott-like struggle against insurmountable debts, and at the time of his death in 1869 his literary reputation was probably at its lowest point. Interest in him revived a generation later, as it commonly does.

Like many epoch-making works, the 1820 volume contained little that would have been altogether new to its first audience. (Ten months before its appearance, Lamartine himself had written in a private letter: 'There's nothing in it to attract the slightest attention or popularity—nothing grand; nothing new, or very little . . . ') In the famous opening poem, 'Isolation', the subject-matter is the traditional one of eighteenth-century poetry: love and the loss of love, landscape, religion. The verse-forms are equally eighteenth-century: smooth, regular, end-stopped lines with the sense laid out symmetrically in quatrains: 'here' this (two lines), 'there' that (two more lines); 'if' this (two lines), 'then' that (two more lines). The vocabulary is eighteenth-century; indeed, whole phrases are borrowed or half-recalled from minor poets of the recent past—this idiom, we are told, can be found in Delille, that in Parny. There is an eighteenth-century fondness for traditional circumlocution: 'the blurred chariot of the queen of night', 'the boundaries of its sphere', 'the fountain to which I aspire'. All these things were thoroughly consistent with the literary fashions of the time. In literature, Marmontel had declared, 'objects should be veiled from the eyes by a vagueness and temperance of expression'; and Lamartine himself believed that 'poetry weeps well and sings well, but it describes poorly'.

Lamartine never turned his back on his poetic antecedents, as a Rimbaud or even a Verlaine might strive to do; but he did develop, and to present him only as the author of the three or four most familiar *Meditations* is to misrepresent his achievement. His vocabulary and syntax remained essentially eighteenth-century, but his handling of them became more relaxed and more fluid: the paragraph of 'The Infinite in the Skies' beginning 'Que le séjour de l'homme est divin...' (ll. 39–62) has often been cited as a model in this respect. He also became more relaxed—and more adventurous—in his use of form; many of his later poems abandon the fixed stanza-patterns of the *Meditations* and vary metrically as their train of thought varies. In the *Poetic and Religious Harmonies* of 1830, with its forty-eight separate poems arranged in four 'books', we find one of the earliest successful examples of the method of construction which Baudelaire was to use so effectively in *The Flowers of Evil* and Hugo in his mature volumes: the loosely ordered poem-sequence, where each piece can be read on its own, and yet gains further significance from its place in the whole. The earlier sets of *Meditations*, by contrast, are simply miscellaneous poem-collections in the old manner.

What was new in the 1820 *Meditations* was the personal tone of voice—a tone familiar enough in prose in those days (it had been heard in Chateaubriand and Rousseau), but not in verse. 'The public', as Lamartine later wrote, 'saw a human being instead of a book.' So, in 'Isolation', mountain, river, sun, and moon are presented not for their own sakes, as Roucher or Saint-Lambert might have presented them a generation earlier, but solely for the sake of their effect on the speaker: 'Yet my soul, unmoved by this pleasant view, | Feels neither charmed with it nor comforted.' Indeed, not only in the *Meditations* but throughout Lamartine's poetry the material world is utterly subordinated to the human being who observes it. It seems fluid, insubstantial, evanescent. The poems' recurrent images are distant sounds, passing streams, varying shadows, hills waveringly reflected in water, stars indistinctly seen through atmospheric haze. There is no outward solidity, security, or permanence anywhere; everything around the observer is fleeting and disappointing.

> In its blue waves, harmonious Ether drapes
> With purer fluid all the highland capes;
> Each crased peak, each half-extinguished trace,
> Seemingly swims in air, flutters in space,
> As we see, rippling in the liquid floor
> Of sleeping seas, the phantom of their shore.

The use of language itself is slightly blurred, as though the object under discussion isn't clearly visualized: from what possible line of sight, for instance, could the 'shore' of a sea be seen reflected in its 'floor'? Nothing is quite distinct or quite discrete in this poetry; everything is on the point of dissolving into something else.

The same could be said of personal relationships. There are stray fragments of biography in the *Meditations*, and if we piece them together, we can almost build them into a 'story': the speaker has loved someone; he has returned to their appointed meeting-place, but she has not; without her, all of nature has become worthless to

him ('One creature goes . . . all is depopulated'), and he looks only
for death. Yet the fragments are never pieced together by the poet
himself; the 'story' is never quite told; the 'someone' is never named,
never really described—even in 'The Lake', where her presence is
most vividly felt, we are shown only a pair of feet and a disembodied
voice.

Yet to place too much stress on this particular side of Lamartine is
to restrict his achievement. He is not the poet of gently monotonous
misery portrayed by the older anthologists, with their concentration
on 'Isolation' and 'The Lake' to the exclusion of all else. Even within
'Isolation' and 'The Lake' he is not such a poet: when his poems
mourn the insubstantiality of the universe, they do so in images of
rhythm, of a regular or recurrent motion—the rise and fall of waves,
the annual cycle of the seasons, the daily circuit of the sun, the
diminution and extension of shadows; the poet's sense of loss and
dissolution stands in constant tension with an underlying sense of a
deeper pattern and regularity. He writes not of unmitigated decline,
but of decline counterbalanced, decline set against growth, abun-
dance, activity: 'Nature and all that quickens her' rushing desper-
ately towards the 'great Whole' ('The West'), 'suns of countless
grades' and 'floods of live creatures' humiliating the reflective obser-
ver ('The Infinite in the Skies'). The same effect is seen in the
versification itself: its melancholy is played off against the richness
of its word-music and the rhythmic patterning of its metre. The
result is a curious shot-silk effect which is one of the perennial
fascinations of Lamartinian verse. It is not that 'the style sings of
growth, the message is decay', but that even as the style sings of
decay, it sings of growth in the same breath; and the proportions of
the two, the balance between them, may seem to change and fluctu-
ate before the eyes when the same poem is read on different
occasions.

Hugo

Victor Hugo was born in 1802. His father was an army officer, and
the boy followed the Napoleonic campaigns in Italy and Spain; but
his mother was a royalist and a Catholic, and so, at first (with charac-
teristic zeal), was her son. Several volumes of *Odes* (1822–8) estab-
lished his reputation and traced his increasing dissatisfaction with
the constraints of conservatism—in literature and in other matters.

During the next decade he became the acknowledged leader of the French Romantic movement, not only in poetry (with *Orientalia* (*Les Orientales*), 1829, and four subsequent volumes), but also in fiction (*The Last Day of a Condemned Man*, 1828; *Notre-Dame de Paris*, 1831) and drama (*Hernani*, 1830; *Ruy Blas*, 1838). The death of his 19-year-old daughter Léopoldine at Villequier in 1843 silenced him for some years as a poet, but not as a public speaker: he had entered politics and was becoming a prominent advocate of republicanism and radical social reform. When Napoleon III seized power in 1851 Hugo led the opposition to the new dictatorship; he was exiled to the Channel Islands, where he issued political satires (*The Empire in the Pillory* (*Les Châtiments*), 1853), personal lyrics (*Contemplations* (*Les Contemplations*), 1856), 'miniature epics' (*The Legend of the Ages* (*La Légende des siècles*), First Series, 1859), novels (*Les Misérables*, 1862; *Toilers of the Sea*, 1866), and literary criticism (*William Shakespeare*, 1864). In 1870, on the fall of Napoleon III, he returned to France in triumph and continued to generate huge quantities of prose and verse, including *The Art of Being a Grandfather* (*L'Art d'être grand-père*, 1877) and the remainder of *The Legend of the Ages* (1877–83). A stroke in 1878 ended his creative career, but so great was the backlog of material in manuscript that the flow of new Hugo publications continued, virtually without diminution, until 1902: four new volumes of verse appeared in 1879–81, *The End of Satan* (*La Fin de Satan*, posthumously) in 1886, *God* (*Dieu*) in 1891, and so on; even the *Last Gleanings* (*Dernière Gerbe*, 1902) were far from being actually the last, and impressive new Hugo fragments were still appearing in print for the first time a hundred years after his death. In his final years he became an immensely popular figure—not only among the usual reading public—and his funeral procession in 1885 attracted larger crowds than any European writer's has ever done.

It might seem, at first glance, that his career ran parallel to Lamartine's. In politics both began as strict royalists and developed into republican antagonists of Napoleon III; in religion both began as orthodox Roman Catholics and came to see religious orthodoxies as obstacles to the knowledge of God; in poetry both began as imitators of the eighteenth century and became leaders of the French Romantic movement—the première of Hugo's play *Hernani* is as familiar a date in the history of that movement as the publication of Lamartine's *Poetic Meditations* ten years earlier.

Yet at all these points of comparison, Hugo's position is the more extreme. Lamartine's *Poetic Meditations* attracted attention; Hugo's *Hernani* caused a riot. On the rise of Napoleon III, Lamartine withdrew into private life; Hugo went into exile in the Channel Islands, never to return to France as long as the new régime lasted. Most of Lamartine's political poems (see, for example, 'The Lizard') are relatively short and characterized by a resigned irony; Hugo's *The Empire in the Pillory* contains 7,000 lines of passionately felt satire. Lamartine's appraisal of the Roman Catholic priesthood in *Jocelyn* was severe enough for the work to be placed on the Papal Index; yet it is far less scathing than 'Momotombo's Reasons' or dozens of other Hugolian poems on the subject.

Hugo is an extremist. In politics, in religion, he never does anything by halves; and the same is true in poetry. He delights in primary colours, striking contrasts, towering heights and unfathomable chasms, brilliant lights and Cimmerian darknesses. As his critics complained and he cheerfully acknowledged, he loves antithesis. The antithesis may be built up slowly over the whole span of a poem ('Sound, sound forever, trumpet-calls of thought...'); or it may be condensed in a single phrase, a single striking oxymoron ('the sea's sinister sheep'). What is unusual, in either case, is the intensity of the poet's emotional involvement in *both* sides of the antithesis, an intensity no doubt fuelled by his personal experiences, by the death of his daughter, by his exile to the Channel Islands. In every angel he sees his dead child ('The Bridge'); in every authority-figure he sees Napoleon III ('Momotombo's Reasons'). The responses run so deep that they can be evoked even by very indirect stimuli, and therefore a situation will commonly trigger two or more conflicting sympathies at different levels. In 'After the Battle' both the Spaniard and the Frenchman attract his support to varying extents, the former for being a victim of tyranny, the latter for refusing to take vengeance like a tyrant. In 'Jeanne was holed up' Grandfather both leads the people to ruin like an emperor, and incites them to insurrection like a Victor Hugo. In 'Conscience' the poet both hunts Cain down because he is an avatar of Napoleon III, and identifies with him because he is an exile. He enters so wholeheartedly into the hidden currents and countercurrents that move within his characters, 'good' and 'evil' alike, that they seem to breathe and feel and live from the inside, from the very depths of their being—however extreme their beliefs may be, and however superficially implausible their situations.

In 'More About God (But With Some Reservations)' he offers a characteristic defence of his art. Do we complain that Hugolian poetry is 'wild, unseemly, extravagant'? that it runs too frequently to extremes—'antitheses everywhere'? that it 'never knows when to stop'? He replies that he is simply holding the mirror up to Nature, as great poets have always done. Nature is wild, unseemly, extravagant; Nature has antitheses everywhere; Nature never knows when to stop. As for his extreme characters, his Cains and Boazes—why, declares Hugo, the universe is full of Cains and Boazes; only a Baculard or a Nonotte (Hugo suggests at the end of the poem) would fail to notice it!

An English-language reader may recall George Santayana's defence of Dickens in *Soliloquies in England* (1922): 'When people say that Dickens exaggerates, it seems to me that they can have no eyes and no ears. The world is a perpetual caricature of itself . . . There *are* such people; we are such people ourselves in our true moments, in our veritable impulses; but we are careful to stifle and to hide those moments from ourselves and from the world.' Yet Hugo, characteristically, goes further than Santayana. His work, he would have said, extreme though it may be, is not extreme enough. No writer's work is extreme enough; no writer's work can be. No possible human language is extreme enough to do justice to the reality; as he says in 'The Trumpet of Judgement':

> Oh, in the human mind, where everything
> Wavers and scatters, where language itself
> Has no unstammered word, where dawn arises
> Like a wound—in this mind, trembling as it
> Ventures to prophesy—how can it all
> Be pictured, how imagined...

The poet's quest is endless and impossible, for he is nothing more than a 'gleam-led larva', and he is in pursuit of something 'invisible . . . nameless and unenvisaged'—something of which he can catch, at most, only faint glimmers, 'vague luminescences'. Let him rise every morning and write hundreds of lines before breakfast; let him heap poem on poem and volume on volume; let him accumulate a lifetime's output of 156,000 lines of verse (not counting a massive pile of verse dramas); let him supplement it with novels over a thousand pages long; let him die at the end of it all, and be drawn into the presence of God—still, at the very best, he will be able to recognize only 'something indescribable . . . of which I felt doubtful'; still, at the very best, he will cry out: 'I still know nothing.'

Baudelaire

Charles Baudelaire was born in 1821; his father died six years later, and his mother then married a distinguished army officer whom the boy came to detest. As an adult Baudelaire led a debt-ridden, bohemian existence in squalid surroundings, writing art criticism and translating Edgar Allan Poe. Hardly any of his poems appeared in journals until 1855, and when they were first collected as *The Flowers of Evil* (*Les Fleurs du mal*, 1857), he and his publisher were successfully prosecuted for indecency: six poems were banned and the edition was withdrawn from sale. A revised edition, omitting the six offensive items but adding many of Baudelaire's finest poems, appeared in 1861. By this time he was already beginning to suffer the first symptoms of a progressive neurological disease (perhaps neurosyphilis), and he died in 1867 after a year of paralysis and dysphasia. He is remembered mainly for *The Flowers of Evil*, but his prose poems and private journals, both dating mainly from the early 1860s, are also of considerable interest.

There is nothing comfortable about Baudelaire. The very title of his volume speaks of *Evil*; in the opening poem ('To the Reader') he mentions not only 'evil' and 'sin', but also 'Satan' and 'the Devil': 'The Devil pulls on all our strings.' The book's condemnation of the human condition is so searching, so radical, that a reader may want to draw back from it, to dilute it somehow, to feel that the poet can't possibly mean what he is saying. But no; this is not mere fairy-tale language or a mere manner of speaking; it is absolutely in earnest. In a famous letter to Flaubert (26 June 1860), Baudelaire finds it 'utterly impossible to account for some of man's impulsive thoughts or actions, without the hypothesis that an evil force outside himself is intervening'—however 'scandalous', he says, such a suggestion might seem to modern-day thinkers. When George Sand 'claims that true Christians don't believe in hell' he is genuinely, and deeply, horrified; you find him returning to the subject in note after note of his private journals. 'The Sand woman has a vested interest in fancy-ing that hell doesn't exist,' he declares; and again: 'Her moral views have as much profundity and subtlety as a washerwoman's or a hired prostitute's . . . She has good reasons for wanting to do away with hell'; and again: 'It's the Devil who has persuaded her to put her faith in *her kind heart* and *her good sense*, so that she can persuade all the other prize idiots to put their faith in theirs.' 'The Devil's cun-ningest trick is to convince you that he doesn't exist,' he says in the prose-poem 'The Generous Gambler'.

How deeply, and how seriously, Baudelaire himself believes in the existence of the Devil, the corruption of humanity, and the utter unreliability of kind-heartedness and 'good sense' may be seen on almost any page of his poems. The 'Seven Old Men', for instance, 'come from . . . hell'; they are a 'parade from hell'; yet there isn't the slightest suggestion that they are creatures of fairy-tale or fiction. On the contrary, they are absolutely real. If they are 'ghosts', they are ghosts that 'tug the stroller's sleeve' 'in daylight'. They are set in a landscape sharply and precisely observed, one that any nineteenth-century city-dweller might encounter any day, where streets are 'shaken by rumbling carts', where a 'rainy sky' matches the colour of 'yellowed rags', and where 'houses, rendered taller by the mist, | Seemed to be towering wharves at riverside'. Through this utterly real landscape the men themselves stalk with equal reality:

> His spine made a right angle with his legs
> So neatly that his cane, the final touch,
> Gave him the figure and the clumsy step
>
> Of some sick beast, or a three-legged Jew.
> In snow and filth he made his heavy way,
> As if his old shoes trampled on the dead
> In hatred, not indifference to life.

It is impossible to say, in such a poem, where the earthly finishes and the infernal begins. The two realms are inextricably associated, and are treated with equal seriousness: and the poet moves easily back and forth between the material and the immaterial ('despite their feeble-ness, | These monsters smacked of all eternity'), with an air not of indulging in poetic rhetoric, but of stating simple matters of fact.

This should not surprise anyone who has pondered the sonnet

'Correspondences'. Baudelaire sees an intimate and exact relation between the material and the immaterial realms: things in the one 'correspond' to things in the other. In his essay on Wagner he maintains that, 'ever since the day when God ordained the universe as a complex and indivisible whole', colours have corresponded to sounds, and both to abstract ideas, by a 'reciprocal analogy'. Elsewhere, writing on Hugo, he cites with approval the Swedenborgian doctrine that 'everything—shape, motion, number, colour, scent—in the *spiritual* realm as well as the *natural*—is significant, reciprocal, converse, *corresponding*'. Thus, at any moment the poet may draw an analogy between things from one plane and things from another—not to invent 'poetic images', but to equate what is inherently equal: 'yellowed rags' and a 'rainy sky', snow in the streets and corpses in a graveyard, the external 'stage-set' and the 'actor's soul', flowing sap and passing mysteries. No one conceptual stratum is felt to be more 'real' than any other.

'The Seven Old Men' ends with an impulse to take flight from its corrupt universe—one of many such impulses in the *Flowers of Evil*; but the attempt, as so often, proves to be 'vain': 'my soul danced in circles like a hull | Dismasted, on a monstrous shoreless sea!' The immediately preceding poem, 'The Swan', is full of such would-be escapees: Andromache by the 'empty tomb' and 'fraudulent Simois'; the swan trying to bathe in the 'dried out ditch'; the

> negress, thin and tubercular,
> Treading in the mire, searching with haggard eye
> For palm trees she recalls from splendid Africa,
> Somewhere behind a giant barrier of fog.

Often, as here, the flight is towards something remembered, a 'lost something' from the past: the 'old recollections' of 'The Cracked Bell', the 'living light of summer gone too soon' in 'Autumn Song', the memory of a lost love in the final lines of 'The Carcass' and 'Harmony of Evening'. In other poems it is a flight towards some realm never previously visited, some exotic region known only from travellers' tales: the utopian 'land to write songs about' of the 'Voyage to Cythera', or the less specific 'there' of 'Invitation to the Voyage'. The last and longest of the *Flowers*, 'Voyaging', surveys the phenomenon in detail. But the past can never be recaptured (it is 'something they may not find | Ever, ever again'), and the utopia, if reached, always proves to be 'a poor land after all'. The inhabitants of Baudelaire's poems are trapped in the world of evil and cannot escape from it. Satan has 'vaporized' their willpower and lulled their 'captive soul'; their limbs must move in whatever direction his strings pull them.

In many of the *Flowers of Evil* there is yet another impulse to escape—something that we might call a flight towards women. Women, in these poems, are mysterious creatures, 'animals' as alien as cats; and 'we love women', Baudelaire writes in his journals, 'in so far as they are strangers to us'. They offer yet another exotic utopia, a 'languorous Asia' or a 'scorching Africa' ('Head of Hair') 'resembling' the Eastern lands to which the speaker longs to flee with them ('Invitation to the Voyage'). Like such lands, they are best seen from and kept at a distance (as the poems show, this is no conventional desire for erotic possession, any more than Baudelaire's fascination with foreign lands is a desire for real-life travel expeditions). But despite all distancing strategies, the creatures can't be kept 'strangers' for ever; inevitably, with repeated contact, they become more familiar, less alien; and then they become just as disappointing as Africa or Asia do:

> Like desert sands and skies she is as well,
> As unconcerned with human misery,
> Like the long networks of the ocean's swells
> Unfolding with insensibility.
>
> Her polished eyes are made of charming stones,
> And in her essence, where the natures mix
> Of holy angel and the ancient sphinx,
>
> Where all is lit with gold, steel, diamonds,
> A useless star, it shines eternally,
> The sterile woman's frigid majesty.

Thus, says Baudelaire in his journals, 'the eternal Venus (caprice, hysteria, fantasy) is another of the Devil's seductive manifestations'. Whereas 'invocation of God (or spirituality) is a longing to climb higher, invocation of Satan (or animality) is a delight in going downwards'—and 'love for women must be attributed to the latter'. If we indulge in a 'love foolishly displaced from God onto created things', then we must suffer the consequences: 'the animal-worshipper is always deceived in his idol.' At first, from a distance, the beloved creature may seem to offer the 'eternal warmth' of the heavens ('Head of Hair'); later, on closer acquaintance, she becomes merely 'one step further into hell'. At least three times in the *Flowers of Evil* this cycle of attraction and repulsion is traced; one female love-object after another is pursued, and all alike end in disillusion.

Very little 'invocation of God' occurs in the world of these poems; its inhabitants are too will-paralysed to escape from Satan in that direction. Where any God is mentioned at all he is usually one created by humanity in its own image, for its own self-indulgent ends—and is more often abused than invoked; as we are told in 'Voyaging', religions

> Climb skyward on their saints, who it is said
> Indulge their lusts with hairshirts, or with nails,
> As dainty fops sprawl on a feather bed.
>
> Drunk on her genius, Humanity,
> Mad now as she has always been, or worse,
> Cries to her God in raging agony:
> 'Master, my image, damn you with this curse!'

But even that much acknowledgement of the divine is unusual. More often the world's inhabitants merely gaze blankly, and vainly, into the invisible: 'What in the Skies can these men hope to find?' ('The Blind'). The 'Correspondences' in the universe are scarcely perceptible to human beings: they are 'shadowy', 'heard from afar', speaking to us only 'sometimes' and with a 'confusing speech'. Such correspondences, Baudelaire tells us in his essay on Hugo, are clear or obscure 'in proportion to the purity, good will or insight innate in different souls'—and, if human souls are lacking in purity, good will, and insight, how can they hope to perceive the ordained analogies of the universe?

Verlaine

Paul Verlaine was born in 1844 and sent his first known poem to Hugo at the age of 14. His first two volumes, *Saturnian Poems* (*Poèmes saturniens*, 1866) and *Fêtes galantes* (1869), were generally well received; but the third, *La Bonne Chanson* (1870), was overshadowed by the Franco-Prussian War, and the fourth, *Songs Without Words* (*Romances sans paroles*, 1874), by his public disgrace. He had married in 1870, but he and his wife had little in common, and in 1872 he ran away with the young Rimbaud to England. The turbulent relationship between the two poets ended in July 1873, when Verlaine shot Rimbaud in the wrist and was arrested. He was sentenced to two years' imprisonment, and his wife obtained a judicial separation. While in prison he became a devout Roman Catholic, as his next volume, *Wisdom* (*Sagesse*, 1880), attests; it is said to have sold eight copies. However, during the next few years Verlaine began to attract a cult following, and the earlier poems collected in *Once Upon a Time* (*Jadis et naguère*, 1884) were widely discussed. *Wisdom* became the first volume of a religious tetralogy, but its three successors—*Love* (*Amour*, 1888), *In Parallel* (*Parallèlement*, 1889), and *Happiness* (*Bonheur*, 1891)—revealed a striking decline in his poetic skills: he was now struggling against alcoholism, multiple physical problems (between 1886 and his death he spent about half of each year in hospital), and a chaotic personal life. When he applied for membership of the French Academy in 1893 even his friends thought it was a joke, and he attracted not a single vote. He was, however, voted 'Prince of Poets' by his peers in 1894, and his work—especially *Songs Without Words* and *Wisdom*—was much admired by younger readers. He died in 1896.

Baudelaire's *Flowers of Evil* were written, slowly and gradually, over a quarter of a century; yet on the whole they are notably consistent in both style and content—so consistent that it is often hard to say, from internal evidence alone, whether a given poem dates from 1842 or 1859. By contrast, there are many different Verlaines. There is the relatively impersonal craftsman seen in some of the early *Saturnian Poems*; the wry eighteenth-century pasticheur of the *Fêtes galantes*; the naive singer of courtship in *La Bonne Chanson*; the impressionist of *Songs Without Words*; the devout Catholic of *Wisdom*; the blatant sinner of *In Parallel*; the advocate of simplicity and plain speech in the final *Epigrams*—but succinct characterizations of this kind inevitably oversimplify the matter: conflicting styles and conflicting beliefs are often seen within a single volume, especially if the volume was compiled over an extended period of time.

One Verlaine, though not the only one, is seen in his 'Art of

Poetry'—a Verlaine, probably, of about 1874, shortly after the completion of *Songs Without Words* and contemporary with the earliest parts of *Wisdom*. This Verlaine calls for a poetry that is 'vague' and 'light', achieved by the use of unexpected rhythms ('no more one-two-one-twos') and obliquely chosen wording ('no . . . pinpoint definitions'); a poetry that is full of 'nuance' rather than 'colour'; a poetry that puts music first and rejects everything redolent of 'lit'ritcher'. There is a certain sly fun in all this, for the poem practises, and yet doesn't quite practise, its own precepts. 'Who will denounce that criminal, Rhyme?' it asks, carefully rhyming as it does so. The 'vague', similarly, turns out to be not utter imprecision, but a blend of the *précis* and the *indécis*, and the poem's line of argument, though it drifts rather lazily between point and point, is always perfectly lucid: all things considered, this little 'art of poetry' is no more erratically arranged or illogically reasoned than either Horace's or Boileau's. (By contrast, imagine an 'art of poetry' written by Rimbaud—or look at his 'Morning of Drunkenness', which is probably as close to one as anything he could have produced.) Yet in many ways the poem does illustrate what it preaches: there is no shortage of 'music' in its verse; its rhythms are certainly not 'one-two-one-twos' (it uses nine-syllable lines, unusual in earlier French poetry); its phrasing is often far from conventional 'lit'ritcher' ('Grip eloquence by the throat and squeeze it to death') and is sometimes, in the original French, a mere offhand gesture in the general direction of the thought ('Que ton vers soit la chose envolée | Qu'on sent...'). Above all, it illustrates its own last stanza: it 'rides its luck'; it's a playful thing chasing the promise of the moment without too earnest a concern for structure or absolute consistency.

That point needs to be stressed, because the poem has often been taken as a solemn manifesto of Verlaine's invariable faith; by 1890 its author was already obliged to insist: 'Don't take the "Art of Poetry" too seriously; after all, it's only a song, and I'VE NEVER DONE ANY THEORIZING!' 'Music', admittedly, is often 'put first and foremost' in Verlaine's writing: its overt influence can be seen equally in the early 'Autumn Song' with its plangent violin-vowels, and in the relatively late 'Parsifal' with its sonorous imitation of 'Ô ces voix d'enfants chantant dans la cupole' ('And then, those children's voices singing in the dome'). And rhyme is always used—Verlaine (not surprisingly, given his love of assonance and musicality) insisted on it—though often in a careless or half-hearted way: the poet never strives to match the virtuosity of a Hugo or a Banville in this realm. He rhymes 'langoureuse' with 'amoureuse' and 'vaguement' with 'quasiment'. He rhymes on trivial, insignificant words—'the' in 'Autumn Song', 'his' and 'so' in 'Colombine'. These are not simply accidents or signs of impatience with technique: easy, 'weak' rhymes, like imprecisions of wording, can be an asset in a kind of poetry that is designed to appear slightly out of focus.

'Vagueness'—at least vagueness of sense—is less ubiquitous. It is most prominent in *Songs Without Words* and the early poems of *Wisdom*. In such poems a landscape may be sketched in, but its features are often indistinct, hazily seen and hazily worded: 'green-tinged . . . fade . . . half-light . . . question-marks on everything . . . somewhere a bird. . . faint. . . fade' (all these phrases come from one short piece, 'Brussels: Simple Frescos I'). Emotions are similarly hazy: 'I drift in languor . . . hardly even sad', for instance, in the same poem. Often there seems to be someone else present, someone who may even be addressed directly yet who is left so shadowy that he/she may be identified by one commentator as Verlaine's wife, by a second as Rimbaud, and by a third as Verlaine's cousin Élisa. Every-thing is drawn with blurry contours, coloured in pastel shades, and only half illuminated.

Yet this is far from being Verlaine's only manner. In the *commedia dell'arte* poems of *Fêtes galantes*, such as 'Weird as Puppets' and 'Colombine', various sharply observed characters—all of them familiar stereotypes—interact in definite ways and from visible, if conflicting, motives. In 'On the Grass', too, the speakers' characters are quite distinct—so distinct that nearly all the bits of dialogue can be assigned to their rightful owners even in the absence of speech-prefixes—and the setting is perfectly clear—so clear that it can be recognized even in the absence of stage-directions. 'Parsifal' not only sketches the mood and emotional ambience of Wagner's opera but manages to summarize a remarkable amount of its plot in fourteen lines. And each of these poems seems as distinctively Verlainian as anything in *Songs Without Words* or *Wisdom*. By the time of the final *Epigrams* Verlaine has travelled so far from the 'Art of Poetry' that we find him emphatically *denouncing* imprecision and obscurity in literature:

> I like books that are read and known,
> I prize words that are definite,
> I worship the plain Cross alone:
> A stake with Jesus Christ on it.

Admittedly, few readers have ever felt these final poems to be 'distinctively Verlainian'. However, what seems uncharacteristic in them is not the change of belief; it is the loss of inventiveness in the poet's use of language. By this stage of his career alcoholic brain damage had affected Verlaine's literary skills in the way it usually does: the broad outlines were still there, but most of the 'fine tuning', the feel for nuance and delicacy, had vanished. The results, in most readers' eyes, are greeting-card verse rather than poetry.

The sense of play, however—of 'riding one's luck'—never deserts him, even in his last volumes: in his preface to the *Epigrams* he reminds posterity for one final time that his work has been 'nothing more than a game'. He is the most playful of the poets in this anthology. To him, a poem—however famous it might be, and however earnestly its meanings might be debated—is always 'only a song'. Does this suggest a tendency to take the easy way out—to avoid profundities? Perhaps. Verlaine, unlike the other poets in the present volume, tends to be patronized by literary critics. There is seldom much sense of conflicts overcome or truths hard-won in his poems; and their limits may be even more obvious when they are printed with Baudelaire's work on one side and Rimbaud's on the other. Yet in this respect, as in so many others, it is dangerous to generalize about him. The great middle-period poems of *Wisdom* (those written around 1875, such as 'Beauty of women...' and 'The humble life...') struggle between old and new ways of thinking, between flesh and spirit, truth and temptation, without underplaying either the power of the temptation or the necessity of shunning it if the truth is to be attained; their reluctance to be content with pat answers may owe something to Baudelaire, yet they remain Verlaine, and (unlike the late *Epigrams*) quintessential Verlaine. If we feel inclined to patronize this idle luck-rider and song-singer, perhaps it shows that we have not yet appreciated the full range of his work.

Rimbaud

Arthur Rimbaud was born in 1854 and by the age of 16 had become a foul-mouthed, foul-tempered, foul-smelling rebel, writing copious sardonic verses and hoping to revolutionize the world. In August 1871 he sent some of his poems (including 'Cheated Heart') to Verlaine, who immediately asked to see him. Their brief, passionate, and hostile relationship, noted above, seems to have stimulated both writers to greater literary adventurousness; Rimbaud, indeed, apparently abandoned rhyme altogether thereafter, writing only free verse ('Seascape') and prose poetry. Five hundred copies of *A Season in Hell* (*Une Saison en enfer*) were printed in October 1873 but not offered for sale; the *Illuminations* and the rhymed poems remained in manuscript. After Verlaine's arrest in August 1873 Rimbaud drifted back and forth across Europe for a number of years, and in 1880 arrived in Abyssinia, where he worked for ten years as a trader and gun-runner. He had given up literature entirely; though his poems were now starting to attract attention in France, he himself regarded them with total contempt. By 1891 he had developed a tumour of the right knee and returned to France, where his leg was amputated; but his illness rapidly progressed, and he died before the end of the year. Astonishing to the last, he is said to have amazed a priest in his final weeks by the depth of his religious faith. Whatever the significance of that episode, it reminds us that he was never one to remain content with a previous viewpoint, or to tread in his own former footsteps.

It's impossible to read Rimbaud's poems without reflecting that they are the work of an adolescent. They were written in a sudden torrent, between the ages of 15 and 19 (or thereabouts); virtually nothing earlier survives except dutiful school exercises in Latin, and virtually nothing later except pedestrian letters to his family. The poems rebel against all forms of authority: schoolteachers, librarians, officials, poets, God, and (perhaps above all) the creature once described by their writer as 'la *mother*'. Eventually, with self-destructive logic, they rebel against their own authority, and the torrent runs dry.

'Asleep in the Valley', early (1870) and conventionally arranged though it is, already displays many of the characteristic elements of Rimbaud's universe. Nature and civilization are at war in it, and their conflict is painted in primary colours: 'nature' is all warmth and childhood and sleep, 'civilization' all cruelty and adulthood and bloodshed. The scene is studied with a passionate irony kept (barely) under glacial control, and driven by an intense compassion for the victims of civilization and convention.

The same elements, though deployed in more complex ways, are prominent in the work of Rimbaud's remaining two or three years as a poet. On the one hand there is an abiding love of, and delight in, sunshine and sleep and rivers and rural landscapes in general ('Blackcurrant River', 'Dawn'); on the other, there is an abiding detestation of cruelty and insensitivity, the Hotel Splendide and the modern metropolis ('City', 'After the Flood'). The writer is struggling desperately to escape from the second realm and take flight into the first; how desperately, may be seen from pieces as diverse as 'Drunken Boat' and 'Departure'—or indeed from the history of his life from 1870 to 1880, which is the story of one flight after another.

For a while, in 1871 and 1872, he seems almost to think that Arthur Rimbaud has found the cure for the world's ailments. A famous letter of 15 July 1871 sets out his position:

> I say that you have to be a *seer* [*voyant*], you have to make yourself a *seer*. The Poet makes himself a *seer* by a long vast rational *disordering* of *all the senses*. All the types of love and suffering and madness; he searches himself, he eradicates all the poisons inside himself, retaining only their quintessences. Indescribable torment—in which he needs all his faith, all his superhuman power—in which he becomes the great sick and criminal and damned person of the whole human race,—and the supreme Thinker! Because he reaches the *unknown*! Because he has cultivated his soul (which was rich already) more than anyone has!

By 'the Poet' he means, of course, himself. A few previous writers have been 'seers' to some extent: Baudelaire particularly, Lamartine sometimes, Hugo in his later work, a few others; but all of them were 'strangled by the old form' of poetry; 'to invent from the unknown, you need new forms'. 'Author, creator, poet—no such person has ever yet existed!' Arthur Rimbaud, it seems, is to be the first one.

Among the poems, perhaps 'Morning of Drunkenness' stands closest to this letter. In it, too, an 'unheard-of work' is accomplished by a 'drunkenness' which has 'method', and in spite of 'tortures' and 'poison'. Indeed, in many respects the poem takes us further than the letter. The letter had hinted at a social function of poetry, though its details were left vague: 'Poetry will no longer keep in time with action; it *will be ahead of it*.' The 'new forms', so the letter said, were to be accompanied by 'new ideas'. Here the poem is more specific: 'The tree of good and evil shall be buried in darkness . . . tyrannical decencies shall be exiled, so that we may introduce our love of utmost purity.' Rimbaud seems to have believed at this time that he was on the point of doing away with good and evil and creating a new, immensely superior world-order.

Few of the poems, however, are as optimistic about the grand scheme as 'Morning of Drunkenness' and the letter of 15 July 1871. Even the boat that escapes from 'tyrannical decencies' so exuberantly in the early stages of 'Drunken Boat', later confesses to a longing for 'Europe's ancient parapets'. And throughout both the *Illuminations* and the *Season in Hell* the proposed new 'wisdom' struggles for survival. In 'Sales', for instance, exuberance is undercut by a pervasive tinge of self-mockery. 'Unsuspected things', things 'never heard before', are up for sale in this poem—'the opportunity, the only one, to free our senses', and the like. The poem's 'unsuspected things' recall the 'unheard-of' things proclaimed in 'Morning of Drunkenness', and the extraordinary panache of the sales pitch recalls 'Drunken Boat'. Yet the very fact that it *is* a sales pitch seems to devalue the commodities on offer ('For sale anarchy for the masses...'); and many of the commodities themselves have a glib and tawdry superficiality worthy of the most up-to-the-minute holiday resort: 'dwelling-places and migrations, sports, perfect magic, perfect comforts, and the noise, the movement and the future they create...'.

The self-mockery reaches its height in the 'Night in Hell'. 'Poison' (or at least its quintessence) had been a possible source of enlightenment in 'Morning of Drunkenness', but here it brings only damnation. The speaker may talk of having 'glimpsed . . . salvation'; he may call on the poor, the workers, the little children, to 'trust' in him, as they would in a saviour—but every such statement is attacked, indeed destroyed, by sardonic counter-statement. What he has attained has been not salvation, but the opposite. His supposed wisdom has been a 'false conversion'. His talents ('I have all the talents'), his 'noble ambitions', his aspirations for a different way of life ('negro songs, Eastern dancing-girls')—all these things have been futile. His life has been 'only sweet madness'.

Early readers, who were sure that the *Illuminations* had been written before the *Season in Hell*, tended to see a straight chronological progression in these poems: the earlier volume was full of optimism about the power of his art to revitalize humanity, the later one expressed the inevitable reaction. But the dates of the *Illuminations* are very uncertain, and with the exception of a few pieces like 'Morning of Drunkenness', little in either volume seems to be written in a spirit of unalloyed optimism. The collapse of the 'new ideas' is everywhere imminent. On the whole, the impression is of a mind veering back and forth in frustration, now emphatically declaring that 'wisdom' has indeed been attained, now, even more emphatically, dismissing the enterprise as nonsense. Eventually the later view becomes permanent, and Rimbaud turns his back on his art for ever. Yet his rejection of literature seems to have been embodied within his pursuit of literature (however erratically, and with whatever hesitations and fluctuations) for some years before he fell silent.

The 'new ideas', in fact, are the least valuable things in this poetry; and the poetry knows it. They remain at an abstract, unimaginative level; they ring as hollow as political campaign speeches, on which indeed Rimbaud seems at times to have modelled them: 'tyrannical decencies shall be exiled'; 'I have the truth and see justice'; 'the opportunity, the only one, to free our senses'. The (relative) weakness of the writing at such points shows how uneasy the writer himself is about his visionary plan, how far he is from trusting his own party promises. He really has no new scheme of salvation to offer; all he has is a constant exasperation at the world he sees around him, coupled with a desperate feeling that there *ought* to be some alternative. The real strength of his poems lies in the strain between the opposing forces, and especially in the incidental flashes of imagery that break forth, over and over again, when they come into conflict: wash-houses ringed with German poplars, Madame *** installing her piano in the Alps, Crime whimpering in the muck of the street. The tensions underlying 'Asleep in the Valley' continued to generate what was strongest in his poetry to the last.

Mallarmé

Stephane Mallarmé, the descendant of (in his own words) 'an uninterrupted succession of civil servants', was born in Paris in 1842 and led a life remarkably devoid of superficial excitement. He married in 1863, taught English at a number of provincial and Parisian schools, translated Edgar Allan Poe, and published occasional poems, while working towards a great 'Book' ('Livre') of which no substantial trace survives. The poems seem to have been mere by-products of this project, written at desultory intervals, and nearly half of them (including the 'Faun', 'Sea Breeze', 'Saint', and 'With her pure nails...') date from very early in his career (1862–7: though most underwent significant later revision). They were finally collected in 1899, a year after his death.

Mallarmé, as everyone knows, is a 'difficult' writer; and the difficulties are not superficial or detachable things; they are essential components of his art. Contrast, in this respect, Rimbaud: there are obscurities in Rimbaud, but many of them look like accidents—things caused by some characteristic momentary carelessness or impatience: you feel that the writer could have said perfectly well what 'ring' (in 'Night in Hell') or what 'small, terrible tree' (in 'Farewell') he had in mind, if only he had happened to be in a mood to do so. But Mallarmé does nothing casually or on impulse. When he withholds information, or when his meaning is hard to unravel, it seems a deliberate part of his system. He could not make it clearer; and he would not if he could. Where Rimbaud's obscurities are wayward and erratic, Mallarmé's are planned and coherent. In his article 'Mystery in Literature' he says that 'there has to be something arcane in the depths of all things; I firmly believe that something abstruse (i.e. enclosed and concealed) dwells within what is commonplace'. We see this, he argues, in nature, in the heavens, in music; why should we object if we see it in poetry as well? 'Everything that is holy and seeks to remain holy shrouds itself in mystery,' he says. A demand that poets should write with 'ever-gushing lucidity' would deprive them of the opportunity to express these 'holy', 'arcane' things, and would reduce their work to the level of the newspaper.

There are indeed some passages where Mallarmé appears to set out his views simply and clearly—almost in the prose of a newspaper

editorial; and it might seem sensible for a reader to start there. Here
is one of them, from a letter written in April 1866:

Yes, *I know it*—we are nothing more than empty forms of matter; but we
are truly sublime, because we have invented God and our soul. So sublime,
my friend, that I want to stage for myself this spectacle of matter, con-
scious that it exists, and yet rushing frantically into the Dream which (it
knows) doesn't exist—singing of the Soul and all such divine impressions
that have built up within us since the earliest times, and proclaiming,
before the Nothingness that is real, these glorious falsehoods!

Material things, according to Mallarmé (at least the prose Mallarmé
of 1866), are the only things that 'exist' and are 'real'; yet they are
'Nothingness' and 'empty'—they have no meaning and no value.
Only immaterial things are 'glorious' and 'divine', even though they
'don't exist' as the material things do. Contrasts of this type play an
important part in Mallarmé's poetry; and therefore it is tempting to
claim that the 1866 letter says 'the same thing' as the poetry, except
in a more lucid and comprehensible form.

Yet a Mallarmé whose verse had been written in that plain,
newspaper-editorialish style would no longer be remembered as a
poet; at most, he might have a certain documentary interest for
students of the history of thought. His best poetry derives its power
from the points at which it *differs* from a passage like the one above;
it gains strength from the fact that it is *not* written in 'plain
language'.

> When the shade threatened with the fatal decree
> that old Dream, my bones' craving and their blight,
> pained to die under the funereal height
> it bowed its doubt-less plumage deep in me.
>
> Splendour—ebony hall where, to allure
> a king, illustrious wreaths writhe in their doom—
> you are merely a pride lied by the gloom
> to the faith-dazzled Solitary viewer.
>
> Yes, Earth has cast into this night afar
> the startling mystery of sheer dazzlingness
> beneath dread aeons darkening it less.

Space, its own peer, whether it fail or grow
rolls in this tedium trivial fires to show
the genius kindled by a festive star.

Here, as in the letter, empty forms of matter (the 'trivial fires' of
'Space', for instance) are contrasted with the glorious falsehood of an
'old Dream'—but how much richer, how much more convincing, the
scene has become in the poem! The letter ostensibly drew a sharp
contrast between material and immaterial things: the former were
said to be empty though existing, the latter glorious though non-
existent; yet both were discussed in the same plain prose and lit by
the same clear light. The poem, on the other hand, is full of chiaro-
scuro. Its contrasts are not merely asserted, but embodied in the
grain and substance of its writing, so that its style follows—indeed,
clings to—the movement of its thought: the opening lines, for
instance, are shadowy, contorted, and flecked with obscure hints of
death ('fatal', 'funereal', 'die', 'doom'), whereas the final line is glow-
ing and resoundingly positive: 'the genius kindled by a festive star.'

Part of the strength of the poem, compared to the letter, lies in the
things it *avoids* saying. It 'shrouds itself in mystery'; many of its
details are dimly lit and uncertain, and a few of them simply cannot
be understood without more information than Mallarmé has sup-
plied (the identity of the 'king' in line 6, for example, is nowhere
revealed; numerous guesses can be—and have been!—made, but the
poem itself contains nothing to confirm any of them). Yet, by appear-
ing to say less it actually says more. The poem's 'trivial fires' and
'illustrious wreaths' may be less clear cut and less easily comprehen-
sible than the letter's 'empty forms of matter', yet their resonances
go deeper, their perspectives extend further. They convey a sense not
only of emptiness, but also of superficial glitter and apparent impres-
siveness; and they express the tentative, half-glimpsed insights of a
mere human observer, not the smooth omnisciences of a newspaper
columnist. Again, the poem gestures obliquely towards the Dream
('that old Dream') without attempting to define or elucidate it, and it
remains mysterious and evocative—dreamlike, in fact. The letter
attempts to bring it out into the cold light of day, to spell it out in
plain newspapery prose, or at least to give plain newspapery
examples of it ('God and our soul')—with the result that it loses its
dreamlike quality and becomes cheap and prosaic. In the letter we

see how much Mallarmé was a creature limited to his time and place, a contemporary of Comte, Renan, and Samuel Butler; in the poem his concerns might be those of Pindar or Dante, and as a result he speaks for all time.

Thus, no plain prose restatement of the substance of a Mallarmé poem—not even by Mallarmé himself—can be taken as a fair representation of its sense. The sense of the poem is the poem itself, with its obscurities as well as its clarities. Where the poem speaks of 'trivial fires', the reader should not reduce them to 'empty forms of matter'; where the poem says 'that old Dream', the reader should not interpret it as 'God and our soul'. This is not to say that paraphrases and plain prose restatements (whether by Mallarmé himself or by someone else) have no uses; we ourselves have attempted some in the notes at the back of this volume. But all such attempts should be regarded merely as preliminary scaffolding—scaffolding which fails to make contact with the underlying edifice at some points, and which extends absurdly far beyond it at others. When the edifice itself has been erected in the reader's mind, everything around it should be discarded, and it alone should be left. To the poems themselves we must ultimately return—even, or especially, when they seem most obscure, and when the temptation to depart from them is consequently greatest.

NOTE ON THE TEXT AND TRANSLATION

Anthologies of the conventional type, printing three or four poems by each of a large number of writers, have their place; but they suffer from a disadvantage memorably expressed by Hugh MacDiarmid: the disadvantage that 'cheek by jowl with Shakespeare and Milton must go . . . the incredibly small' (he names 'Waring' and Toke Lynch, Wathen Mark Call and Menella Bute Smedley). For most purposes, English-speaking readers would probably find a moderate-sized selection of Hugos and Baudelaires and Rimbauds more useful than a volume that interspersed two or three poems by each with a comparable number by (say) Banville, Coppée, Jean Moréas, and Francis Jammes. This was recognized long ago by H. E. Berthon, and his *Nine French Poets 1820–1880* (London, 1937), which 'deliberately left out of account the minor poets, in order to devote all available space to the few really great' ones, has had various successors. But those were French-only volumes; the present anthology applies the principle in a bilingual format.

Naturally, notions of the 'really great' vary: Berthon, for instance, included Musset and Vigny, yet ommited Rimbaud. The six nineteenth-century French poets in this volume are certainly among those who are most widely read and most frequently studied today. Furthermore, they are arguably the ones who have had the greatest historical influence on the course of French poetry; and between them they present a good cross-section of the varied styles and concerns of the century, early and late. But nobody should suppose that they are the only 'great' poets of the century, or even the 'best' ones.

In choosing individual poems by our six poets, we have aimed for variety—for a mixture of the lyric and the satiric, the narrative and the philosophical. Long poems as well as short ones are represented, since many of these writers worked mainly in large-scale forms. We have tried to include as many of the standard favourites as possible, though in a few cases, such as that of Hugo, there is little agreement as to which poems are the writer's 'best'. (Louis Aragon's celebrated Hugo selection consists almost entirely of 'political' poems, Jean Gaudon's of 'visionary' ones; the two volumes have scarcely an item in common!) In such cases we have tried not to follow any one party line, but to cater for a variety of tastes.

Nineteenth-century French poets seldom expected (or wanted) their work to be printed exactly as it stood in the original manuscript. Most of them used punctuation rather sparsely and unsystematically when writing; they expected such accidentals to be standardized by an editor before publication (which is not to say that editors could do whatever they liked: the 1859 edition of the *Légende des siècles* incurred Hugo's displeasure because it introduced capitals where he did *not* want them). Our copy-text, therefore, has usually been not a manuscript but an edition (generally the last) known to have been approved by its author: for Hugo, the *ne varietur* edition prepared by his close associate and literary executor Paul Meurice (Paris, 1880–5), which Hugo unequivocally approved in preference to its various predecessors, and the comparable edition of his posthumous *Dieu* (Paris, 1891), again prepared (as Hugo had requested) by Meurice; for Baudelaire, the second edition of *Les Fleurs du mal* (Paris, 1861); for Mallarmé, the volume of *Poésies* (Brussels, 1899) prepared shortly before his death. Where nineteenth-century texts vary but the author's preferences are unclear (this is the case with Lamartine and Verlaine, both of whom were erratic proof-readers and frequent victims of unauthorized editorial changes), we have arbitrarily adopted the same policy as the latest Pléiade editions—Lamartine, *Œuvres poétiques complètes*, edited by Marius-François Guyard (Paris, 1963), and Verlaine, *Œuvres poétiques complètes*, edited by Yves-Gérard Le Dantec, revised by Jacques Borel (Paris, 1962)—though with a few necessary corrections. The result is that our text follows the first editions except in the selections from Lamartine's *Méditations poétiques* (ninth edition, 1823) and Verlaine's *Sagesse* and *Amour* (second editions, 1889 and 1892 respectively). Rimbaud poses a different problem. Except, perhaps, for the *Saison en enfer*, none of his works was printed in a form he approved, so an edition must generally be based on manuscripts; but his manuscripts are littered with idiosyncratic spellings and punctuations—and which of those (if any) would he have allowed an editor to change? Since we cannot answer that question, we have (like most recent editors) preserved all his 'misspellings' as they stand.

Except for Hugo's unfinished 'Le Seuil du gouffre' ('The

Threshold of the Abyss'), all poems are printed complete. All editorial insertions are enclosed in square brackets.

Identifiable errors have been corrected. In the case of 'Le Seuil du gouffre' this has far-reaching consequences; thanks mainly to the various publications of René Journet and Guy Robert, we now know far more about the state of this poem at the time of Hugo's death than Meurice did in 1891, or indeed than Journet and Robert themselves did when they prepared their own edition in 1961, during the earliest phase of their labours. The present edition is the first to present the poem's opening section in the form which Hugo finally preferred, and to reconstruct as much of the crucial concluding section as the available materials will permit. Where Hugo's own final preferences cannot be determined from his surviving papers (e.g. where two alternative drafts of a line or phrase are left undeleted), we have naturally followed the choices made by Meurice (or, in the few passages not printed in 1891, by his most immediate successors).

The English translations of Baudelaire and Verlaine are drawn from the standard Oxford World's Classics editions: Charles Baudelaire, *The Flowers of Evil*, translated by James McGowan (Oxford, 1993), and Paul Verlaine, *Selected Poems*, translated by Martin Sorrell (Oxford, 1999); both volumes include a full account of the translators' policies. The language is present-day English; rhyme is sometimes used (where, in the translator's judgement, it would enhance rather than damage the rendering); the sense of the original French has been reproduced fairly closely, except when this would result in ugly, unreadable, or ineffective English. The translations of Rimbaud are from Professor Sorrell's forthcoming Rimbaud volume in the same series (Oxford, 2001). For Lamartine, Hugo, and Mallarmé, we have adopted a broadly similar policy, though with variations from poet to poet, to suggest something of the differences between the originals. (We did not want Lamartine to look more modern than Baudelaire, or Mallarmé more casual than Verlaine!) Hugo and Mallarmé are often regarded as (for very different reasons) the two most untranslatable poets in the French language; as Harold Bloom says, 'There are no adequate translations of Hugo's poetry, and there are not likely to be any' (*Victor Hugo* (New York, 1988), 2), while the old joke about Mallarmé being 'untranslatable even into French' has lost none of its shrewdness with the passage of the years. English renderings can only hint at the character of these notoriously elusive poems.

We are indebted to many readers, and especially to Oxford's anonymous reviewers, for valuable improvements, both in the choice of poems for inclusion and in the English translations. (Where different readers preferred different options, we have tried to do what appeared to suit the majority.) The quality of Judith Luna's editorial work has been a constant joy and encouragement to us. Finally, to Drs Warner and Erica Quarles de Quarles, and Dr and Mrs H. J. Blackmore, our debts go far beyond the confines of the present project—and perhaps even further beyond our ability to express.

SELECT BIBLIOGRAPHY

LAMARTINE

Translations

Alphonse de Lamartine, *Poetical Meditations/Méditations poétiques*, trans. Gervase Hittle (Lewiston, NY, 1993). Bilingual.
—— *Jocelyn: A Romance in Verse*, trans. Hazel Patterson Stuart (New York, 1954).

Critical Studies

Mary Ellen Birkett, *Lamartine and the Poetics of Language* (Lexington, Ky., 1982).
J. C. Ireson, *Lamartine: A Revaluation* (Hull, 1969).
Charles M. Lombard, *Lamartine* (New York, 1973).

Biographies

William Fortescue, *Alphonse de Lamartine: A Political Biography* (London, 1983).
H. Remson Whitehouse, *The Life of Lamartine*, 2 vols. (Boston, 1918).

HUGO

Translations

Victor Hugo, *The Last Day of a Condemned Man and Other Prison Writings*, trans. Geoff Woollen (Oxford, 1992).
—— *Notre-Dame de Paris*, trans. Alban Krailsheimer (Oxford, 1993).
—— *Poems*, trans. Sir George Young (London, 1901).
—— *The Distance, the Shadows*, trans. Harry Guest (London, 1981).
—— *Les Misérables*, trans. Lee Fahnestock and Norman MacAfee (New York, 1987).

Critical Studies

John Porter Houston, *Victor Hugo*, revised edn. (Boston, 1988).
J. C. Ireson, *Victor Hugo: A Companion to His Poetry* (Oxford, 1997).

Biographies

Adèle Hugo, *Victor Hugo by a Witness of his Life*, trans. Charles E. Wilbour (New York, 1863).
André Maurois, *Victor Hugo*, trans. Gerard Hopkins (London, 1956).
Graham Robb, *Victor Hugo* (London, 1997).

BAUDELAIRE

Translations

Charles Baudelaire, *The Flowers of Evil*, trans. James McGowan (Oxford, 1993). Bilingual.
—— *The Prose Poems and La Fanfarlo*, trans. Rosemary Lloyd (Oxford, 1991).
—— *Intimate Journals*, trans. Christopher Isherwood (London, 1930).

Critical Studies

Walter Benjamin, *Charles Baudelaire: A Lyric Poet in the Era of High Capitalism*, trans. Harry Zohn (London, 1973).
Alison Fairlie, *Baudelaire: Les Fleurs du mal* (London, 1960).
F. W. Leakey, *Baudelaire: Les Fleurs du mal* (Cambridge, 1992).

Biographies

Claude Pichois and Jean Ziegler, *Baudelaire*, trans. Graham Robb (London, 1989).
Jean-Paul Sartre, *Baudelaire*, trans. Martin Turnell (London, 1964).
Enid Starkie, *Baudelaire* (London, 1957).

VERLAINE

Translation

Paul Verlaine, *Selected Poems*, trans. Martin Sorrell (Oxford, 1999). Bilingual.

Critical Studies

Antoine Adam, *The Art of Paul Verlaine*, trans. Carl Morse (New York, 1963).
C. Chadwick, *Verlaine* (London, 1973).

Biographies

Edmond Lepelletier, *Paul Verlaine*, trans. Elsie M. Lang (New York, 1909).
A. E. Carter, *Verlaine: A Study in Parallels* (Toronto, 1965).

RIMBAUD

Translation

Arthur Rimbaud, *Selected Poems*, trans. Martin Sorrell (Oxford, forthcoming, 2001). Bilingual.

Critical Studies

W. M. Frohock, *Rimbaud's Poetic Practice* (Oxford, 1963).
C. A. Hackett, *Rimbaud: A Critical Introduction* (Cambridge, 1981).
F. C. St. Aubyn, *Arthur Rimbaud*, revised edn. (Boston, 1988).

Biographies

Pierre Petitfils, *Rimbaud*, trans. Alan Sheridan (Charlottesville, Va., 1987).
Enid Starkie, *Rimbaud*, revised edn. (London, 1961).

MALLARMÉ

Translation

Stephane Mallarmé, *Collected Poems*, trans. Henry Weinfield (Berkeley, Calif., 1994). Bilingual.

Critical Studies

Malcolm Bowie, *Mallarmé and the Art of Being Difficult* (Cambridge, 1978).
Robert Greer Cohn, *Toward the Poems of Mallarmé* (Berkeley, Calif., 1965).
Thomas M. Williams, *Mallarmé and the Language of Mysticism* (Athens, Ga., 1970).

Biography

Gordon Millan, *Mallarmé: A Throw of the Dice* (London, 1994).

FURTHER READING IN OXFORD WORLD'S CLASSICS

Flaubert, Gustave, *Madame Bovary*, trans. Gerard Hopkins.
Huysmans, Joris-Karl, *Against Nature (A Rebours)*, trans. Margaret Mauldon, ed. Nicholas White.
Sand, George, *The Master Pipers*, trans. Rosemary Lloyd.

CHRONOLOGY

1789 French Revolution.

1790 21 October: birth of Alphonse-Marie-Louis de Lamartine, at Mâcon.

1794 Fall of Robespierre; Lamartine's father is among the imprisoned aristocrats set free.

1799 Napoleon Bonaparte seizes power.

1802 26 February: birth of Victor-Marie Hugo, at Besançon.

1809–12 Hugo's father is a colonel (later general) in the Napoleonic army in Spain.

1814 Restoration of the Bourbon monarchy; Lamartine serves in Louis XVIII's bodyguard.

1815 Napoleon returns from exile (Lamartine takes refuge in Switzerland); battle of Waterloo.

1816 Lamartine's meeting with Julie Charles at Aix-les-Bains.

1817 August–September: Lamartine waits for Julie at Aix, in vain.
18 December: death of Julie Charles.

1820 Publication of Lamartine's *Poetic Meditations* (*Méditations poétiques*; enthusiastically reviewed by Hugo); Lamartine becomes secretary to the French embassy at Naples.

1821 9 April: birth of Charles-Pierre Baudelaire, in Paris.

1822 Publication of Hugo's first volume, *Odes and Other Poems* (*Odes et poésies diverses*).

1829 Publication of Hugo's *Orientalia* (*Les Orientales*); Lamartine is elected to the French Academy.

1830 First performance of Hugo's play *Hernani*; publication of Lamartine's *Poetic and Religious Harmonies* (*Harmonies poétiques et religieuses*).
July: Overthrow of the Bourbon monarchy; constitutional monarchy established under Louis-Philippe.

1831 Publication of Hugo's novel *Notre-Dame de Paris*.

1836 Publication of Lamartine's verse novel *Jocelyn*.

1841 Hugo is elected to the French Academy.

1842 18 March: birth of Stephane Mallarmé, in Paris.

1843 4 September: Hugo's 19-year-old daughter Léopoldine and her husband are drowned in a boating accident at Villequier.

1844 30 March: birth of Paul-Marie Verlaine, at Metz.

1845 First magazine publication of a poem by Baudelaire.

1848 24 February: overthrow of Louis-Philippe's government;

establishment of the Second Republic, with Lamartine as effective head of government till June.

4 June: Hugo is elected to the Constituent Assembly.

1849   Subscribers' Edition of Lamartine's works, including the *Further Poetic Meditations* (*Méditations poétiques inédites*).

1851   2 December: Napoleon III seizes power; Hugo is exiled from France and takes refuge in Belgium, Jersey (1852–5), and Guernsey (1855–70).

1853   Publication of Hugo's *The Empire in the Pillory* (*Les Châtiments*).

1854   20 October: birth of Jean-Arthur Rimbaud, at Charleville-Mézières.

1855–6   Hugo writes *God* (*Dieu*, not published till 1891).

1856   Publication of Hugo's *Contemplations* (*Les Contemplations*).

1857   Publication of Baudelaire's *The Flowers of Evil* (*Les Fleurs du mal*); Baudelaire is convicted of offences against public decency. (Hugo to Baudelaire, 30 August: 'you have just been awarded one of the few honours that the present French Government has the power to bestow.')

1858   Verlaine writes to Hugo, enclosing his earliest surviving verses.

1859   Publication of the First Series of Hugo's *The Legend of the Ages* (*La Légende des siècles*).

1861   Second edition of Baudelaire's *The Flowers of Evil*.

1862   First magazine publication of poems by Mallarmé; publication of Hugo's *Les Misérables*, enthusiastically received by the public but reviewed rather severely by Lamartine ('a swan trying to bite', says Hugo).

1863   First meeting of Verlaine and Mallarmé; they remain firm friends thereafter.

1864   One of Mallarmé's early prose poems attracts Baudelaire's attention ('clever, but not quite true', he remarks in his journal).

1866   Baudelaire collapses; development of paralysis and dysphasia.

Publication of Verlaine's first volume, *Saturnian Poems* (*Poèmes saturniens*).

1867   16 February: death of Verlaine's beloved cousin Élisa.

31 August: death of Baudelaire, in Paris; Verlaine attends the funeral.

1869   Publication of Verlaine's *Fêtes galantes* (an unusually delighted Hugo writes to Verlaine, praising the 'many deft and clever things' in it).

28 February: death of Lamartine, in Paris.

1870   First magazine publication of a poem by Rimbaud; publication of Verlaine's *La Bonne Chanson*.

         19 July: Napoleon III declares war on Prussia.

         11 August: Verlaine marries Mathilde Mauté (1853–1914).

         31 August: defeat of the French army at Sedan.

         4 September: proclamation of the Third Republic; Napoleon III flees to England.

         5 September: Hugo returns to France.

1871   March–May: the Paris Commune, bloodily suppressed by the end of May.

         10 September: Rimbaud arrives in Paris, where he stays with Verlaine and his wife, aggravating an already troubled domestic situation.

1872   July: Verlaine deserts his wife and travels with Rimbaud to Belgium, then to England.

1873   April–May: Rimbaud on his mother's farm at Roche.

         May–July: Verlaine and Rimbaud together again in England and Belgium.

         10 July: during one of their quarrels Verlaine shoots Rimbaud, wounding him in the wrist; he is sentenced to two years' imprisonment.

         October: Rimbaud's *A Season in Hell* (*Une Saison en enfer*) is printed, but not distributed for sale.

1874   Publication of Verlaine's *Songs Without Words* (*Romances sans paroles*).

         June: Verlaine is converted to Roman Catholicism.

1875   Verlaine is released from prison; he meets Rimbaud for the last time at Stuttgart, then works as a schoolteacher in England for two years.

1875–80 Rimbaud travels widely (Germany, Italy, Austria, the Netherlands, Indonesia, Sweden, Denmark, Aden).

1876   Publication of Mallarmé's *A Faun in the Afternoon* (*L'Après-midi d'un faune*, limited edition).

1877   Publication of Hugo's *The Art of Being a Grandfather* (*L'Art d'être grand-père*) and the New Series of *The Legend of the Ages*.

1878   Hugo suffers a severe cerebrovascular stroke; he writes very little new work thereafter.

1880   Publication of Verlaine's *Wisdom* (*Sagesse*).

         13 December: Rimbaud arrives in Abyssinia, where he stays till 1891, working as a trader.

1883   Publication of the Last Volume and Definitive Edition of Hugo's *The Legend of the Ages*; publication of Verlaine's *Les*

Poètes maudits, prose studies drawing attention to three little-known poets: Rimbaud, Mallarmé, and Tristan Corbière.

1884   Publication of Verlaine's *Once Upon a Time* (*Jadis et naguère*).

1885   22 May: death of Victor Hugo, in Paris.

1886   Publication of Hugo's *The End of Satan* (*La Fin de Satan*) and (without the author's knowledge) Rimbaud's *Illuminations*.

1888   Publication of Verlaine's *Love* (*Amour*).

1889   Publication of Verlaine's *In Parallel* (*Parallèlement*).

1891   Publication of Hugo's *God* and Verlaine's *Happiness* (*Bonheur*). February: Rimbaud, suffering from a malignant tumour of the knee, returns to France.

        10 November: death of Rimbaud, at Marseilles.

1894   Publication of Verlaine's last volumes of poetry, *In Limbo* (*Dans les limbes*) and *Epigrams* (*Épigrammes*).

1896   8 January: death of Verlaine, in Paris; Mallarmé gives a speech at his funeral.

1898   9 September: death of Mallarmé, at Valvins.

1899   Publication of Mallarmé's *Poems* (*Poésies*).

1902   Publication of Hugo's *Last Gleanings* (*Dernière gerbe*).

SIX FRENCH POETS
OF THE
NINETEENTH CENTURY

ALPHONSE DE LAMARTINE

from *Méditations poétiques*

1. L'Isolement

Souvent sur la montagne, à l'ombre du vieux chêne,
Au coucher du soleil, tristement je m'assieds;
Je promène au hasard mes regards sur la plaine,
Dont le tableau changeant se déroule à mes pieds.

Ici, gronde le fleuve aux vagues écumantes: 5
Il serpente, et s'enfonce en un lointain obscur;
Là, le lac immobile étend ses eaux dormantes
Où l'étoile du soir se lève dans l'azur.

Au sommet de ces monts couronnés de bois sombres,
Le crépuscule encor jette un dernier rayon;   10
Et le char vaporeux de la reine des ombres
Monte, et blanchit déjà les bords de l'horizon.

Cependant, s'élançant de la flèche gothique,
Un son religieux se répand dans les airs,
Le voyageur s'arrête, et la cloche rustique   15
Aux derniers bruits du jour mêle de saints concerts.

Mais à ces doux tableaux mon âme indifférente
N'éprouve devant eux ni charme, ni transports,
Je contemple la terre, ainsi qu'une ombre errante:
Le soleil des vivants n'échauffe plus les morts.   20

De colline en colline en vain portant ma vue,
Du sud à l'aquilon, de l'aurore au couchant,
Je parcours tous les points de l'immense étendue,
Et je dis: Nulle part le bonheur ne m'attend.

TRANSLATED BY E. H. AND A. M. BLACKMORE

from *Poetic Meditations*

Isolation

On the mountain, in the old oak's domain,
Often at dusk I sadly take my seat,
And glance haphazardly across the plain
Whose varied scene unfolds beneath my feet.

Here growls the river with its frothy surge:
It winds far off, and vanishes from view;
There the calm lake extends its sleeping verge
Where evening's star arises in the blue.

On these dark woods crowning the mountains' height
Twilight is sending out its final ray,
While the blurred chariot of the queen of night
Rises, and pales the skyline far away.

Meanwhile the ringing of a Gothic bell
Casts a religious sound across the breeze;
The traveller pauses, and the rustic knell
With day's last noise blends sacred harmonies.

Yet my soul, unmoved by this pleasant view,
Feels neither charmed with it nor comforted;
I see the earth as wandering spirits do:
The sun of the living never warms the dead.

Vainly from hill to hill, look where I may,
From south to north, from dawn to dusk, I stare;
I scan the whole of the vast realm, and say:
'There is no happiness for me anywhere.'

Que me font ces vallons, ces palais, ces chaumières?   25
Vains objets dont pour moi le charme est envolé;
Fleuves, rochers, forêts, solitudes si chères,
Un seul être vous manque, et tout est dépeuplé.

Que le tour du soleil ou commence ou s'achève,
D'un œil indifférent je le suis dans son cours;   30
En un ciel sombre ou pur qu'il se couche ou se lève,
Qu'importe le soleil? je n'attends rien des jours.

Quand je pourrais le suivre en sa vaste carrière,
Mes yeux verraient partout le vide et les déserts;
Je ne désire rien de tout ce qu'il éclaire,   35
Je ne demande rien à l'immense univers.

Mais peut-être au delà des bornes de sa sphère,
Lieux où le vrai soleil éclaire d'autres cieux,
Si je pouvais laisser ma dépouille à la terre,
Ce que j'ai tant rêvé paraîtrait à mes yeux?   40

Là, je m'enivrerais à la source où j'aspire,
Là, je retrouverais et l'espoir et l'amour,
Et ce bien idéal que toute âme désire,
Et qui n'a pas de nom au terrestre séjour!

Que ne puis-je, porté sur le char de l'aurore,   45
Vague objet de mes vœux, m'élancer jusqu'à toi;
Sur la terre d'exil pourquoi resté-je encore?
Il n'est rien de commun entre la terre et moi.

Quand la feuille des bois tombe dans la prairie,
Le vent du soir s'élève et l'arrache aux vallons;
Et moi, je suis semblable à la feuille flétrie: 50
Emportez-moi comme elle, orageux aquilons!

What are these vales, towers, cottages to me?
Vain things, whose charm for me has long abated;
Streams, rocks, woods—places loved and solitary—
One creature goes... all is depopulated.

Whether the passing sun may set or rise,
With an indifferent eye I watch its way;
It comes or goes, through clear or cloudy skies—
No matter! I have no hope any day.

If I could follow it throughout its flights,
Everywhere I should see voids, wastes, and worse;
I care for none of all the things it lights,
I ask for nothing of the universe.

Yet perhaps past the boundaries of its sphere,
Where the true Sun enlightens other skies,
If I could leave my trappings on earth here,
What I have dreamed might stand before my eyes.

Filled at the fountain to which I aspire,
There I might find both hope and love once more—
The ideal goodness that all souls desire,
Which never can be named on this world's shore!

O that, within Dawn's chariot, I were sent
To the dim object of my longings there!
Why linger in the land of banishment?
The earth and I have nothing that we share.

When forest leaves fall in the open waste,
The night wind, rising, blows them from the vales;
And I am such a leaf, dry and debased:
Sweep me away like them, you stormy gales!

VI. Le Vallon

Mon cœur, lassé de tout, même de l'espérance,
N'ira plus de ses vœux importuner le sort;
Prêtez-moi seulement, vallons de mon enfance,
Un asile d'un jour pour attendre la mort.

Voici l'étroit sentier de l'obscure vallée: 5
Du flanc de ces coteaux pendent des bois épais
Qui, courbant sur mon front leur ombre entremêlée,
Me couvrent tout entier de silence et de paix.

Là, deux ruisseaux cachés sous des ponts de verdure
Tracent en serpentant les contours du vallon;   10
Ils mêlent un moment leur onde et leur murmure,
Et non loin de leur source ils se perdent sans nom.

La source de mes jours comme eux s'est écoulée;
Elle a passé sans bruit, sans nom, et sans retour:
Mais leur onde est limpide, et mon âme troublée   15
N'aura pas réfléchi les clartés d'un beau jour.

La fraîcheur de leurs lits, l'ombre qui les couronne,
M'enchaînent tout le jour sur les bords des ruisseaux;
Comme un enfant bercé par un chant monotone,
Mon âme s'assoupit au murmure des eaux.   20

Ah! c'est là qu'entouré d'un rempart de verdure,
D'un horizon borné qui suffit à mes yeux,
J'aime à fixer mes pas, et, seul dans la nature,
A n'entendre que l'onde, à ne voir que les cieux.

J'ai trop vu, trop senti, trop aimé dans la vie,   25
Je viens chercher vivant le calme du Léthé;
Beaux lieux, soyez pour moi ces bords où l'on oublie:
L'oubli seul désormais est ma félicité.

The Valley

Tired of all things—with even hope put by—
My heart asks nothing more that fate can give;
Only, you vales in which I used to live,
Grant me a day's rest while I wait to die.

Here is the valley's path, obscure and small:
Across its slopes dense hanging woods are spread.
Their tangled shadows bend above my head,
And silence and repose envelop all.

There, two brooks wander, hidden under green
Bridges, and trace the valley's winding ground;
Briefly they blend their water and their sound,
Then, near their source, pass nameless from the scene.

Like theirs, my own life's source has flowed away,
Has passed without a name, silent and whole;
Their stream is clear, though—while my troubled soul
Never mirrors the gleam of one fine day.

The sparkle of their beds, their crowning shades,
Chain me to the streams' borders all day long;
Like a child lulled by a monotonous song,
My soul is soothed by murmuring cascades.

Ah! there, where all around green ramparts rise,
Where only close horizons can be viewed,
I love to pause in Nature's solitude,
To hear and see nothing but surge and skies.

I have known too much passion, love, and fret;
Now, living, I am seeking Lethe's peace.
May these fair banks be where my memories cease:
My sole remaining joy is to forget.

Mon cœur est en repos, mon âme est en silence!
Le bruit lointain du monde expire en arrivant,   30
Comme un son éloigné qu'affaiblit la distance,
A l'oreille incertaine apporté par le vent.

D'ici je vois la vie, à travers un nuage,
S'évanouir pour moi dans l'ombre du passé;
L'amour seul est resté: comme une grande image   35
Survit seule au réveil dans un songe effacé.

Repose-toi, mon âme, en ce dernier asile,
Ainsi qu'un voyageur, qui, le cœur plein d'espoir,
S'assied avant d'entrer aux portes de la ville,
Et respire un moment l'air embaumé du soir.   40

Comme lui, de nos pieds secouons la poussière;
L'homme par ce chemin ne repasse jamais:
Comme lui, respirons au bout de la carrière
Ce calme avant-coureur de l'éternelle paix.

Tes jours, sombres et courts comme des jours d'automne,   45
Déclinent comme l'ombre au penchant des coteaux;
L'amitié te trahit, la pitié t'abandonne,
Et, seule, tu descends le sentier des tombeaux.

Mais la nature est là qui t'invite et qui t'aime;
Plonge-toi dans son sein qu'elle t'ouvre toujours;   50
Quand tout change pour toi, la nature est la même,
Et le même soleil se lève sur tes jours.

De lumière et d'ombrage elle t'entoure encore;
Détache ton amour des faux biens que tu perds;
Adore ici l'écho qu'adorait Pythagore,   55
Prête avec lui l'oreille aux célestes concerts.

Suis le jour dans le ciel, suis l'ombre sur la terre,
Dans les plaines de l'air vole avec l'aquilon,
Avec les doux rayons de l'astre du mystère
Glisse à travers les bois dans l'ombre du vallon.   60

My soul is quiet, and my heart is clear!
The world's far noise, on its way to me, dies,
Like a faint sound which distance nullifies,
Carried on breezes to a doubtful ear.

From here I see life, through a misty steam,
Vanishing in the shadow of the past;
Love alone remains: as, alone, one vast
Image stays, when we waken from a dream.

Rest, then, my soul, within this final lair,
Like travellers of hopeful spirit, who
Sit at the town gates before passing through,
And breathe awhile the scented evening air.

Let us, like them, shake the dust from our shoes—
For people never pass again this way—
And breathe, like them, this calm at close of day,
To which an everlasting peace ensues.

Your days, like autumn days, dim, quickly flown,
Decline as shadows on the hillsides do;
Friendship betrays, pity abandons you,
You tread the road down to the grave alone.

Yet Nature kindly cares for you always;
Cling to the breast she constantly bestows;
When all things alter, Nature never goes,
The same sun still keeps rising on your days.

With light and dark she swathes you steadfastly;
Sever your love from fading lies; revere
The echo, like Pythagoras; and hear,
As he did, the celestial harmony.

In the sky pursue light, on the earth shade;
With the wind, fly the airy realms afar;
With the soft rays of the mysterious star,
Slip through the woods into the darkened glade.

Dieu, pour le concevoir, a fait l'intelligence;
Sous la nature enfin découvre son auteur!
Une voix à l'esprit parle dans son silence,
Qui n'a pas entendu cette voix dans son cœur?

XIII. Le Lac

Ainsi, toujours poussés vers de nouveaux rivages,
Dans la nuit éternelle emportés sans retour,
Ne pourrons-nous jamais sur l'océan des âges
      Jeter l'ancre un seul jour?

O lac! l'année à peine a fini sa carrière,   5
Et près des flots chéris qu'elle devait revoir,
Regarde! je viens seul m'asseoir sur cette pierre
      Où tu la vis s'asseoir!

Tu mugissais ainsi sous ces roches profondes,
Ainsi tu te brisais sur leurs flancs déchirés,   10
Ainsi le vent jetait l'écume de tes ondes
      Sur ses pieds adorés.

Un soir, t'en souvient-il? nous voguions en silence;
On n'entendait au loin, sur l'onde et sous les cieux,
Que le bruit des rameurs qui frappaient en cadence   15
      Tes flots harmonieux.

Tout à coup des accents inconnus à la terre
Du rivage charmé frappèrent les échos:
Le flot fut attentif, et la voix qui m'est chère
      Laissa tomber ces mots: 20

« O temps! suspends ton vol, et vous, heures propices!
      Suspendez votre cours:
Laissez-nous savourer les rapides délices
      Des plus beaux de nos jours!

God made the intellect to know the whole:
In Nature, find her Author if you will!
A voice speaks to the heart when all is still:
Who never heard that voice within his soul?

The Lake

So, driven to new shores incessantly,
Into eternal darkness swept away,
Are we never to anchor on time's sea
    Even for one sole day?

O lake, although a year has scarcely flown,
To the waves she was due to see again
I alone come to sit upon this stone
    Where she was sitting then!

You rolled beneath those rocks in the same way;
On the same rugged banks you used to beat;
And from your surge the wind tossed the same spray
    About her lovely feet.

One night, beneath the skies, far from the shores—
Do you recall?—we sailed without a word;
Only the rowers, beating rhythmic oars
    On murmuring waves, were heard.

Then tones that Earth had never learnt to tell
Suddenly echoed on the spellbound sea:
The surge attended, and these sayings fell
    From the voice dear to me:

'You favourable hours, pause in your flight!
    O time, pause on your way!
Let us enjoy the transient delight
    Of this our fairest day!

« Assez de malheureux ici-bas vous implorent,   25
        Coulez, coulez pour eux;
Prenez avec leurs jours les soins qui les dévorent,
        Oubliez les heureux.

« Mais je demande en vain quelques moments encore,
        Le temps m'échappe et fuit;   30
Je dis à cette nuit: Sois plus lente; et l'aurore
        Va dissiper la nuit.

« Aimons donc, aimons donc! de l'heure fugitive,
        Hâtons-nous, jouissons!
L'homme n'a point de port, le temps n'a point de rive;   35
        Il coule, et nous passons! »

Temps jaloux, se peut-il que ces moments d'ivresse,
Où l'amour à longs flots nous verse le bonheur,
S'envolent loin de nous de la même vitesse
        Que les jours du malheur?   40

Eh quoi! n'en pourrons-nous fixer au moins la trace?
Quoi! passés pour jamais! quoi! tout entiers perdus!
Ce temps qui les donna, ce temps qui les efface,
        Ne nous le rendra plus!

Éternité, néant, passé, sombres abîmes,   45
Que faites-vous des jours que vous engloutissez?
Parlez: nous rendrez-vous ces extases sublimes
        Que vous nous ravissez?

O lac! rochers muets! grottes! forêt obscure!
Vous, que le temps épargne ou qu'il peut rajeunir,   50
Gardez de cette nuit, gardez, belle nature,
        Au moins le souvenir!

Qu'il soit dans ton repos, qu'il soit dans tes orages,
Beau lac, et dans l'aspect de tes riants coteaux,
Et dans ces noirs sapins, et dans ces rocs sauvages   55
        Qui pendent sur tes eaux.

'Enough unhappy creatures pray to you;
    For them, flow and be spent:
Remove their days, remove their sufferings too;
    Leave those who are content.

'But vainly do I beg time to delay;
    It slips away in flight;
I ask tonight to linger on—yet day
    Must dissipate the night.

'Then let us love—enjoy without a pause
    The hour so quickly gone!
Man has no harbour, and time has no shores;
    It flows, and we pass on.'

Cruel time, can such hours of intoxication,
When love pours happiness so lavishly,
Pass from us with as quick a transformation
    As days of misery?

What! can we never keep, at least, some traces?
Vanished for ever? all lost in the black?
Can the time that gave then, and now effaces,
    Never once bring them back?

Eternity, void, past—dark cavities—
What do you do with days you swallow thus?
Will you never restore the ecstasies
    That you have snatched from us?

Lake, silent rocks, caves, forests dark and deep,
Whom time has spared, or whom it can revive,
Keep at least some of that night, Nature—keep
    Its memory alive!

Let it be in your calms and in your storms,
Fair lake, and in the smilings at your verge,
And in the black pines, and the rocky forms
    That overhang your surge!

Qu'il soit dans le zéphyr qui frémit et qui passe,
Dans les bruits de tes bords par tes bords répétés,
Dans l'astre au front d'argent qui blanchit ta surface
    De ses molles clartés.   60

Que le vent qui gémit, le roseau qui soupire,
Que les parfums légers de ton air embaumé,
Que tout ce qu'on entend, l'on voit ou l'on respire,
    Tout dise: Ils ont aimé!

XXIX. L'Automne

Salut! bois couronnés d'un reste de verdure!
Feuillages jaunissants sur les gazons épars!
Salut, derniers beaux jours! le deuil de la nature
Convient à la douleur et plaît à mes regards!

Je suis d'un pas rêveur le sentier solitaire,   5
J'aime à revoir encor, pour la dernière fois,
Ce soleil pâlissant, dont la faible lumière
Perce à peine à mes pieds l'obscurité des bois!

Oui, dans ces jours d'automne où la nature expire,
A ses regards voilés, je trouve plus d'attraits,   10
C'est l'adieu d'un ami, c'est le dernier sourire
Des lèvres que la mort va fermer pour jamais!

Ainsi, prêt à quitter l'horizon de la vie,
Pleurant de mes longs jours l'espoir évanoui,
Je me retourne encore, et d'un regard d'envie   15
Je contemple ses biens dont je n'ai pas joui!

Terre, soleil, vallons, belle et douce nature,
Je vous dois une larme aux bords de mon tombeau;
L'air est si parfumé! la lumière est si pure!
Aux regards d'un mourant le soleil est si beau!   20

Let it be in the breeze that stirs and goes,
In the sounds that resound beside your stream,
In the silver-browed star that lights your flows
    With such a gentle gleam!

And let the reeds that sigh, the winds that keen,
The light scent of your fragrant air above,
Let all things that are breathed, or heard, or seen,
    Declare: 'Yes—they did love!'

Autumn

Welcome, woods crowned with sparse remains of green,
Yellowing leafage on the scanty lawn!
Last fine days, welcome! such a dismal scene
Pleases my taste—is fit for those who mourn!

I trace the lone path with a pensive tread;
I love—for the last time—to see again
This pale sun where I walk, struggling to shed
Its feeble light into the dusky glen!

Yes, in these autumn days, when Nature dies,
Her fading glances rather gladden me—
A friend's last greeting, the last smile to rise
On lips that death will close eternally!

So, grieving for lost hopes of longer days,
As I am drawing near life's boundary-line
I turn again, and with an envious gaze
I view the blessings that were never mine.

Earth, sun, vales—Nature, fair and marvellous—
I mourn you from the margin of the tomb;
To dying eyes, the sun is glorious!
The light is pure! the air has such perfume!

Je voudrais maintenant vider jusqu'à la lie
Ce calice mêlé de nectar et de fiel!
Au fond de cette coupe où je buvais la vie,
Peut-être restait-il une goutte de miel?

Peut-être l'avenir me gardait-il encore   25
Un retour de bonheur dont l'espoir est perdu?
Peut-être dans la foule, une âme que j'ignore
Aurait compris mon âme, et m'aurait répondu?...

La fleur tombe en livrant ses parfums au zéphire;
A la vie, au soleil, ce sont là ses adieux;   30
Moi, je meurs; et mon âme, au moment qu'elle expire,
S'exhale comme un son triste et mélodieux.

from *Harmonies poétiques et religieuses*

II.ii. L'Occident

Et la mer s'apaisait, comme une urne écumante
Qui s'abaisse au moment où le foyer pâlit,
Et retirant du bord sa vague encor fumante,
Comme pour s'endormir, rentrait dans son grand lit;

Et l'astre qui tombait de nuage en nuage   5
Suspendait sur les flots un orbe sans rayon,
Puis plongeait la moitié de sa sanglante image,
Comme un navire en feu qui sombre à l'horizon;

Et la moitié du ciel pâlissait, et la brise
Défaillait dans la voile, immobile et sans voix,   10
Et les ombres couraient, et sous leur teinte grise
Tout sur le ciel et l'eau s'effaçait à la fois;

Now I would rather empty to the last
This drink of mixed ambrosia and gall!
In the cup where I drained life in the past,
Could drops of honey linger after all?

Perhaps, stored in the future, might still be
Some happiness when hope has all gone by;
Within the crowd, a soul unknown to me
Might understand my soul, and might reply...

The falling blossom leaves the breeze her scent;
To life, to sunlight, that is her farewell;
I too die; and my soul, as it is spent,
Breathes out its mournful and melodious knell.

from *Poetic and Religious Harmonies*

The West

And, as a boiling vessel cools once more
When the fire fades, the sea was quieted:
Drawing its still-white surge back from the shore
As if for sleep, it entered its vast bed;

And the sun, falling through the cloud-banks, lay
Suspended on the waves, a rayless sphere;
Then, as a burning ship sinks far away,
Its blood-red disc half dropped past the frontier;

And half the heavens faded, and the breeze
Failed in the air, still, and without a sigh;
Shadows rushed in, and their grey draperies
Effaced all things at sea and in the sky;

Et dans mon âme, aussi pâlissant à mesure,
Tous les bruits d'ici-bas tombaient avec le jour,
Et quelque chose en moi, comme dans la nature,   15
Pleurait, priait, souffrait, bénissait tour à tour!

Et vers l'occident seul, une porte éclatante
Laissait voir la lumière à flots d'or ondoyer,
Et la nue empourprée imitait une tente
Qui voile sans l'éteindre un immense foyer;   20

Et les ombres, les vents, et les flots de l'abîme,
Vers cette arche de feu tout paraissait courir,
Comme si la nature et tout ce qui l'anime
En perdant la lumière avait craint de mourir!

La poussière du soir y volait de la terre,   25
L'écume à blancs flocons sur la vague y flottait;
Et mon regard long, triste, errant, involontaire,
Les suivait, et de pleurs sans chagrin s'humectait.

Et tout disparaissait; et mon âme oppressée
Restait vide et pareille à l'horizon couvert,   30
Et puis il s'élevait une seule pensée,
Comme une pyramide au milieu du désert!

O lumière! où vas-tu? Globe épuisé de flamme,
Nuages, aquilons, vagues, où courez-vous?
Poussière, écume, nuit! vous, mes yeux! toi, mon âme!   35
Dites, si vous savez, où donc allons-nous tous?

A toi, grand Tout! dont l'astre est la pâle étincelle,
En qui la nuit, le jour, l'esprit, vont aboutir!
Flux et reflux divin de vie universelle,
Vaste océan de l'Être où tout va s'engloutir!...   40

And in my own soul, fading comparably,
All worldly noises sank down with the day;
And, as in Nature, something deep in me
Began to weep and bless and ache and pray.

Westward alone one gate was prominent,
Revealing light rippling with gold attire,
And the encrimsoned cloud was like a tent
That veils but does not quench a mighty fire;

The shadows, the gulf-waves, the winds astir—
Toward that fiery arch all seemed to fly,
As if Nature and all that quickens her,
Losing the light, was now afraid to die!

The twilit dust sped to it from the ground,
The white spray on the waves went rolling there;
And my slow, sad gaze, idly straying round,
Grew moist with tears painless and unaware.

And all things vanished, and my troubled soul
Remained as vacant as the shrouded land;
Then one thought rose up solitary and whole,
Like a great pyramid in the desert sand.

O light—spent globe of fire—where do you go?
Clouds, winds, and waves, where are you running thus?
Dust, spray, night—eyes, soul of mine—if you know,
Tell us where we are going, all of us!

To you, great Whole! The sun is your dim glow,
In you night, day, and spirit meet their end—
Ubiquitous life's sacred ebb and flow,
Vast sea of Being, in which all must blend!...

II.iv. L'Infini dans les cieux

C'est une nuit d'été; nuit dont les vastes ailes
Font jaillir dans l'azur des milliers d'étincelles;
Qui, ravivant le ciel comme un miroir terni,
Permet à l'œil charmé d'en sonder l'infini;
Nuit où le firmament, dépouillé de nuages,   5
De ce livre de feu rouvre toutes les pages!
Sur le dernier sommet des monts, d'où le regard
Dans un double horizon se répand au hasard,
Je m'assieds en silence, et laisse ma pensée
Flotter comme une mer où la lune est bercée.   10

L'harmonieux Éther, dans ses vagues d'azur,
Enveloppe les monts d'un fluide plus pur;
Leurs contours qu'il éteint, leurs cimes qu'il efface,
Semblent nager dans l'air et trembler dans l'espace,
Comme on voit jusqu'au fond d'une mer en repos   15
L'ombre de son rivage onduler sous les flots!
Sous ce jour sans rayon, plus serein qu'une aurore,
A l'œil contemplatif la terre semble éclore;
Elle déroule au loin ses horizons divers
Où se joua la main qui sculpta l'univers!   20
Là, semblable à la vague, une colline ondule,
Là le coteau poursuit le coteau qui recule,
Et le vallon, voilé de verdoyants rideaux,
Se creuse comme un lit pour l'ombre et pour les eaux;
Ici s'étend la plaine, où, comme sur la grève,   25
La vague des épis s'abaisse et se relève;
Là, pareil au serpent dont les nœuds sont rompus,
Le fleuve, renouant ses flots interrompus,
Trace à son cours d'argent des méandres sans nombre,
Se perd sous la colline et reparaît dans l'ombre;   30
Comme un nuage noir, les profondes forêts
D'une tache grisâtre ombragent les guérets,
Et plus loin, où la plage en croissant se reploie,
Où le regard confus dans les vapeurs se noie,
Un golfe de la mer, d'îles entrecoupé,   35

The Infinite in the Skies

A summer night—a night whose wide-spread wings
Strike in the azure myriad sparkling things;
Freshening the tarnished mirror of the sky,
Showing its boundlessness to the tranced eye;
A night when the unclouded firmament
Opens that fire-book to its full extent!
On the mountaintop, from which sight strays out
Across the dual horizon round about,
I sit in silence, letting my thoughts spread
Like waters where the moon is quieted.

In its blue waves, harmonious Ether drapes
With purer fluid all the highland capes;
Each erased peak, each half-extinguished trace,
Seemingly swims in air, flutters in space,
As we see, rippling in the liquid floor
Of sleeping seas, the phantom of their shore.
Beneath this rayless light calmer than dawn,
To meditative eyes Earth seems reborn;
Her various far horizons are unfurled—
The playthings of the hand that shaped the world!
There, like a wave, a hilltop drifts and glides;
Mountainsides chase receding mountainsides;
Valleys meanwhile, in verdant folds arrayed,
Hollow themselves like beds for stream and shade;
Here spreads the plain, where, as on the sea's shore,
Whole waves of wheat plunge down and rise once more;
There, like a serpent with disjointed bends,
The river links its disconnected ends,
Weaves countless loops into its silver braid,
Sinks at the hill, reappears in the glade;
While massive forest depths, like a black cloud,
Darken the furrows with a greyish shroud,
And further off, where the shore bends and twists,
Where sight grows blurred and vanishes in mists,
An ocean gulf with islands specked and strewn—

Des blancs reflets du ciel par la lune frappé,
Comme un vaste miroir, brisé sur la poussière,
Réfléchit dans l'obscur des fragments de lumière.

Que le séjour de l'homme est divin, quand la nuit
De la vie orageuse étouffe ainsi le bruit!   40
Ce sommeil qui d'en haut tombe avec la rosée
Et ralentit le cours de la vie épuisée,
Semble planer aussi sur tous les éléments,
Et de tout ce qui vit calmer les battements;
Un silence pieux s'étend sur la nature,   45
Le fleuve a son éclat, mais n'a plus son murmure,
Les chemins sont déserts, les chaumières sans voix,
Nulle feuille ne tremble à la voûte des bois,
Et la mer elle-même, expirant sur sa rive,
Roule à peine à la plage une lame plaintive;   50
On dirait, en voyant ce monde sans échos,
Où l'oreille jouit d'un magique repos,
Où tout est majesté, crépuscule, silence,
Et dont le regard seul atteste l'existence,
Que l'on contemple en songe, à travers le passé,   55
Le fantôme d'un monde où la vie a cessé!
Seulement, dans les troncs des pins aux larges cimes,
Dont les groupes épars croissent sur ces abîmes,
L'haleine de la nuit, qui se brise parfois,
Répand de loin en loin d'harmonieuses voix,   60
Comme pour attester, dans leur cime sonore,
Que ce monde, assoupi, palpite et vit encore.

Un monde est assoupi sous la voûte des cieux?
Mais dans la voûte même où s'élèvent mes yeux,
Que de mondes nouveaux, que de soleils sans nombre,   65
Trahis par leur splendeur, étincellent dans l'ombre!
Les signes épuisés s'usent à les compter,
Et l'âme infatigable est lasse d'y monter!
Les siècles, accusant leur alphabet stérile,
De ces astres sans fin n'ont nommé qu'un sur mille;   70
Que dis-je! Aux bords des cieux, ils n'ont vu qu'ondoyer
Les mourantes lueurs de ce lointain foyer;

Pale glints of heaven lit up by the moon—
Like a vast mirror broken on the ground,
In the gloom scatters scraps of light around.

How godlike man's state is, when night transforms
Into such murmurs all life's noisy storms!
This sleep that falls from heaven with the dew,
Relaxing life's exhausted avenue,
Seems to suffuse the elements, and bring
Calm to the pulse of every living thing.
Throughout creation sacred peace is spread:
Streams shimmer on, and yet no sound is shed;
Paths are deserted, houses have no speech,
Not a leaf trembles on the lofty beech;
The sea itself, expiring on its strand,
Scarcely rolls one soft ripple to the land.
Seeing this world where not an echo flows,
Where ears enjoy a magical repose,
Where all is majesty, dusk, silence, distance,
Where sight alone bears witness to existence,
We might seem to be dreaming—looking on
Some ghostly past world from which life has gone!
Only, among the parasol pine-trees' bases
Growing in scattered groups on these vast spaces,
The night's breath now and then begins to break,
And spreads harmonious accents in its wake—
Seemingly, through those echoing boughs, avers
That in its sleep this world still lives and stirs.

One world—asleep beneath the vaulted skies?
Yet in that vault, to which I lift my eyes,
How many new worlds, suns of countless grades,
Exposed in splendour, sparkle through the shades!
Symbols are spent, exhausted, in their count;
The tireless soul grows tired of the amount!
Ages, convicting their vain alphabet,
Have scarcely named one in a thousand yet—
Have seen, flickering on the fringe of space,
Mere last gleams from this far-off fireplace:

Là l'antique Orion des nuits perçant les voiles,
Dont Job a le premier nommé les sept étoiles;
Le navire fendant l'Éther silencieux,　　　　　　　　75
Le bouvier dont le char se traîne dans les cieux,
La lyre aux cordes d'or, le cygne aux blanches ailes,
Le coursier qui du ciel tire des étincelles,
La balance inclinant son bassin incertain,
Les blonds cheveux livrés au souffle du matin,　　　　80
Le bélier, le taureau, l'aigle, le sagittaire,
Tout ce que les pasteurs contemplaient sur la terre,
Tout ce que les héros voulaient éterniser,
Tout ce que les amants ont pu diviniser,
Transporté dans le ciel par de touchants emblèmes,　　85
N'a pu donner des noms à ces brillants systèmes.
Les cieux pour les mortels sont un livre entr'ouvert,
Ligne à ligne à leurs yeux par la nature offert;
Chaque siècle avec peine en déchiffre une page,
Et dit: Ici finit ce magnifique ouvrage:　　　　　　90
Mais sans cesse le doigt du céleste écrivain
Tourne un feuillet de plus de ce livre divin,
Et l'œil voit, ébloui par ces brillants mystères,
Étinceler sans fin de plus beaux caractères!
Que dis-je? A chaque veille, un sage audacieux　　　95
Dans l'espace sans bords s'ouvre de nouveaux cieux;
Depuis que le cristal qui rapproche les mondes
Perce du vaste Éther les distances profondes,
Et porte le regard dans l'infini perdu,
Jusqu'où l'œil du calcul recule confondu,　　　　　100
Les cieux se sont ouverts comme une voûte sombre
Qui laisse en se brisant évanouir son ombre;
Ses feux multipliés plus que l'atome errant
Qu'éclaire du soleil un rayon transparent,
Séparés ou groupés, par couches, par étages,　　　105
En vagues, en écume, ont inondé ses plages,
Si nombreux, si pressés, que notre œil ébloui,
Qui poursuit dans l'espace un astre évanoui,
Voit cent fois dans le champ qu'embrasse sa paupière
Des mondes circuler en torrents de poussière!　　　110
Plus loin sont ces lueurs que prirent nos aïeux

Ancient Orion piercing veils of night,
Whose seven stars Job was the first to cite;
The ship that through calm Ether passes by,
The herdsman whose cart trundles through the sky,
The lyre with golden strings, the white-winged swan,
The winged horse drawing heaven's glimmers on,
The scales tilting their balance to and fro,
The locks of hair set where the dawn winds blow,
Eagle and archer, ram and bull and goat—
All things that earthly shepherds used to note,
All that wise men wished to immortalize,
All that could be adored by lovers' eyes,
Raised to the sky with poignant allegories,
Have failed to name these bright confederacies.
To mortals, the skies are an opening book;
Nature allows them, line by line, to look;
Each century struggles to comprehend
A page, and says: 'Here the great work must end!'
Yet in this sacred volume, age by age,
The heavenly writer's hand turns one more page,
Where eyes dazed by such arcane splendours see
More glorious letters glittering endlessly!
Each night, indeed, bold sages in some place
Are opening new skies in boundless space;
And since the crystal that brings worlds nearby
Has pierced the distant depths of the vast sky
And led our baffled sight so far away
We draw back from the total in dismay,
The heavens have parted like a sombre sphere
That shatters till its shadows disappear;
Their fires, more numerous than the drifting gleams
Which the sun lights with its transparent beams,
Dispersed or grouped, in different beds and floors,
In waves, in sprays, have flooded all their shores,
Packed so profusely that our dazzled gaze,
Seeking one lost star in the heavenly maze,
Sees constantly, within its field of view,
Countless worlds whirl in a torrential dew!
Beyond lie the gleams which—our fathers said—

Pour les gouttes du lait qui nourrissait les dieux;
Ils ne se trompaient pas: ces perles de lumière,
Qui de la nuit lointaine ont blanchi la carrière,
Sont des astres futurs, des germes enflammés   115
Que la main toujours pleine a pour les temps semés,
Et que l'esprit de Dieu, sous ses ailes fécondes,
De son ombre de feu couve au berceau des mondes.
C'est de là que, prenant leur vol au jour écrit,
Comme un aiglon nouveau qui s'échappe du nid,   120
Ils commencent sans guide et décrivent sans trace
L'ellipse radieuse au milieu de l'espace,
Et vont, brisant du choc un astre à son déclin,
Renouveler des cieux toujours à leur matin.

Et l'homme cependant, cet insecte invisible,   125
Rampant dans les sillons d'un globe imperceptible,
Mesure de ces feux les grandeurs et les poids,
Leur assigne leur place et leur route et leurs lois,
Comme si, dans ses mains que le compas accable,
Il roulait ces soleils comme des grains de sable!   130
Chaque atome de feu que dans l'immense Éther
Dans l'abîme des nuits l'œil distrait voit flotter,
Chaque étincelle errante aux bords de l'empyrée,
Dont scintille en mourant la lueur azurée,
Chaque tache de lait qui blanchit l'horizon,   135
Chaque teinte du ciel qui n'a pas même un nom,
Sont autant de soleils, rois d'autant de systèmes,
Qui, de seconds soleils se couronnant eux-mêmes,
Guident, en gravitant dans ces immensités,
Cent planètes brûlant de leurs feux empruntés,   140
Et tiennent dans l'Éther chacune autant de place
Que le soleil de l'homme en tournant en embrasse,
Lui, sa lune et sa terre, et l'astre du matin,
Et Saturne obscurci de son anneau lointain!

Oh! que tes cieux sont grands! et que l'esprit de l'homme   145
Plie et tombe de haut, mon Dieu! quand il te nomme!
Quand, descendant du dôme où s'égaraient ses yeux,
Atome, il se mesure à l'infini des cieux,

Were drops of milk from which the gods were fed;
Nor, indeed, were they wrong: these beads of light
Brightening the carriageway of distant night
Are future stars, luminous seedlings sown
By the ever-full Hand for times unknown;
The Spirit of God, beneath her fertile wings,
Broods in her fiery shade these infant things.
Then, taking flight on the appointed day,
As from the nest an eaglet flies away,
They describe, with no guide, and with no trace,
Radiant ellipses in the midst of space;
Their motion shatters stars about to die,
And yet renews the ever-dawning sky.

Nevertheless, man—that invisible mite
Crawling the cracks of a globe lost to sight—
Measures the weights and sizes of such flames,
Assigns them paths and places, laws and names,
As if, within his compass-burdened hand,
He could roll suns around like grains of sand!
Each fiery atom which the eye sees dance
In the abyss of night, the vast expanse,
Each spark that wanders the empyrean height
Or glimmers, dying, with an azure light,
Each drop of milk whitening the heavens' frame,
Each tinge of sky that lacks even a name—
They all are suns, all kings of territories,
Crowning themselves with solar deputies,
Drawing through their vast realms a whirling flight
Of myriad planets lit with borrowed light,
And filling, in the Ether, as much space
As our whole solar system would embrace:
The sun, its moon, its earth, the morning star,
And Saturn darkened with its rings afar!

Such mighty heavens! the human spirit is awed,
Bows down, and falls down, when it names you, Lord!
Descending from the vault with dazzled eyes,
Measuring its speck against the boundless skies,

Et que, de ta grandeur soupçonnant le prodige,
Son regard s'éblouit, et qu'il se dit: Que suis-je?   150
Oh! que suis-je, Seigneur! devant les cieux et toi?
De ton immensité le poids pèse sur moi,
Il m'égale au néant, il m'efface, il m'accable,
Et je m'estime moins qu'un de ces grains de sable,
Car ce sable roulé par les flots inconstants,   155
S'il a moins d'étendue, hélas! a plus de temps;
Il remplira toujours son vide dans l'espace
Lorsque je n'aurai plus ni nom, ni temps, ni place;
Son sort est devant toi moins triste que le mien,
L'insensible néant ne sent pas qu'il n'est rien,   160
Il ne se ronge pas pour agrandir son être,
Il ne veut ni monter, ni juger, ni connaître,
D'un immense désir il n'est point agité;
Mort, il ne rêve pas une immortalité!
Il n'a pas cette horreur de mon âme oppressée,   165
Car il ne porte pas le poids de ta pensée!

Hélas! pourquoi si haut mes yeux ont-ils monté?
J'étais heureux en bas dans mon obscurité,
Mon coin dans l'étendue et mon éclair de vie
Me paraissaient un sort presque digne d'envie;   170
Je regardais d'en haut cette herbe; en comparant,
Je méprisais l'insecte et je me trouvais grand;
Et maintenant, noyé dans l'abîme de l'être,
Je doute qu'un regard du Dieu qui nous fait naître
Puisse me démêler d'avec lui, vil, rampant,   175
Si bas, si loin de lui, si voisin du néant!
Et je me laisse aller à ma douleur profonde,
Comme une pierre au fond des abîmes de l'onde;
Et mon propre regard, comme honteux de soi,
Avec un vil dédain se détourne de moi,   180
Et je dis en moi-même à mon âme qui doute:
Va, ton sort ne vaut pas le coup d'œil qu'il te coûte!
Et mes yeux desséchés retombent ici-bas,
Et je vois le gazon qui fleurit sous mes pas,
Et j'entends bourdonner sous l'herbe que je foule   185
Ces flots d'êtres vivants que chaque sillon roule:

Sensing your wondrous majesty on high,
With blinded gaze it asks: 'Who, Lord, am I?'
Before you and your skies, what must I be?
Your sheer immensity is crushing me—
It makes me nothing—fells me where I stand—
I find myself less than a grain of sand,
For if that sand, rolled by the drifting slime,
Has less extent, it has, alas! more time!
It still will occupy its niche in space
When I have no more name, or time, or place;
Its fate in your eyes is less sad than mine:
Unaware it is naught, it cannot pine,
It never struggles wretchedly to grow,
It never strives to rise, discern, or know;
It suffers from no great desires; and, dead,
It dreams no immortality ahead!
It lacks the terrors that oppress my soul;
It is crushed by no sense of your control!

Why did I raise my eyes so loftily?
I was happy in my obscurity;
My spark of life, my corner within space,
Seemed, then, an almost enviable case;
I looked down on the grass; measured my state,
Despised the insects, and judged myself great.
Now, plunged in fathomless depths of life, I fear
To our Creator's gaze I must appear
No different from them; crawling, ill-wrought,
So low, so far from him, so nearly naught!
I steep myself in my deep misery
Like a stone in the chasms of the sea;
To contemplate myself causes me pain:
I turn away in mockery and disdain,
Telling my soul lost in its ignorance:
'Your fortunes are not worth a second glance!'
But then my dried eyes look again below;
I see the lawn flowering where I go;
I hear, buzzing beneath the grass I tread,
Floods of live creatures in each furrow-bed:

Atomes animés par le souffle divin,
Chaque rayon du jour en élève sans fin,
La minute suffit pour compléter leur être,
Leurs tourbillons flottants retombent pour renaître,   190
Le sable en est vivant, l'Éther en est semé,
Et l'air que je respire est lui-même animé;
Et d'où vient cette vie, et d'où peut-elle éclore,
Si ce n'est du regard où s'allume l'aurore?
Qui ferait germer l'herbe et fleurir le gazon,   195
Si ce regard divin n'y portait son rayon?
Cet œil s'abaisse donc sur toute la nature,
Il n'a donc ni mépris, ni faveur, ni mesure,
Et devant l'infini pour qui tout est pareil,
Il est donc aussi grand d'être homme que soleil!   200
Et je sens ce rayon m'échauffer de sa flamme,
Et mon cœur se console, et je dis à mon âme:
Homme ou monde à ses pieds, tout est indifférent,
Mais réjouissons-nous, car notre maître est grand!

Flottez, soleils des nuits, illuminez les sphères;   205
Bourdonnez sous votre herbe, insectes éphémères;
Rendons gloire là-haut, et dans nos profondeurs,
Vous par votre néant, et vous par vos grandeurs,
Et toi par ta pensée, homme! grandeur suprême,
Miroir qu'il a créé pour s'admirer lui-même,   210
Écho que dans son œuvre il a si loin jeté,
Afin que son saint nom fût partout répété.
Que cette humilité qui devant lui m'abaisse
Soit un sublime hommage, et non une tristesse;
Et que sa volonté, trop haute pour nos yeux,   215
Soit faite sur la terre, ainsi que dans les cieux!

Specks kindled by the breath of Deity,
Raised up by rays of sunlight boundlessly.
A moment is sufficient for their store:
Their whirling hordes fall and are born once more;
Sand bristles with such creatures, space is rife,
The very air I breathe is full of life.
How is that life derived, how is it born,
If not from the Eye that illumes the dawn?
How would the grass grow, how would the lawn flower,
But for the rays of that Infinite Power?
That Eye looks down on nature one and all,
Then, without favouring great or scorning small;
Before the Infinite, all is as one:
A human is no smaller than a sun!
I feel that fire warming me with its ray;
My heart is soothed, and to my soul I say:
'To him, no man or world has any weight;
Let us rejoice, though, for our Lord is great!'

Night's stars, illuminate the spheres—flow on;
Buzz in the grass, insects so quickly gone!
Give glory in the depths and in the height,
You by your worthlessness, you by your might,
And you, man, by your thought—mightier still,
A mirror he made to reflect his will,
A far-off echo in his works, set there
For his pure name to resound everywhere!
May this lowliness that abases me
Be homage to him, and not misery;
And may his will, too lofty for our eyes,
Be done on earth, as it is in the skies!

from *Méditations poétiques inédites*

XIII.   Le Lézard

Sur les ruines de Rome (1846)

Un jour, seul dans le Colisée,
Ruine de l'orgueil humain,
Sur l'herbe de sang arrosée
Je m'assis, *Tacite* à la main.

Je lisais les crimes de Rome,   5
Et l'empire à l'encan vendu,
Et, pour élever un seul homme,
L'univers si bas descendu.

Je voyais la plèbe idolâtre,
Saluant les triomphateurs,   10
Baigner ses yeux sur le théâtre
Dans le sang des gladiateurs.

Sur la muraille qui l'incruste,
Je recomposais lentement
Les lettres du nom de l'Auguste   15
Qui dédia le monument.

J'en épelais le premier signe;
Mais, déconcertant mes regards,
Un lézard dormait sur la ligne
Où brillait le nom des Césars.   20

Seul héritier des sept collines,
Seul habitant de ces débris,
Il remplaçait sous ces ruines
Le grand flot des peuples taris.

from *Further Poetic Meditations*

The Lizard

On the ruins of Rome (1846)

Once, in the Colosseum—that
Tottering ruin of human pride—
On the blood-sprinkled grass I sat
Alone, Tacitus by my side.

I read about imperial crime,
Rome auctioned off by lot and span,
The whole world lowered to the slime
To elevate a single man.

Then I could see mobs idolize
And venerate their subjugators:
Here, on this stage, they bathed their eyes
In the blood of the gladiators.

On the wall's crusted residue
I spelled out (somewhat hit-or-miss)
The name of the Augustus who
Dedicated the edifice.

I could decipher the first signs;
But, interfering with my sight,
A lizard slept upon the lines
Where Caesar's name had once shone bright.

The sole heir of the seven hills,
The wreckage's sole denizen,
It replaced, on those cracks and rills,
The now-dry teeming flood of men.

Sorti des fentes des murailles,   25
Il venait, de froid engourdi,
Réchauffer ses vertes écailles
Au contact du bronze attiédi.

Consul, César, maître du monde,
Pontife, Auguste, égal aux dieux,   30
L'ombre de ce reptile immonde
Éclipsait ta gloire à mes yeux!

La nature a son ironie:
Le livre échappa de ma main.
O Tacite, tout ton génie   35
Raille moins fort l'orgueil humain!

Crawling out of the wall's entrails
It had come, numbed with the cold air,
To heat once more its greenish scales
Against the warm bronze metal there.

Consul, Augustus, Caesar, King,
Pontiff matching the gods in might,
The shadow of that unclean thing
Blotted your glory from my sight!

Nature has her own sense of wit.
I let the book fall from my side;
The powers of Tacitus never hit
So hard a blow at human pride.

VICTOR HUGO

from *Les Orientales*

XXVIII. Les Djinns

Murs, ville,
Et port,
Asile
De mort,
Mer grise   5
Où brise
La brise,
Tout dort.

Dans la plaine
Naît un bruit.   10
C'est l'haleine
De la nuit.
Elle brame
Comme une âme
Qu'une flamme   15
Toujours suit.

La voix plus haute
Semble un grelot.
D'un nain qui saute
C'est le galop.   20
Il fuit, s'élance,
Puis en cadence
Sur un pied danse
Au bout d'un flot.

TRANSLATED BY E. H. AND A. M. BLACKMORE

from *Orientalia*

The Djinns

Port, walls
And keeps,
Death's halls
And deeps,
Grey seas
Where breeze
Now flees:
All sleeps.

From the verge
Of the flow
Sighs emerge—
Night-airs blow
And they toll
Like a soul
On patrol
With a glow.

The loudest sounds
Are like a sleigh—
An elf who bounds
And skips away.
He leaps and flows,
In rhythmic throes
Springs on his toes
Across the spray.

La rumeur approche,   25
L'écho la redit.
C'est comme la cloche
D'un couvent maudit,
Comme un bruit de foule
Qui tonne et qui roule,   30
Et tantôt s'écroule
Et tantôt grandit.

Dieu! la voix sépulcrale
Des Djinns!... —Quel bruit ils font!
Fuyons sous la spirale   35
De l'escalier profond!
Déjà s'éteint ma lampe;
Et l'ombre de la rampe,
Qui le long du mur rampe,
Monte jusqu'au plafond.   40

C'est l'essaim des Djinns qui passe,
Et tourbillonne en sifflant.
Les ifs, que leur vol fracasse,
Craquent comme un pin brûlant.
Leur troupeau lourd et rapide,   45
Volant dans l'espace vide,
Semble un nuage livide
Qui porte un éclair au flanc.

Ils sont tout près!—Tenons fermé
Cette salle où nous les narguons.   50
Quel bruit dehors! Hideuse armée
De vampires et de dragons!
La poutre du toit descellée
Ploie ainsi qu'une herbe mouillée,
Et la vieille porte rouillée   55
Tremble à déraciner ses gonds.

Now the knell grows near,
Echoes and entwines
Like the bells we hear
At accursèd shrines.
Like a noisy crowd
Thundering and proud,
Sometimes it grows loud,
Sometimes it declines.

O God! the ghostly sound
Of Djinns!—and how they blare!
Quick! let's escape around
The sunken spiral stair!
Oh, I have lost my light!
The shadow of the flight
Covers the wall—goes right
Up to the open air.

Swarms of Djinns are going past,
And they swirl and whirl and whine.
Yew-trees, shattered by the blast,
Crackle like a blazing pine.
In a huddle, quick and wide,
Through the empty space they glide,
Like a pale cloud at whose side
Sudden bolts of lightning shine.

They are so close!—Let's keep the place
Shut tight, and we'll defy them all.
The noise out there! A dreadful race,
Vampires and dragons—how they bawl!
And how the broken roof-beam heaves,
Sags like a mass of sodden leaves,
While the old rusty door-frame reaves
Its hinges, quaking, from the wall!

Cris de l'enfer! voix qui hurle et qui pleure!
L'horrible essaim, poussé par l'aquilon,
Sans doute, ô ciel! s'abat sur ma demeure.
Le mur fléchit sous le noir bataillon.   60
La maison crie et chancelle penchée,
Et l'on dirait que, du sol arrachée,
Ainsi qu'il chasse une feuille séchée,
Le vent la roule avec leur tourbillon!

Prophète! si ta main me sauve   65
De ces impurs démons des soirs,
J'irai prosterner mon front chauve
Devant tes sacrés encensoirs!
Fais que sur ces portes fidèles
Meure leur souffle d'étincelles,   70
Et qu'en vain l'ongle de leurs ailes
Grince et crie à ces vitraux noirs!

Ils sont passés!—Leur cohorte
S'envole et fuit, et leurs pieds
Cessent de battre ma porte   75
De leurs coups multipliés.
L'air est plein d'un bruit de chaînes,
Et dans les forêts prochaines
Frissonnent tous les grands chênes,
Sous leur vol de feu pliés!   80

De leurs ailes lointaines
Le battement décroît,
Si confus dans les plaines,
Si faible que l'on croit
Ouïr la sauterelle   85
Crier d'une voix grêle,
Ou pétiller la grêle
Sur le plomb d'un vieux toit.

Infernal cries! voices that weep and roar!
The horrible swarm, driven by the gale,
Heavens! is surely beating at my door!
The walls, before their black battalions, quail!
The bent house shudders with a hideous sound,
As if it's been uprooted from the ground
And some great wind is tossing it around
Like a dry leaf, so much they swirl and flail!

Prophet, if your hand saves me now
From all these unclean fiends of night,
I shall prostrate my naked brow
Before your holy censers' sight!
Ordain it that this faithful door
Withstands the blast of sparks they pour,
And that in vain their wing and claw
On the dark windows shriek and smite!

They are past!—Their mighty ranks
Flee; no longer do their feet
Buffet on the door's old planks
With a multifarious beat.
Sounds of shackles fill the sky;
Great oaks in the woods nearby
Wilt and waver, as they fly
Past with such a fiery heat!

The beatings of their wings
Distantly faint and fail—
Such far-off feeble things,
You'd think that in the vale
You heard grasshoppers stir
And purr their spindly purr,
Or that old lead roofs were
Spattered with sprays of hail.

D'étranges syllabes
Nous viennent encor: 90
Ainsi, des Arabes
Quand sonne le cor,
Un chant sur la grève
Par instants s'élève,
Et l'enfant qui rêve   95
Fait des rêves d'or.

  Les Djinns funèbres,
  Fils du trépas,
  Dans les ténèbres
  Pressent leurs pas;   100
  Leur essaim gronde:
  Ainsi, profonde,
  Murmure une onde
  Qu'on ne voit pas.

    Ce bruit vague   105
    Qui s'endort,
    C'est la vague
    Sur le bord;
    C'est la plainte
    Presque éteinte   110
    D'une sainte
    Pour un mort.

      On doute
      La nuit...
      J'écoute:—   115
      Tout fuit,
      Tout passe;
      L'espace
      Efface
      Le bruit.   120

Still they come and go,
Those strange murmurings;
So, when Arabs blow
Horn-calls, music sings
Out across the stream's
Furthermost extremes,
While babes in their dreams
Dream of golden things.

Djinns of the tomb,
Sons of the dead,
In the deep gloom
Quicken their tread,
And cry and keen:
So, from serene
Waters, unseen
Whispers are shed.

This dim knell
Is a wave
Of calm swell
In a cave,
Or the plaint,
Very faint,
Of a saint
At a grave.

So dark
A place!
Yet hark:—
No trace,
None found;
The sound
Is drowned
In space.

from *Les Châtiments*

I.V. Cette nuit-là

Trois amis l'entouraient. C'était à l'Élysée.
On voyait du dehors luire cette croisée.
Regardant venir l'heure et l'aiguille marcher,
Il était là, pensif; et, rêvant d'attacher
Le nom de Bonaparte aux exploits de Cartouche,   5
Il sentait approcher son guet-apens farouche.
D'un pied distrait dans l'âtre il poussait le tison,
Et voici ce que dit l'homme de trahison:
—« Cette nuit vont surgir mes projets invisibles.
Les Saint-Barthélemy sont encore possibles.   10
Paris dort, comme au temps de Charles de Valois;
Vous allez dans un sac mettre toutes les lois,
Et par-dessus le pont les jeter dans la Seine. »—
O ruffians! bâtards de la fortune obscène,
Nés du honteux coït de l'intrigue et du sort!   15
Rien qu'en songeant à vous mon vers indigné sort,
Et mon cœur orageux dans ma poitrine gronde
Comme le chêne au vent dans la forêt profonde!

Comme ils sortaient tous trois de la maison Bancal,
Morny, Maupas le grec, Saint-Arnaud le chacal,   20
Voyant passer ce groupe oblique et taciturne,
Les clochers de Paris, sonnant l'heure nocturne,
S'efforçaient vainement d'imiter le tocsin;
Les pavés de Juillet criaient: à l'assassin!
Tous les spectres sanglants des antiques carnages,   25
Réveillés, se montraient du doigt ces personnages;
La Marseillaise, archange aux chants aériens,
Murmurait dans les cieux: aux armes, citoyens!
Paris dormait, hélas! et bientôt, sur les places,
Sur les quais, les soldats, dociles populaces,   30
Janissaires conduits par Reybell et Sauboul,

from *The Empire in the Pillory*

That Night

Three friends were with him at the Élysée;
Their lighted room was visible far away.
Watching the hour come near, the clock proceed,
And sensing the approach of his vile deed,
There he stood, pensive, deep in thought, and made
Bonaparte's name embrace Bill Sikes's trade.
He gave the glowing fire a casual poke,
And in these terms the Man of Treachery spoke:
"Tonight my secret goals will all be won.
Bartholomew Massacres can still be done.
As in those days, Paris is fast asleep;
You can bag all the laws in one big heap,
Run to the bridge, and drop them in the Seine.'
O ruffians! whorish Fortune's bastard strain,
Born when Deceit had squalid sex with Fate!
At the mere thought of you I turn irate;
The beating heart within me howls and cries
Like mighty forest oaks when storm-winds rise!

They left the house of ill repute, those three:
Sneak Maupas, jackal Saint-Arnaud, Morny.
Seeing this pack of perfidy and crime,
The city spires that rang their nightly chime
Tried vainly to produce a tocsin's sound;
'Murderers!' cried the pavements all around.
The bleeding ghosts of ancient massacres woke,
And with their fingers pointed at these folk;
Archangel Marseillaise, who sings on high,
Hummed her 'Arm yourselves, citizens!' in the sky.
And yet, alas! Paris remained asleep;
And soon, everywhere, soldiers tame as sheep,
Reibell's and Sauboul's rowdies, overcome

Payés comme à Byzance, ivres comme à Stamboul,
Ceux de Dulac, et ceux de Korte et d'Espinasse,
La cartouchière au flanc et dans l'œil la menace,
Vinrent, le régiment après le régiment,   35
Et le long des maisons ils passaient lentement,
A pas sourds, comme on voit les tigres dans les jongles
Qui rampent sur le ventre en allongeant leurs ongles;
Et la nuit était morne, et Paris sommeillait
Comme un aigle endormi pris sous un noir filet.   40

Les chefs attendaient l'aube en fumant leurs cigares.

O cosaques! voleurs! chauffeurs! routiers! bulgares!
O généraux brigands! bagne, je te les rends!
Les juges d'autrefois pour des crimes moins grands
Ont brulé la Voisin et roué vif Desrues!   45

Éclairant leur affiche infâme au coin des rues
Et le lâche armement de ces filous hardis,
Le jour parut. La nuit, complice des bandits,
Prit la fuite, et, traînant à la hâte ses voiles,
Dans les plis de sa robe emporta les étoiles   50
Et les milles soleils dans l'ombre étincelant,
Comme les sequins d'or qu'emporte en s'en allant
Une fille, aux baisers du crime habituée,
Qui se rhabille après s'être prostituée!

II.iii. Souvenir de la nuit du 4

L'enfant avait reçu deux balles dans la tête.
Le logis était propre, humble, paisible, honnête;
On voyait un rameau bénit sur un portrait.
Une vieille grand'mère était là qui pleurait.
Nous le déshabillions en silence. Sa bouche,   5
Pâle, s'ouvrait; la mort noyait son œil farouche;
Ses bras pendants semblaient demander des appuis.
Il avait dans sa poche une toupie en buis.

By cash and drink as at Byzantium,
Those Korte, Dulac, and Espinasse supplied,
Hate in their eyes and powder at their side,
Appeared, regiment after regiment,
And with a slow tread through the streets they went
As jungle tigers go, on silent paws,
Slithering low and spreading out their claws;
The night was glum, and Paris slumbered yet—
A sleeping eagle caught in a dark net.

The leaders watched for dawn and smoked cigars.

Thieves, Cossacks, Bulgars, torturers, hussars!
Brigandier-generals! clap them all in cages!
For lesser felonies, judges of past ages
Burnt Monvoisin, broke Desrues on the wheel!

Day, lighting these bold rogues' cowardly steel
And their cheap posters on street corners, broke.
Night—that accomplice of all thieving folk—
Snatched up her veils, made off on the alert,
And took the stars in the folds of her skirt,
Those thousand suns shimmering through the shade,
Like the gold sequins taken by some jade
Hardened to vice, when she gets dressed once more
    After she's played the whore.

The Night of the Fourth: A Recollection

The child had got two bullets in the head.
The place was humble, tidy, decent, with a palm-branch over a holy
   picture;
And an old grandmother was there.
She wept.
We undressed the lad in silence. His mouth was livid:
Pale, and hung open. Death had numbed his startled eyes;
His arms were dangling—seemed to want support; and in his pocket
There was a boxwood top.

On pouvait mettre un doigt dans les trous de ses plaies.
Avez-vous vu saigner la mûre dans les haies?   10
Son crâne était ouvert comme un bois qui se fend.
L'aïeule regarda déshabiller l'enfant,
Disant:—Comme il est blanc! approchez donc la lampe.
Dieu! ses pauvres cheveux sont collés sur sa tempe!—
Et quand ce fut fini, le prit sur ses genoux.   15
La nuit était lugubre; on entendait des coups
De fusil dans la rue où l'on en tuait d'autres.
—Il faut ensevelir l'enfant, dirent les nôtres,
Et l'on prit un drap blanc dans l'armoire en noyer.
L'aïeule cependant l'approchait du foyer,   20
Comme pour réchauffer ses membres déjà roides.
Hélas! ce que la mort touche de ses mains froides
Ne se réchauffe plus aux foyers d'ici-bas!
Elle pencha la tête et lui tira ses bas,
Et dans ses vieilles mains prit les pieds du cadavre.   25
—Est-ce que ce n'est pas une chose qui navre!
Cria-t-elle; monsieur, il n'avait pas huit ans!
Ses maîtres, il allait en classe, étaient contents.
Monsieur, quand il fallait que je fisse une lettre,
C'est lui qui l'écrivait. Est-ce qu'on va se mettre   30
A tuer les enfants maintenant? Ah! mon Dieu!
On est donc des brigands? Je vous demande un peu,
Il jouait ce matin, là, devant la fenêtre!
Dire qu'ils m'ont tué ce pauvre petit être!
Il passait dans la rue, ils ont tiré dessus.   35
Monsieur, il était bon et doux comme un Jésus.
Moi je suis vieille, il est tout simple que je parte;
Cela n'aurait rien fait à monsieur Bonaparte
De me tuer au lieu de tuer mon enfant!—
Elle s'interrompit, les sanglots l'étouffant.   40
Puis elle dit, et tous pleuraient près de l'aïeule:
—Que vais-je devenir à présent toute seule?
Expliquez-moi cela, vous autres, aujourd'hui.
Hélas! je n'avais plus de sa mère que lui.
Pourquoi l'a-t-on tué? je veux qu'on me l'explique.   45

You could have put a finger through the wound-holes.
Have you ever seen blackberries bleeding in the hedgerows?
His skull was open: split like a tree-trunk. Grandmother
Watched the boy being undressed;
'He's very pale', she said; 'bring the light nearer.
Goodness, his poor hair—it's stuck to his temples!'
Afterwards she took him on her knees.
It was very dark then; you could still
Hear shooting outside in the street: others were being killed there.
People told her the boy had to be wrapped,
And took a white sheet out of the walnut cupboard.
She brought him to the fire,
As if to warm his limbs—they were stiff already.
Ah, but something that Death has touched with its cold fingers
Will never warm at any fire on earth!
She bent her head and bared his feet,
Took them in her gnarled hands.
'Wouldn't it break your heart', she cried;
'Why, sir, he wasn't eight years old.
His teachers—he went to school—were pleased with him.
Why, sir, whenever I had to do a letter,
He was the one that wrote it. So, they're starting
To kill the children, are they? Lord above!
They're just bandits, and that's the truth. I ask you—
Only this morning he was playing over there by the window!
To think they killed a little boy like that, as good as Jesus, sir!
He was out in the street, they shot at him.
Me, I'm an old thing; if I go, that's natural;
It wouldn't have made any difference to Monsieur Bonaparte
If I'd been the one they killed, instead of my boy!'—
She broke off—
The sobs stifled her;
Everyone around her was in tears too.
Then she added: 'What am I going to do now, all alone?
Tell me that. Why did they kill him?
He was all I had left of his poor mother.
Why did they kill him? I want to be told.

L'enfant n'a pas crié vive la République. —
Nous nous taisions, debout et graves, chapeau bas,
Tremblant devant ce deuil qu'on ne console pas.

Vous ne compreniez point, mère, la politique.
Monsieur Napoléon, c'est son nom authentique,   50
Est pauvre, et même prince; il aime les palais;
Il lui convient d'avoir des chevaux, des valets,
De l'argent pour son jeu, sa table, son alcôve,
Ses chasses; par la même occasion, il sauve
La famille, l'église et la société;   55
Il veut avoir Saint-Cloud, plein de roses l'été,
Où viendront l'adorer les préfets et les maires;
C'est pour cela qu'il faut que les vieilles grand'mères,
De leurs pauvres doigts gris que fait trembler le temps,
Cousent dans le linceul des enfants de sept ans.   60

IV.i. *Sacer esto*

Non, liberté! non, peuple, il ne faut pas qu'il meure!
Oh! certes, ce serait trop simple, en vérité,
Qu'après avoir brisé les lois, et sonné l'heure
Où la sainte pudeur au ciel a remonté;

Qu'après avoir gagné sa sanglante gageure,   5
Et vaincu par l'embûche, et le glaive, et le feu;
Qu'après son guet-apens, ses meurtres, son parjure,
Son faux serment, soufflet sur la face de Dieu;

Qu'après avoir traîné la France, au cœur frappée,
Et par les pieds liée, à son immonde char,   10
Cet infâme en fût quitte avec un coup d'épée
Au cou comme Pompée, au flanc comme César!

Non! il est l'assassin qui rôde dans les plaines.
Il a tué, sabré, mitraillé sans remords,
Il fit la maison vide, il fit les tombes pleines,   15
Il marche, il va, suivi par l'œil fixe des morts;

He never cheered for the Republic.'—
All of us stood with hats off, silent and solemn,
And trembled at this inconsolable sorrow.

You don't understand politics, madame.
Monsieur Napoléon—that's his true name—
Is poor, yet he's a prince; well, he likes palaces;
It suits him to have horses, valets, money for
His gambling and his private rooms, his dinners and his
    hunting-parties; and, furthermore, he's doing it
To save the church, the family, society;
He wants Saint-Cloud full of roses in summer,
And mayors and prefects coming to bow down to him;
That's why it's necessary for old grandmothers
With grey and trembling fingers
To wrap shrouds around seven-year-old children.

Set Him Apart!

No, Liberty! People, he must not die!
It would be all too simple, all too nice,
If—after the offence, the hue and cry
That drove poor Virtue back to Paradise,

After his so-triumphant strategies,
Conquests by fire and sword-thrust and disgrace,
After his tricks, murders, and treacheries,
His perjured vows that slap God in the face,

When France is dragged behind his chariot-wheel,
Struck to the core, and with her ankles tied—
The wretch could be rewarded with cold steel,
Pompey- or Caesar-style, in throat or side!

No! he stabbed, sabred, slew, remorselessly;
Now the assassin wanders through the plain;
He emptied homes, he filled the cemetery;
Now he walks in the set gaze of the slain.

A cause de cet homme, empereur éphémère,
Le fils n'a plus de père et l'enfant plus d'espoir,
La veuve à genoux pleure et sanglote, et la mère
N'est plus qu'un spectre assis sous un long voile noir;   20

Pour filer ses habits royaux, sur les navettes
On met du fil trempé dans le sang qui coula;
Le boulevard Montmartre a fourni ses cuvettes,
Et l'on teint son manteau dans cette pourpre-là.

Il vous jette à Cayenne, à l'Afrique, aux sentines,   25
Martyrs, héros d'hier et forçats d'aujourd'hui!
Le couteau ruisselant des rouges guillotines
Laisse tomber le sang goutte à goutte sur lui;

Lorsque la trahison, sa complice livide,
Vient et frappe à sa porte, il fait signe d'ouvrir;   30
Il est le fratricide! il est le parricide!—
Peuples, c'est pour cela qu'il ne doit pas mourir!

Gardons l'homme vivant. Oh! châtiment superbe!
Oh! s'il pouvait un jour passer par le chemin,
Nu, courbé, frissonnant, comme au vent tremble l'herbe,   35
Sous l'exécration de tout le genre humain!

Étreint par son passé tout rempli de ses crimes,
Comme par un carcan tout hérissé de clous,
Cherchant les lieux profonds, les forêts, les abîmes,
Pâle, horrible, effaré, reconnu par les loups;   40

Dans quelque bagne vil n'entendant que sa chaîne,
Seul, toujours seul, parlant en vain aux rochers sourds,
Voyant autour de lui le silence et la haine,
Des hommes nulle part et des spectres toujours;

Vieillissant, rejeté par la mort comme indigne,   45
Tremblant sous la nuit noire, affreux sous le ciel bleu...
Peuples, écartez-vous! cet homme porte un signe;
Laissez passer Caïn! il appartient à Dieu.

Because of this ephemeral emperor
Sons have no fathers, children have no hopes;
Widows bow weeping; mothers are no more
Than seated ghosts shrouded in long black copes;

The spindle for his ceremonial stole
Spun fabric that was steeped in squandered blood;
The Boulevard Montmartre supplied the bowl,
His cloaks were dipped into that crimson mud;

He casts to foreign deserts and ravines
Yesterday's heroes—criminals today!
Over him, from the reddened guillotines,
The blood is dripping drop by drop away;

When livid treason, rushing to his side,
Knocks on his door, he opens at its cry;
He is the fratricide, the parricide—
And, for that very reason, must not die!

Keep him alive—a splendid punishment!
Oh, let him simply roam the open space,
Trembling like windswept grasses, bared, and bent
Beneath the curses of the human race!

Gripped by his past replete with felonies
As by a fetter spiked from end to end,
Seeking deep places, chasms, clustered trees,
Pale, horrid, scared—one that the wolves call friend—

Hearing, in some vile hole, only his chain,
Crying to deaf rocks, ever solitary,
Seeing around him silence and disdain,
People nowhere, and ghosts incessantly;

Dreading the blue sky, fearful of the dark,
Ageing, yet spurned by death as a mere clod—
Nations, keep back! this person bears a mark:
Let Cain go by, for he belongs to God.

VII.i. « Sonnez, sonnez toujours... »

Sonnez, sonnez toujours, clairons de la pensée.

Quand Josué rêveur, la tête aux cieux dressée,
Suivi des siens, marchait, et, prophète irrité,
Sonnait de la trompette autour de la cité,
Au premier tour qu'il fit le roi se mit à rire;   5
Au second tour, riant toujours, il lui fit dire:
—Crois-tu donc renverser ma ville avec du vent?
A la troisième fois l'arche allait en avant,
Puis les trompettes, puis toute l'armée en marche,
Et les petits enfants venaient cracher sur l'arche,   10
Et, soufflant dans leur trompe, imitaient le clairon;
Au quatrième tour, bravant les fils d'Aaron,
Entre les vieux créneaux tout brunis par la rouille,
Les femmes s'asseyaient en filant leur quenouille,
Et se moquaient jetant des pierres aux hébreux;   15
A la cinquième fois, sur ces murs ténébreux,
Aveugles et boiteux vinrent, et leurs huées
Raillaient le noir clairon sonnant sous les nuées;
A la sixième fois, sur sa tour de granit
Si haute qu'au sommet l'aigle faisait son nid,   20
Si dure que l'éclair l'eût en vain foudroyée,
Le roi revint, riant à gorge déployée,
Et cria:—Ces hébreux sont bons musiciens!—
Autour du roi joyeux, riaient tous les anciens
Qui le soir sont assis au temple et délibèrent.   25

A la septième fois, les murailles tombèrent.

'Sound, sound forever...'

Sound, sound forever, trumpet-calls of thought!

When pensive Joshua marched to and fro—
The wrathful prophet with the flock he brought,
Sounding the trumpet around Jericho—
At his first passing, the king merely grinned;
The second day, he sent to him and said:
'Do you mean to demolish the town with wind?'
On the third day—as the ark went ahead,
Trumpets and soldiers following—small boys
Rushed up to spit upon the holy place,
And blew their hooters like the trumpet's noise;
On the fourth day, deriding Aaron's race,
Over the ancient rust-browned city heights
Women seated themselves to spin their thread,
And threw stones, scoffing, at the Israelites;
The fifth day, on those dark walls overhead
Appeared the lame and blind, and with their sour
Howls mocked the sombre trumpet's earthy shriek;
While, the sixth day, upon his granite tower—
So high that eagles nested at its peak,
So hard no lightning ravaged it at all—
The king came back; he laughed openly then,
And cried: 'These Hebrews are quite musical!'
And when he laughed, so did the wise old men
Who counsel nightly in the temple halls.

And on the seventh day, down fell the walls.

from *Les Contemplations*

IV.xiv. « Demain, dès l'aube... »

Demain, dès l'aube, à l'heure où blanchit la campagne,
Je partirai. Vois-tu, je sais que tu m'attends.
J'irai par la forêt, j'irai par la montagne.
Je ne puis demeurer loin de toi plus longtemps.

Je marcherai les yeux fixés sur mes pensées,   5
Sans rien voir au dehors, sans entendre aucun bruit,
Seul, inconnu, le dos courbé, les mains croisées,
Triste, et le jour pour moi sera comme la nuit.

Je ne regarderai ni l'or du soir qui tombe,
Ni les voiles au loin descendant vers Harfleur,   10
Et quand j'arriverai, je mettrai sur ta tombe
Un bouquet de houx vert et de bruyère en fleur.

IV.xv. A Villequier

Maintenant que Paris, ses pavés et ses marbres,
Et sa brume et ses toits sont bien loin de mes yeux;
Maintenant que je suis sous les branches des arbres,
Et que je puis songer à la beauté des cieux;

Maintenant que du deuil qui m'a fait l'âme obscure   5
    Je sors, pâle et vainqueur,
Et que je sens la paix de la grande nature
    Qui m'entre dans le cœur;

from *Contemplations*

'Tomorrow, when the meadows grow...'

Tomorrow, when the meadows grow
Bright with the dawn, I'll leave. I know
   That you'll be waiting for me. Through
Forest and mountain-pass I'll go.
   No longer can I keep from you.

I'll walk with eyes fixed on my heart,
   Seeing nothing all around,
   Hearing not the slightest sound,
Back curved, hands crossed, sad, unknown, and apart;
     And day will be
     Like night to me.

I'll watch neither the fall of evening fraught
With gold, nor the far sails go down to port;
     And when I've come,
There on your grave I'll set a wreath:
Fresh holly-sprays, and flowering heath.

At Villequier

Now that the city with its masonrics,
Marbles, and mists, has vanished from my eyes—
Now that beneath the branches of the trees
I can survey the beauty of the skies—

Now that from all the grief that dimmed my soul,
   Pale, conquering, I depart,
And feel the very peace of nature roll
   Into my inmost heart—

Maintenant que je puis, assis au bord des ondes,
Ému par ce superbe et tranquille horizon,   10
Examiner en moi les vérités profondes
Et regarder les fleurs qui sont dans le gazon;

Maintenant, ô mon Dieu! que j'ai ce calme sombre
    De pouvoir désormais
Voir de mes yeux la pierre où je sais que dans l'ombre   15
    Elle dort pour jamais;

Maintenant qu'attendri par ces divins spectacles,
Plaines, forêts, rochers, vallons, fleuve argenté,
Voyant ma petitesse et voyant vos miracles,
Je reprends ma raison devant l'immensité;   20

Je viens à vous, Seigneur, père auquel il faut croire;
    Je vous porte, apaisé,
Les morceaux de ce cœur tout plein de votre gloire
    Que vous avez brisé;

Je viens à vous, Seigneur! confessant que vous êtes   25
Bon, clément, indulgent et doux, ô Dieu vivant!
Je conviens que vous seul savez ce que vous faites,
Et que l'homme n'est rien qu'un jonc qui tremble au vent;

Je dis que le tombeau qui sur les morts se ferme
    Ouvre le firmament;   30
Et que ce qu'ici-bas nous prenons pour le terme
    Est le commencement;

Je conviens à genoux que vous seul, père auguste,
Possédez l'infini, le réel, l'absolu;
Je conviens qu'il est bon, je conviens qu'il est juste   35
Que mon cœur ait saigné, puisque Dieu l'a voulu!

Je ne résiste plus à tout ce qui m'arrive
    Par votre volonté.
L'âme de deuils en deuils, l'homme de rive en rive,
    Roule à l'éternité.   40

Now that I can sit here beside the sea
And by the calm horizon feel reborn,
Examining the furthest truths in me,
And noticing the flowers on the lawn—

Now, Lord my God, that I have gained the deep
    Peace to look unafraid
At the stone where she will, I know it, sleep
    Forever in the shade—

Now that, touched by the sacred scenes of plain,
Rock, forest, valley, silver stream, I see
My weakness and your wonders, and regain
My senses before their immensity—

I come in faith to you, Father of Days,
    And bring to you the scattered
Pieces, Lord, of a heart filled with your praise
    Which you yourself have shattered;

I come, Lord, and confess that you are true,
Gentle, and merciful, and never fail;
I grant that you alone know what you do,
That man is a reed shaken by the gale;

I know that tombs shut on mortality
    Open in heaven's heart;
I know that what on earth we take to be
    The ending, is the start;

Kneeling I grant that you alone, august
Father, are real and infinite; I know,
I grant that it was good, that it was just,
When my heart bled, because God willed it so.

All of the things that you have planned for me
    Now I resist no more.
From grief to grief, souls reach eternity;
    People, from shore to shore.

Nous ne voyons jamais qu'un seul côté des choses;
L'autre plonge en la nuit d'un mystère effrayant.
L'homme subit le joug sans connaître les causes.
Tout ce qu'il voit est court, inutile et fuyant.

Vous faites revenir toujours la solitude   45
    Autour de tous ses pas.
Vous n'avez pas voulu qu'il eût la certitude
    Ni la joie ici-bas!

Dès qu'il possède un bien, le sort le lui retire.
Rien ne lui fut donné, dans ses rapides jours,   50
Pour qu'il s'en puisse faire une demeure, et dire:
C'est ici ma maison, mon champ et mes amours!

Il doit voir peu de temps tout ce que ses yeux voient;
    Il vieillit sans soutiens.
Puisque ces choses sont, c'est qu'il faut qu'elles soient;   55
    J'en conviens, j'en conviens!

Le monde est sombre, ô Dieu! l'immuable harmonie
Se compose des pleurs aussi bien que des chants;
L'homme n'est qu'un atome en cette ombre infinie,
Nuit où montent les bons, où tombent les méchants.   60

Je sais que vous avez bien autre chose à faire
    Que de nous plaindre tous,
Et qu'un enfant qui meurt, désespoir de sa mère,
    Ne vous fait rien, à vous.

Je sais que le fruit tombe au vent qui le secoue,   65
Que l'oiseau perd sa plume et la fleur sa parfum;
Que la création est une grande roue
Qui ne peut se mouvoir sans écraser quelqu'un;

Les mois, les jours, les flots des mers, les yeux qui pleurent,
    Passent sous le ciel bleu;
Il faut que l'herbe pousse et que les enfants meurent;   70
    Je le sais, ô mon Dieu!

Always we see things only from one side;
The other lies in night and mysteries.
Without knowing the cause, man must abide
The yoke; fleeting and vain is all he sees.

In all his steps you make him solitary
        Wherever he may go.
You never wish him to have certainty
        Or joy, on earth below!

Any good thing he has, fate takes away;
He receives nothing every fleeting year
For him to make his dwelling of, and say:
'My house, my property, my love is here!'

Briefly his eyes must see what they can see;
        Unaided he grows old;
And since these things are thus, so they must be:
        Yes, that is what I hold!

The world is dark; its changeless harmony
Is woven, part of songs, and part of cries;
Man is an atom in infinity—
The night where wicked fall and good arise.

I know you cannot always pity: there
        Are other things to do;
If children die, or if mothers despair,
        It cannot alter you.

I know, when the wind shakes, the fruit will fall;
Birds lose their feathers, flowers lose their scent.
Creation's great wheel cannot move at all
Without someone beneath it being spent.

Months, days, waves, tears, beneath the clear blue sky
        Must pass and be outpoured;
The grass must grow, and children needs must die—
        I know it, O my Lord!

Dans vos cieux, au delà de la sphère des nues,
Au fond de cet azur immobile et dormant,
Peut-être faites-vous des choses inconnues   75
Où la douleur de l'homme entre comme élément.

Peut-être est-il utile à vos desseins sans nombre
    Que des êtres charmants
S'en aillent, emportés par le tourbillon sombre
    Des noirs événements.   80

Nos destins ténébreux vont sous des lois immenses
Que rien ne déconcerte et que rien n'attendrit.
Vous ne pouvez avoir de subites clémences
Qui dérangent le monde, ô Dieu, tranquille esprit!

Je vous supplie, ô Dieu! de regarder mon âme,   85
    Et de considérer
Qu'humble comme un enfant et doux comme une femme
    Je viens vous adorer!

Considérez encor que j'avais, dès l'aurore,
Travaillé, combattu, pensé, marché, lutté,   90
Expliquant la nature à l'homme qui l'ignore,
Éclairant toute chose avec votre clarté;

Que j'avais, affrontant la haine et la colère,
    Fait ma tâche ici-bas,
Que je ne pouvais pas m'attendre à ce salaire,   95
    Que je ne pouvais pas

Prévoir que, vous aussi, sur ma tête qui ploie
Vous appesantiriez votre bras triomphant,
Et que, vous qui voyiez comme j'ai peu de joie,
Vous me reprendriez si vite mon enfant!   100

Qu'une âme ainsi frappée à se plaindre est sujette,
    Que j'ai pu blasphémer,
Et vous jeter mes cris comme un enfant qui jette
    Une pierre à la mer!

Within your skies, beyond the cloudy sphere,
Deep in the sleeping still blue firmament,
You yet may make some mystery appear
With human suffering as one element;

It may be useful, in your countless plans,
 For creatures of delight
To pass, swept away by dark hurricanes
 And happenings of night.

Our shadowy doom is guided by vast laws;
Nothing can soften them or make them cease.
One single unplanned tenderness of yours
Would disarrange the world, O Lord of peace.

Look on my soul, I ask you, Lord, and see:
 Consider what I do;
Gentle as woman, meek as infancy,
 I come to worship you.

Recall that I have been a labourer
Since dawn. I thought, marched, struggled, fought the fight;
Nature, to those who never knew of her,
I showed, and lightened all things with your light.

Even when faced with anger and offence,
 I did my work below.
How could I have foreseen such recompense,
 And how was I to know

That even you, on my bowed head, would press
Your ever-conquering arm so heavily,
And, knowing I had such small happiness,
Would take my child so quickly back from me?

A stricken soul is prone, Lord, to complain,
 And, as I did, blaspheme,
Throwing you cries as children throw a stone
 Into the ocean-stream.

Considérez qu'on doute, ô mon Dieu! quand on souffre,   105
Que l'œil qui pleure trop finit par s'aveugler,
Qu'un être que son deuil plonge au plus noir du gouffre,
Quand il ne vous voit plus, ne peut vous contempler,

Et qu'il ne se peut pas que l'homme, lorsqu'il sombre
    Dans les afflictions,   110
Ait présente à l'esprit la sérénité sombre
    Des constellations!

Aujourd'hui, moi qui fus faible comme une mère,
Je me courbe à vos pieds devant vos cieux ouverts.
Je me sens éclairé dans ma douleur amère   115
Par un meilleur regard jeté sur l'univers.

Seigneur, je reconnais que l'homme est en délire
    S'il ose murmurer;
Je cesse d'accuser, je cesse de maudire,
    Mais laissez-moi pleurer!   120

Hélas! laissez les pleurs couler de ma paupière,
Puisque vous avez fait les hommes pour cela!
Laissez-moi me pencher sur cette froide pierre
Et dire à mon enfant: Sens-tu que je suis là?

Laissez-moi lui parler, incliné sur ses restes,   125
    Le soir, quand tout se tait,
Comme si, dans sa nuit rouvrant ses yeux célestes,
    Cet ange m'écoutait!

Hélas! vers le passé tournant un œil d'envie,
Sans que rien ici-bas puisse m'en consoler,   130
Je regarde toujours ce moment de ma vie
Où je l'ai vue ouvrir son aile et s'envoler.

Je verrai cet instant jusqu'à ce que je meure,
    L'instant, pleurs superflus!
Où je criai: L'enfant que j'avais tout à l'heure,   135
    Quoi donc! je ne l'ai plus!

Reflect that when we suffer, Lord, we doubt,
And that an eye too full of tears is blind;
A mourner, deep in the black gulf, without
Sight of you—how can you be in his mind,

And how can such a man, when he has been
　　Steeped in humiliations,
Contemplate in his spirit the serene
　　Dark of the constellations?

I, who was feeble as a mother then,
Kneel to you now before your open skies.
In my grief I feel lightened once again,
And see your universe with better eyes.

I know that a man grumbling and perverse
　　Is raving in his sleep;
No longer do I criticize or curse,
　　But let me weep.

Ah! let the tears run down, let the voice moan,
Because you have created people so,
And let me bend over the ice-cold stone
And tell her: 'Here I am—do you still know?'

Let me speak to her, stooping where she lies,
　　When all is silent here,
As if, reopening her heavenly eyes
　　In the night, she could hear!

My gaze keeps turning to the past again;
Nothing on earth can comfort me today.
Incessantly I see the moment when
I watched her spread her wing and fly away;

And I shall see that time until I die—
　　Useless, these tears I pour!—
When I cried out: 'The child I had just now,
　　I don't have any more!'

Ne vous irritez pas que je sois de la sorte,
O mon Dieu! cette plaie a si longtemps saigné!
L'angoisse dans mon âme est toujours la plus forte,
Et mon cœur est soumis, mais n'est pas résigné.   140

Ne vous irritez pas! fronts que le deuil réclame,
    Mortels sujets aux pleurs,
Il nous est malaisé de retirer notre âme
    De ces grandes douleurs.

Voyez-vous, nos enfants nous sont bien nécessaires,   145
Seigneur; quand on a vu dans sa vie, un matin
Au milieu des ennuis, des peines, des misères,
Et de l'ombre que fait sur nous notre destin,

Apparaître un enfant, tête chère et sacrée,
    Petit être joyeux,   150
Si beau, qu'on a cru voir s'ouvrir à son entrée
    Une porte des cieux;

Quand on a vu, seize ans, de cet autre soi-même
Croître la grâce aimable et la douce raison,
Lorsqu'on a reconnu que cet enfant qu'on aime   155
Fait le jour dans notre âme et dans notre maison,

Que c'est la seule joie ici-bas qui persiste
    De tout ce qu'on rêva,
Considérez que c'est une chose bien triste
    De le voir qui s'en va!   160

My God, do not be angry that I fret;
Long indeed has my wound bled unconfined!
The anguish in my soul is stronger yet;
My heart, though it submits, is not resigned.

Do not be pained! We sorrow-laden men,
 We mortals prone to weep,
Find it hard to retrieve our souls again
 When miseries go so deep.

Our children are so needful to us, Lord,
And when, one morning in our life, we see—
Amid our hardship, suffering, discord,
And all the shadows cast by destiny—

A child, a precious, sacred thing, appear—
 A little joyous head,
So pretty, that it seems when she came here
 The heavens were outspread—

When, sixteen years, we watch her grow and flower
In grace and sense, lovely in every part—
When we learn that this other self has power
To bring the day into our home and heart,

And that she is our one continuing
 Joy, as earth's dreams decay—
Consider, Lord, it is so sad a thing
 To see her pass away!

v.xxiii. Pasteurs et troupeaux

Le vallon où je vais tous les jours est charmant,
Serein, abandonné, seul sous le firmament,
Plein de ronces en fleurs; c'est un sourire triste.
Il vous fait oublier que quelque chose existe,
Et, sans le bruit des champs remplis de travailleurs,   5
On ne saurait plus là si quelqu'un vit ailleurs.
Là, l'ombre fait l'amour; l'idylle naturelle
Rit; le bouvreuil avec le verdier s'y querelle,
Et la fauvette y met de travers son bonnet;
C'est tantôt l'aubépine et tantôt le genêt;   10
De noirs granits bourrus, puis des mousses riantes;
Car Dieu fait un poëme avec des variantes;
Comme le vieil Homère, il rabâche parfois,
Mais c'est avec les fleurs, les monts, l'onde et les bois!
Une petite mare est là, ridant sa face,   15
Prenant des airs de flot pour la fourmi qui passe,
Ironie étalée au milieu du gazon,
Qu'ignore l'océan grondant à l'horizon.
J'y rencontre parfois sur la roche hideuse
Un doux être; quinze ans, yeux bleus, pieds nus, gardeuse 20
De chèvres, habitant, au fond d'un ravin noir,
Un vieux chaume croulant qui s'étoile le soir;
Ses sœurs sont au logis et filent leur quenouille;
Elle essuie aux roseaux ses pieds que l'étang mouille;
Chèvres, brebis, béliers, paissent; quand, sombre esprit, 25
J'apparais, le pauvre ange a peur, et me sourit;
Et moi, je la salue, elle étant l'innocence.
Ses agneaux, dans le pré plein de fleurs qui l'encense,
Bondissent, et chacun, au soleil s'empourprant,
Laisse aux buissons, à qui la bise le reprend,   30
Un peu de sa toison, comme un flocon d'écume.
Je passe; enfant, troupeau, s'effacent dans la brume;
Le crépuscule étend sur les longs sillons gris
Ses ailes de fantôme et de chauve-souris;
J'entends encore au loin dans la plaine ouvrière   35
Chanter derrière moi la douce chevrière;

Shepherds and Flocks

This vale—my daily haunt—is a delight:
Serene, deserted, lone in heaven's sight,
All bramble-flowers—it's smiling listlessly.
Makes you forget that other things can be:
But for the sound of workers in the distance,
You wouldn't know that man was in existence.
The shadows all make love there: Nature's idyll
Rejoices; bull- and greenfinch taradiddle;
The warbler sets her bonnet quite askew.
Now hawthorn, now genistra is on view;
Here, rough black granites; there, moss gaily seeding—
God prints the poem plus the variant reading:
If, like old Homer, he goes on a bit,
It's done with flower and forest, peak and pit.
A little pond is there, wrinkling its face,
Acting the high seas when ants pass the place—
Irony in the garden!—a display
Lost on the ocean growling far away.
There, on the dreadful rock, I sometimes meet
A lovely thing—fifteen, blue eyes, bare feet—
Minding her goats. In a ravine her cottage sprawls—
By day an old hut, but a star when evening falls.
Her sisters are indoors spinning their needs.
She wipes her pond-wet feet on the wild reeds;
Goats, rams, ewes browse. When I, grim ghost, appear,
Why, the poor angel smiles at me in fear.
And I wave back—she's such an innocent.
Among the flowers perfuming her with scent
Her lambs are frisking, flushed with the warm sun,
And leaving on the bushes every one
Some tuft of wool—some little fleece of spray.
I go. Child, flock, in mist all pass away.
Over the long grey furrows, evening flings
Its phantom's- or its flittermouse's-wings;
Still, from the toiling plains, I faintly find
The lovely goatherd singing far behind.

Et, là-bas, devant moi, le vieux gardien pensif
De l'écume, du flot, de l'algue, du récif,
Et des vagues sans trêve et sans fin remuées,
Le pâtre promontoire au chapeau de nuées,   40
S'accoude et rêve au bruit de tous les infinis,
Et, dans l'ascension des nuages bénis,
Regarde se lever la lune triomphale,
Pendant que l'ombre tremble, et que l'âpre rafale
Disperse à tous les vents avec son souffle amer   45
La laine des moutons sinistres de la mer.

vi.i. Le Pont

J'avais devant les yeux les ténèbres. L'abîme
Qui n'a pas de rivage et qui n'a pas de cime
Était là, morne, immense; et rien n'y remuait.
Je me sentais perdu dans l'infini muet.
Au fond, à travers l'ombre, impénétrable voile,   5
On apercevait Dieu comme une sombre étoile.
Je m'écriai:—Mon âme, ô mon âme! il faudrait,
Pour traverser ce gouffre où nul bord n'apparaît,
Et pour qu'en cette nuit jusqu'à ton Dieu tu marches,
Bâtir un pont géant sur des millions d'arches.   10
Qui le pourra jamais? Personne! O deuil! effroi!
Pleure!—Un fantôme blanc se dressa devant moi
Pendant que je jetais sur l'ombre un œil d'alarme,
Et ce fantôme avait la forme d'une larme;
C'était un front de vierge avec des mains d'enfant;   15
Il ressemblait au lys que la blancheur défend;
Ses mains en se joignant faisaient de la lumière.
Il me montra l'abîme où va toute poussière,
Si profond que jamais un écho n'y répond;
Et me dit:—Si tu veux, je bâtirai le pont.   20
Vers ce pâle inconnu je levai ma paupière.
—Quel est ton nom? lui dis-je. Il me dit:—La prière.

And there in front the rapt old guardian
Of reef and spray—of weed and flood and span
And ever-restless waves billowing loud—
The shepherd promontory capped with cloud
Leans, pondering to the sound of all infinity,
And, while mists rise with blessings of divinity,
Sees the triumphal moon ascend at last,
As the dark trembles, and a savage blast
Scatters to every wind, with one harsh sweep,
The fleeces of the sea's sinister sheep.

The Bridge

Dark was before my eyes. There lay the abyss
With neither boundary nor precipice,
Dismal, immense; and nothing stirred in it.
I felt lost in the silent infinite.
Across the infrangible veil of dark, afar,
The Lord was visible like a sombre star.
'My soul, my soul,' I wondered, 'how are we
To cross this gulf that has no boundary,
And walk to God in the nocturnal shade?
A vast bridge—myriad arches—must be laid.
Yet who could do it? Alas! Nobody!'
A pale phantom appeared in front of me
While I was looking at the dark in fear.
This phantom had the semblance of a tear;
He seemed a lily guarded by its white,
And from his folded hands there issued light.
He had a virgin's forehead, a child's hand.
Showing the chasm where all dust must land,
So deep that nothing echoes from its bed,
'If you want, I can build the bridge', he said.
I turned to the pale stranger with a stare.
'What is your name?' I asked him. He said: 'Prayer.'

VI.ix.　A la fenêtre pendant la nuit

I

Les étoiles, points d'or, percent les branches noires;
Le flot huileux et lourd décompose ses moires
　　　Sur l'océan blêmi;
Les nuages ont l'air d'oiseaux prenant la fuite;
Par moments le vent parle, et dit des mots sans suite,　　　5
　　　Comme un homme endormi.

Tout s'en va. La nature est l'urne mal fermée.
La tempête est écume et la flamme est fumée.
　　　Rien n'est hors du moment,
L'homme n'a rien qu'il prenne, et qu'il tienne, et qu'il garde.　10
Il tombe heure par heure, et, ruine, il regarde
　　　Le monde, écroulement.

L'astre est-il le point fixe en ce mouvant problème?
Ce ciel que nous voyons fut-il toujours le même?
　　　Le sera-t-il toujours?　　　15
L'homme a-t-il sur son front des clartés éternelles?
Et verra-t-il toujours les mêmes sentinelles
　　　Monter aux mêmes tours?

II

Nuits, serez-vous pour nous toujours ce que vous êtes?
Pour toute vision, aurons-nous sur nos têtes　　　20
　　　Toujours les mêmes cieux?
Dis, larve Aldebaran, réponds, spectre Saturne,
Ne verrons-nous jamais sur le masque nocturne
　　　S'ouvrir de nouveaux yeux?

At the Window in the Dark

I

The stars, gold specks, are piercing the dark leaves;
The oily sea, dismembering its swell, heaves
    Onto the livid deep;
The clouds seem to be taking flight like birds,
And the wind grunts inconsequential words
    Like a man in his sleep.

All passes. Nature is an ill-shut jar;
Storms are spray, and flames vapour. All things are
    Time-bound and transient;
Not one thing can we cling to anywhere;
Ruins, and rotting hour by hour, we stare
    At Earth's dismantlement.

Are stars fixed points in this uncertainty?
Has the sky always been what we now see?
    And will it thus remain?
Are people's brows lit by eternal light?
Will the same sentinels, night after night,
    Survey the same terrain?

II

Will we forever have the nights we do?
Above our foreheads, will there be on view
    Forever the same skies?
Speak, wraith Aldebaran, ghost Saturn, say:
Will the night's visage never once display
    An opening of new eyes?

Ne verrons-nous jamais briller de nouveaux astres? 25
Et des cintres nouveaux, et de nouveaux pilastres
Luire à notre œil mortel,
Dans cette cathédrale aux formidables porches
Dont le septentrion éclaire avec sept torches,
L'effrayant maître-autel? 30

A-t-il cessé, le vent qui fit naître ces roses,
Sirius, Orion, toi, Vénus, qui reposes
Notre œil dans le péril?
Ne verrons-nous jamais sous ces grandes haleines
D'autres fleurs de lumière éclore dans les plaines 35
De l'éternel avril?

Savons-nous où le monde en est de son mystère?
Qui nous dit, à nous, joncs du marais, vers de terre
Dont la bave reluit,
A nous qui n'avons pas nous-mêmes notre preuve, 40
Que Dieu ne va pas mettre une tiare neuve
Sur le front de la nuit?

III

Dieu n'a-t-il plus de flamme à ses lèvres profondes?
N'en fait-il plus jaillir des tourbillons de mondes?
Parlez, Nord et Midi! 45
N'emplit-il plus de lui sa création sainte?
Et ne souffle-t-il plus que d'une bouche éteinte
Sur l'être refroidi?

Quand les comètes vont et viennent, formidables,
Apportant la lueur des gouffres insondables 50
A nos fronts soucieux,
Brûlant, volant, peut-être âmes, peut-être mondes,
Savons-nous ce que font toutes ces vagabondes
Qui courent dans nos cieux?

Are we never to see new stars ablaze,
New arches shining on our mortal gaze,
    New colonnades of space,
In this cathedral whose tremendous spires
Septentrion illumes with seven fires,
    The dread High Altarplace?

Has the wind dropped that bore such flowers to us,
Orion, Sirius, and Hesperus
    That calms our eye in pain?
Are we never to see, in this vast air,
New blooms of light adorning anywhere
    The timeless April plain?

How can we know what the world has concealed?
Who will inform us reeds of the mud-field,
    Worms of the litter-bed
(And if they did, how could we credit them?)
That God will never set a diadem
    Of new gems on Night's head?

III

Have God's vast lips exhausted all their fire?
Can no more worlds spring up at his desire?
    Declare it, North and South!
Does he no longer fill what he has made?
And does he merely blow on its cold shade
    With an extinguished mouth?

When the tremendous comets come and go,
Bringing the gleam of gulfs we cannot know
    Before our anxious eyes—
Perhaps souls, worlds perhaps, that fly and blaze—
How can we tell what those celestial strays
    Are doing in our skies?

Qui donc a vu la source et connaît l'origine? 55
Qui donc, ayant sondé l'abîme, s'imagine
    En être mage et roi?
Ah! fantômes humains, courbés sous les désastres!
Qui donc a dit:—C'est bien, Éternel. Assez d'astres.
    N'en fais plus. Calme-toi!— 60

L'effet séditieux limiterait la cause?
Quelle bouche ici-bas peut dire à quelque chose:
    Tu n'iras pas plus loin?
Sous l'élargissement sans fin, la borne plie;
La création vit, croît et se multiplie; 65
    L'homme n'est qu'un témoin.

L'homme n'est qu'un témoin frémissant d'épouvante.
Les firmaments sont pleins de la séve vivante
    Comme les animaux.
L'arbre prodigieux croise, agrandit, transforme, 70
Et mêle aux cieux profonds, comme une gerbe énorme,
    Ses ténébreux rameaux.

Car la création est devant, Dieu derrière.
L'homme, du côté noir de l'obscure barrière,
    Vit, rôdeur curieux; 75
Il suffit que son front se lève pour qu'il voie
A travers la sinistre et morne claire-voie
    Cet œil mystérieux.

IV

Donc ne nous disons pas:—Nous avons nos étoiles.
Des flottes de soleils peut-être à pleines voiles 80
    Viennent en ce moment;
Peut-être que demain le créateur terrible,
Refaisant notre nuit, va contre un autre crible
    Changer le firmament.

Who knows the source? Who saw its genesis?
Who fancies he has plumbed the whole abyss
    And is its sage or king?
Poor human phantoms, bent by misery,
Saying: 'Enough stars, Lord! Go peaceably!
    Don't add another thing!'

Can mutinous Effect restrict its Cause?
Could any mouth on earth issue such laws—
    'Go thus far, then be gone'?
Boundaries must defer to boundless size;
Creation lives—it grows and multiplies;
    Men are mere lookers-on.

Men are mere lookers-on, timid and small.
A firmament is like an animal,
    Is full of living sap.
The great tree grows, transforms, and rises high;
Like a vast sheaf, across the depths of sky
    Its shady branches wrap.

Creation is in front—God is behind.
Inquisitive prowling man peeps from the blind
    Side of the barrier sky;
Yet he need only lift his brow to see,
Beyond the sinister dim filigree,
    That great mysterious eye.

IV

Never, then, say: 'We have our stars complete.'
Perhaps, right now, a whole fast-sailing fleet
    Of suns is being sent;
The dread Creator may tomorrow give
New nights to us, and with some other sieve
    Replace the firmament.

Qui sait? que savons-nous? Sur notre horizon sombre, 85
Que la création impénétrable encombre
   De ses taillis sacrés,
Muraille obscure où vient battre le flot de l'être,
Peut-être allons-nous voir brusquement apparaître
   Des astres effarés; 90

Des astres éperdus arrivant des abîmes,
Venant des profondeurs ou descendant des cimes,
   Et, sous nos noirs arceaux,
Entrant en foule, épars, ardents, pareils au rêve,
Comme dans un grand vent s'abat sur une grève 95
   Une troupe d'oiseaux;

Surgissant, clairs flambeaux, feux purs, rouges fournaises,
Aigrettes de rubis ou tourbillons de braises,
   Sur nos bords, sur nos monts,
Et nous pétrifiant de leurs aspects étranges; 100
Car dans le gouffre énorme il est des mondes anges
   Et des soleils démons!

Peut-être en ce moment, du fond des nuits funèbres,
Montant vers nous, gonflant ses vagues de ténèbres
   Et ses flots de rayons, 105
Le muet Infini, sombre mer ignorée,
Roule vers notre ciel une grande marée
   De constellations!

from *La Légende des siècles*

II.[ii]. La Conscience

Lorsque avec ses enfants vêtus de peaux de bêtes,
Échevelé, livide au milieu des tempêtes,
Caïn se fut enfui de devant Jéhovah,
Comme le soir tombait, l'homme sombre arriva

Who knows? what can we say? On our dark verge,
That dismal wall battered by Being's surge,
    Strewn with the sacred trees
Of the impenetrably vast creation,
Suddenly we could see some revelation
    Of frightened galaxies—

Of lost stars coming out of the abysses,
Falling from peaks or climbing precipices,
    And into our black doors
Streaming in scattered burning dreamlike herds,
As, in a mighty gale, a flock of birds
    Comes crashing to the shores;

Surging—red furnaces, bright flames, pure fires,
Some ruby-plumes, some whirling cinder-gyres—
    On our peaks and frontiers,
Alarming us with their strange avatars:
For, in the vast gulf, there are angel stars
    And there are demon spheres!

So, at this moment, from the depths of night,
Rising toward us, swelling its waves of light
    And shadow-fluctuations,
The silent Infinite's dark unknown sea
May roll into our sky majestically
    Tide-waves of constellations!

from *The Legend of the Ages*

Conscience

When, with his children clad in animal-skins,
Dishevelled, livid, through the storm-clouds Cain
Had fled the presence of Jehovah,
At nightfall the unhappy man

Au bas d'une montagne en une grande plaine;   5
Sa femme fatiguée et ses fils hors d'haleine
Lui dirent:—Couchons-nous sur la terre, et dormons.—
Caïn, ne dormant pas, songeait au pied des monts.
Ayant levé la tête, au fond des cieux funèbres
Il vit un œil, tout grand ouvert dans les ténèbres,   10
Et qui le regardait dans l'ombre fixement.
—Je suis trop près, dit-il avec un tremblement.
Il réveilla ses fils dormant, sa femme lasse,
Et se remit à fuir sinistre dans l'espace.
Il marcha trente jours, il marcha trente nuits.   15
Il allait, muet, pâle et frémissant aux bruits,
Furtif, sans regarder derrière lui, sans trêve,
Sans repos, sans sommeil. Il atteignit la grève
Des mers dans le pays qui fut depuis Assur.
—Arrêtons-nous, dit-il, car cet asile est sûr.   20
Restons-y. Nous avons du monde atteint les bornes.—
Et, comme il s'asseyait, il vit dans les cieux mornes
L'œil à la même place au fond de l'horizon.
Alors il tressaillit en proie au noir frisson.
—Cachez-moi! cria-t-il; et, le doigt sur la bouche,   25
Tous ses fils regardaient trembler l'aïeul farouche.
Caïn dit à Jabel, père de ceux qui vont
Sous des tentes de poil dans le désert profond:
—Étends de ce côté la toile de la tente.—
Et l'on développa la muraille flottante;   30
Et, quand on l'eut fixée avec des poids de plomb:
—Vous ne voyez plus rien? dit Tsilla, l'enfant blond,
La fille de ses fils, douce comme l'aurore;
Et Caïn répondit:—Je vois cet œil encore!—
Jubal, père de ceux qui passent dans les bourgs   35
Soufflant dans des clairons et frappant des tambours,
Cria:—Je saurai bien construire une barrière.—
Il fit un mur de bronze et mit Caïn derrière.
Et Caïn dit:—Cet œil me regarde toujours!
Hénoch dit:—Il faut faire une enceinte de tours   40
Si terrible, que rien ne puisse approcher d'elle.
Bâtissons une ville avec sa citadelle.
Bâtissons une ville, et nous la fermerons.—

Came to a mountain's foot, in a great plain.
His weary wife and worn-out sons
Said to him: 'Let us lie on the ground, and sleep.'
Cain, who did not sleep, lay before the mountain;
And, having raised his head, in heaven's depths
He saw an eye there in the dark, wide open,
Staring at him intently from the shadows.
'I am too close', he said, and trembled; woke
His sleeping sons, his weary wife, and once more
Took up his dreadful flight into the wilderness.
For thirty days he walked, for thirty nights.
He went, pale, silent, trembling at each sound,
Furtively, without looking back or respite,
Without sleep or repose; and reached the seashore
In the land that was later known as Asshur.
Then he said, 'Let us stop; let us stay here.
Now we have reached the borders of the world.
This refuge is secure.' As he sat down,
He saw the eye there in the dreary heavens,
In the same place, far off, at the horizon.
He shook with a dark shuddering, and cried,
'Hide me!' His sons, their fingers on their lips,
Saw how their troubled ancestor was trembling.
Cain said to Jabal, father of those who dwell
In homes of leather in the wilderness,
'Spread the tent here.' So they unrolled the fluttering
Barricade, weighed it down with iron weights,
And Zillah, the blonde daughter of his sons,
As soft as dawn, said: 'Now you see nothing, surely?'
But Cain replied: 'Still I can see that eye!'
Jubal, father of those who pass through towns
With beat of drum and blast of trumpet, cried:
'I know well how to make a barrier-wall.'
He wrought a bronze screen, and set Cain behind it.
But Cain said: 'Still that eye is watching me!'
Said Enoch: 'We must make a towering bulwark
So terrible, that nothing could approach it.
Come, let us build a town and citadel,
Come, let us build a town, and shut it close.'

Alors Tubalcaïn, père des forgerons,
Construisit une ville énorme et surhumaine.   45
Pendant qu'il travaillait, ses frères, dans la plaine,
Chassaient les fils d'Énos et les enfants de Seth;
Et l'on crevait les yeux à quiconque passait;
Et, le soir, on lançait des flèches aux étoiles.
Le granit remplaça la tente aux murs de toiles,   50
On lia chaque bloc avec des nœuds de fer,
Et la ville semblait une ville d'enfer;
L'ombre des tours faisait la nuit dans les campagnes;
Ils donnèrent aux murs l'épaisseur des montagnes;
Sur la porte on grava: «Défense à Dieu d'entrer.»   55
Quand ils eurent fini de clore et de murer,
On mit l'aïeul au centre en une tour de pierre,
Et lui restait lugubre et hagard.—O mon père!
L'œil a-t-il disparu? dit en tremblant Tsilla.
Et Caïn répondit:—Non, il est toujours là.   60
Alors il dit:—Je veux habiter sous la terre
Comme dans son sépulcre un homme solitaire;
Rien ne me verra plus, je ne verrai plus rien.—
On fit donc une fosse, et Caïn dit: C'est bien!
Puis il descendit seul sous cette voûte sombre.   65
Quand il se fut assis sur sa chaise dans l'ombre
Et qu'on eut sur son front fermé le souterrain,
L'œil était dans la tombe et regardait Caïn.

II.[vi]. Booz endormi

Booz s'était couché de fatigue accablé;
Il avait tout le jour travaillé dans son aire,
Puis avait fait son lit à sa place ordinaire;
Booz dormait auprès des boisseaux pleins de blé.

Ce vieillard possédait des champs de blés et d'orge;   5
Il était, quoique riche, à la justice enclin;
Il n'avait pas de fange en l'eau de son moulin,
Il n'avait pas d'enfer dans le feu de sa forge.

Then Tubal-cain, father of blacksmiths, made
A mighty city, huge and superhuman;
While he was working, in the plain his brothers
Drove off the sons of Enosh and of Seth,
Put out the eyes of all the passers-by,
And, at night, shot their arrows at the stars.
Granite replaced the tent walled round with fabrics;
The blocks were interlinked with iron bonds,
And the town seemed a town of hell: the shadows
Cast by its turrets made the country night.
The walls were thick as mountains; on the gate
They carved these words: 'No entry to the Lord.'
When they had finished closing it and walling,
They set their father in the very centre,
Inside a tower of stone. There he sat, wretched
And miserable. 'Has the eye gone now, father?'
Asked Zillah, trembling. And Cain answered: 'No;
It is still there.' Then he said: 'Let me live
Beneath the earth, a lone man in his tomb;
Nothing will see me there, I shall see nothing.'
They made a pit, and Cain said: 'It is good!'
Then he went down alone to the dark vault.
And when he had been seated in the gloom
And they had shut the crypt above his brain,
The eye was in the tomb and watching Cain.

Boaz Asleep

Overcome by fatigue, there Boaz lay.
He'd laboured all day on his threshing-ground,
Then made his bed in his accustomed way;
And now he slept, with wheat-bags all around.

He was a rich old man, but he was just.
The lands he owned grew wheat and barley well.
The water of his mill contained no dust;
The fire within his forge contained no hell.

Sa barbe était d'argent comme un ruisseau d'avril.
Sa gerbe n'était point avare ni haineuse; 10
Quand il voyait passer quelque pauvre glaneuse:
—Laissez tomber exprès des épis, disait-il.

Cet homme marchait pur loin des sentiers obliques,
Vêtu de probité candide et de lin blanc;
Et, toujours du côté des pauvres ruisselant, 15
Ses sacs de grains semblaient des fontaines publiques.

Booz était bon maître et fidèle parent;
Il était généreux, quoiqu'il fût économe;
Les femmes regardaient Booz plus qu'un jeune homme,
Car le jeune homme est beau, mais le vieillard est grand. 20

Le vieillard, qui revient vers la source première,
Entre aux jours éternels et sort des jours changeants;
Et l'on voit de la flamme aux yeux des jeunes gens,
Mais dans l'œil du vieillard on voit de la lumière.

*

Donc, Booz dans la nuit dormait parmi les siens; 25
Près des meules, qu'on eût prises pour des décombres,
Les moissonneurs couchés faisaient des groupes sombres;
Et ceci se passait dans des temps très anciens.

Les tribus d'Israël avaient pour chef un juge;
La terre, où l'homme errait sous la tente, inquiet 30
Des empreintes de pieds de géants qu'il voyait,
Était encor mouillée et molle du déluge.

*

Comme dormait Jacob, comme dormait Judith,
Booz, les yeux fermés, gisait sous la feuillée;
Or, la porte du ciel s'étant entre-bâillée 35
Au–dessus de sa tête, un songe en descendit.

Et ce songe était tel, que Booz vit un chêne
Qui, sorti de son ventre, allait jusqu'au ciel bleu;
Une race y montait comme une longue chaîne;
Un roi chantait en bas, en haut mourait un dieu. 40

His beard was silvered like an April brook.
In all his fields no hate or meanness lay;
At some poor gleaning-woman he might look—
'Leave a few ears on purpose', he would say.

Clad in white linen and sheer purity
He walked, untouched by any crooked road;
His sacks were open fountains: publicly,
Incessantly, toward the poor they flowed.

An honest master, a good citizen,
Boaz was generous without being flighty.
Girls looked at Boaz more than younger men:
Young men are handsome, but old men are mighty.

Back to their fountainhead old men arise,
Go to eternal Day from passing Night.
You may indeed see fire in young men's eyes,
But in the eyes of old men you see light.

*

So Boaz slept among his labourers.
The millstones stood like ruins; row on row
Beside them lay dark groves of harvesters.
Now, this took place in days of long ago:

A judge in Israel gave the tribes their law;
The earth was soft and moist still from the flood;
Men dwelt in tents, and trembled when they saw
The footprints of the giants in the mud.

*

As Jacob slept or Judith, Boaz lay,
With eyelids closed, beneath the forest's crown.
Now, heaven's gate opened itself halfway
Above his head, and thence a dream came down.

And this was the dream: Boaz saw an oak
Sprout from his loins and rise into the sky,
And up it climbed a mighty chain of folk.
A king sang here; up there, a god would die.

Et Booz murmurait avec la voix de l'âme:
« Comment se pourrait-il que de moi ceci vînt?
Le chiffre de mes ans a passé quatrevingt,
Et je n'ai pas de fils, et je n'ai plus de femme.

« Voilà longtemps que celle avec qui j'ai dormi,   45
O Seigneur! a quitté ma couche pour la vôtre;
Et nous sommes encor tout mêlés l'un à l'autre,
Elle à demi vivante et moi mort à demi.

« Une race naîtrait de moi! Comment le croire?
Comment se pourrait-il que j'eusse des enfants?   50
Quand on est jeune, on a des matins triomphants,
Le jour sort de la nuit comme d'une victoire;

« Mais, vieux, on tremble ainsi qu'à l'hiver le bouleau;
Je suis veuf, je suis seul, et sur moi le soir tombe,
Et je courbe, ô mon Dieu! mon âme vers la tombe,   55
Comme un bœuf ayant soif penche son front vers l'eau. »

Ainsi parlait Booz dans le rêve et l'extase,
Tournant vers Dieu ses yeux par le sommeil noyés;
Le cèdre ne sent pas une rose à sa base,
Et lui ne sentait pas une femme à ses pieds.   60

*

Pendant qu'il sommeillait, Ruth, une moabite,
S'était couchée aux pieds de Booz, le sein nu,
Espérant on ne sait quel rayon inconnu,
Quand viendrait du réveil la lumière subite.

Booz ne savait point qu'une femme était là,   65
Et Ruth ne savait point ce que Dieu voulait d'elle.
Un frais parfum sortait des touffes d'asphodèle;
Les souffles de la nuit flottaient sur Galgala.

L'ombre était nuptiale, auguste et solennelle;
Les anges y volaient sans doute obscurément,   70
Car on voyait passer dans la nuit, par moment,
Quelque chose de bleu qui paraissait une aile.

Then Boaz murmured—in his soul he said:
'Can such things come from me? And if so, how?
My eightieth appointed year has sped;
I have no son—nor a wife either, now:

'Long ago, she with whom I used to sleep
Crossed to you, O Jehovah, from my bed;
And our two souls are still commingled deep,
She being half-alive, and I half-dead.

'Can that be so—a people born from me?
Shall I have children now? How could it hold?
In youth, day springs from night victoriously,
Our dawns are triumphs; but when we are old,

'We toss like trees by winter gales traversed.
Widowed, alone, over me falls the gloom;
And, as an ox bends down to quench its thirst,
I bend, O Lord, my own soul to the tomb.'

In trance and dream thus Boaz spoke, his face
With sleep-drowned eyes raised to Jehovah's seat.
Cedars do not feel roses at their base;
He did not feel a woman at his feet.

*

While he was sleeping, Ruth, a Moabite,
Had lain at Boaz' feet with naked breast,
Trusting that some yet-unknown ray of light,
Some quickening dawn, would soon be manifest.

Boaz knew nothing of her being there,
And Ruth knew nothing of God's plan for her.
Cool tufts of asphodel perfumed the air;
On Galgala, night's breezes were astir.

The dusk was solemn, nuptial, dignified;
Surely dark angels there were hovering:
Now and then, in the shadows, could be spied
A touch of blue that seemed to be a wing.

La respiration de Booz qui dormait,
Se mêlait au bruit sourd des ruisseaux sur la mousse.
On était dans le mois où la nature est douce,   75
Les collines ayant des lys sur leur sommet.

Ruth songeait et Booz dormait; l'herbe était noire;
Les grelots des troupeaux palpitaient vaguement;
Une immense bonté tombait du firmament;
C'était l'heure tranquille où les lions vont boire.   80

Tout reposait dans Ur et dans Jérimadeth;
Les astres émaillaient le ciel profond et sombre;
Le croissant fin et clair parmi ces fleurs d'ombre
Brillait à l'occident, et Ruth se demandait,

Immobile, ouvrant l'œil à moitié sous ses voiles,   85
Quel dieu, quel moissonneur de l'éternel été
Avait, en s'en allant, négligemment jeté
Cette faucille d'or dans le champ des étoiles.

XXVII. L'Inquisition

« Le baptême des volcans est un ancien usage qui remonte aux
premiers temps de la conquête. Tous les cratères du Nicaragua
furent alors sanctifiés, à l'exception du Momotombo, d'où l'on
ne vit jamais revenir les religieux qui s'étaient chargés d'aller y
planter la croix. »

Squier, *Voyage dans l'Amerique du Sud*

LES RAISONS DU MOMOTOMBO

Trouvant les tremblements de terre trop fréquents,
Les rois d'Espagne ont fait baptiser les volcans
Du royaume qu'ils ont en dessous de la sphère;
Les volcans n'ont rien dit et se sont laissé faire,
Et le Momotombo lui seul n'a pas voulu.   5

The sleeper's breathing blended in the ear
With a deep sound of streams on mossy rills.
Nature was gentle at that time of year,
And flowering lilies crowned the distant hills.

The flocks' bells tinkled faintly as they went;
Ruth pondered, Boaz slept; the grass was dank.
Blessings descended from the firmament.
It was the peaceful hour when lions drank.

Ur and Jerimadeth were all at rest;
The stars enamelled heaven's sombre deep;
A slender crescent sparkled in the west
Among those flowers of darkness; half-asleep

Lay Ruth, wondering, her veiled eyes half-parted,
What god, cropping the timeless summer yield,
Had dropped so carelessly as he departed
That golden sickle in the starry field.

The Inquisition

This [the baptism of volcanoes] is an old practice, and the ceremony, it is said, was performed, early after the Conquest, on all the volcanoes in Nicaragua, with the exception of Momotombo, which is still among the unsanctified. The old friars who started for its summit, to set up the cross there, were never heard of again.

Squier, *Travels in Central America*

MOMOTOMBO'S REASONS

As earthquakes happened far too frequently,
Spain's kings had the volcanoes all baptized
Throughout their nether realms beyond the sea.
The summits all said nothing, temporized,
And only Momotombo raised objection.

Plus d'un prêtre en surplis, par le saint-père élu,
Portant le sacrament que l'église administre,
L'œil au ciel, a monté la montagne sinistre;
Beaucoup y sont allés, pas un n'est revenu.

O vieux Momotombo, colosse chauve et nu,   10
Qui songes près des mers, et fais de ton cratère
Une tiare d'ombre et de flamme à la terre,
Pourquoi, lorsqu'à ton seuil terrible nous frappons,
Ne veux-tu pas du Dieu qu'on t'apporte? Réponds.

La montagne interrompt son crachement de lave,   15
Et le Momotombo répond d'une voix grave:

—Je n'aimais pas beaucoup le dieu qu'on a chassé.
Cet avare cachait de l'or dans un fossé;
Il mangeait de la chair humaine; ses mâchoires
Étaient de pourriture et de sang toutes noires;   20
Son antre était un porche au farouche carreau,
Temple sépulcre orné d'un pontife bourreau;
Des squelettes riaient sous ses pieds; les écuelles
Où cet être buvait le meurtre étaient cruelles;
Sourd, difforme, il avait des serpents au poignet;   25
Toujours entre ses dents un cadavre saignait;
Ce spectre noircissait le firmament sublime.
J'en grondais quelquefois au fond de mon abîme.
Aussi, quand sont venus, fiers sur les flots tremblants,
Et du côté d'où vient le jour, des hommes blancs,   30
Je les ai bien reçus, trouvant que c'était sage.
L'âme a certainement le couleur du visage,
Disais-je, l'homme blanc, c'est comme le ciel bleu;
Et le dieu de ceux-ci doit être un très bon dieu.
On ne le verra point de meurtres se repaître.—   35
J'étais content; j'avais horreur de l'ancien prêtre.
Mais quand j'ai vu comment travaille le nouveau,
Quand j'ai vu flamboyer, ciel juste! à mon niveau!
Cette torche lugubre, âpre, jamais éteinte,
Sombre, que vous nommez l'Inquisition sainte,   40

More than one surpliced priest, at the direction
Of Holy Father, bore the sacrament
(One eye on heaven) to the mount's dread vent;
Many went up there, none of them came down.

Old giant Momotombo, bare of crown,
Dreaming beside the seas, making your girth
A smoking flaming diadem on earth,
When at your grim door we come knocking, why
Should you decline the god that we supply?

Mount Momotombo cleared his laval throat,
And gave this answer in a solemn note:

'Little I liked the god they drove away.
He was a miser—buried gold all day;
Used to eat human flesh; and all his breath
Was black with rottenness and blood and death.
His savage temple was a sepulchre
Adorned with a priest-executioner;
Serpents were in his fist, bones at his feet,
And murders were his cruel drink and meat.
The creature was misshapen and unheeding;
Between his teeth some corpse was always bleeding.
There, blackening the glorious sky, was this!
I growled about it down in my abyss.
So when there came, out of the morning light,
Proud on the trembling waves, men who were white,
I welcomed them—it seemed the thing to do.
"The soul's hue must be like the body's hue",
I said; "a white man, that's like a clear sky;
Their god should be a good god"—so thought I;
"We shan't see any murders now, at least."
That pleased me—I'd detested the old priest.
But when I saw the new one do his act,
Setting alight—as big as me, in fact!—
Bitter, grim, dismal, with no intermission,
The fire you call the Holy Inquisition,

Quand j'ai pu voir comment Torquemada s'y prend
Pour dissiper la nuit du sauvage ignorant,
Comment il civilise, et de quelle manière
Le saint-office enseigne et fait de la lumière,
Quand j'ai vu dans Lima d'affreux géants d'osier, 　　　45
Pleins d'enfants, pétiller sur un large brasier,
Et le feu dévorer la vie, et les fumées
Se tordre sur les seins des femmes allumées;
Quand je me suis senti parfois presque étouffé
Par l'âcre odeur qui sort de votre auto-da-fé, 　　　50
Moi qui ne brûlais rien que l'ombre en ma fournaise,
J'ai pensé que j'avais eu tort d'être bien aise;
J'ai regardé de près le dieu de l'étranger,
Et j'ai dit:—Ce n'est pas la peine de changer.

XLIX.[iv].　Après la bataille

Mon père, ce héros au sourire si doux,
Suivi d'un seul housard qu'il aimait entre tous
Pour sa grande bravoure et pour sa haute taille,
Parcourait à cheval, le soir d'une bataille,
Le champ couvert de morts sur qui tombait la nuit. 　　　5
Il lui sembla dans l'ombre entendre un faible bruit.
C'était un espagnol de l'armée en déroute
Qui se traînait sanglant sur le bord de la route,
Râlant, brisé, livide, et mort plus qu'à moitié,
Et qui disait:—A boire, à boire par pitié!— 　　　10
Mon père, ému, tendit à son housard fidèle
Une gourde de rhum qui pendait à sa selle,
Et dit:—Tiens, donne à boire à ce pauvre blessé.—
Tout à coup, au moment où le housard baissé
Se penchait vers lui, l'homme, une espèce de maure, 　　　15
Saisit un pistolet qu'il étreignait encore,
Et vise au front mon père en criant: Caramba!
Le coup passa si près que le chapeau tomba
Et que le cheval fit un écart en arrière.
—Donne-lui tout de même à boire, dit mon père. 　　　20

When I saw Torquemada set to work
Cleansing benighted savages of murk,
Saw how the Holy Office in its might
Civilizes the land and spreads the light,
When I saw Lima's giant wicker frames
Of children crackling over the huge flames,
And fire devouring life itself, and curls
Of smoke wreathing the breasts of burning girls,
When I felt stifled by the stench you make
Every time you burn heretics at the stake—
I who burn only darkness in my furnace—
I saw I should have acted with more sternness.
Viewing the strangers' god at closer range,
"Why", thought I, "bother to make any change?"'

After the Battle

My father—that kind smiling hero—went
With the one hussar whom he most preferred
For his tall stature and cool temperament,
One night, after a battle had occurred,
To ride across the dark field strewn with dead.
He thought he heard a faint noise in the shadows.
There was a Spaniard from the routed army
Crawling in blood beside the road,
Groaning and battered, pale, more than half dead.
'A drink! a drink for pity's sake!' he shouted.
My father, being touched, passed the good hussar
A flask of rum from his saddle;
'Give the poor wounded fellow this', he said.
Suddenly, when the hussar stooped toward him,
The man—a Moor of some kind—snatching up
A little pistol that he had been clutching,
Fired at my father. 'Caramba!' he cried.
The bullet shot the hat clean from his head,
It went so close—and the horse beneath him shied.
'Let him drink all the same', my father said.

LX. La Trompette du jugement

Je vis dans la nuée un clairon monstrueux.

Et ce clairon semblait, au seuil profond des cieux,
Calme, attendre le souffle immense de l'archange.

Ce qui jamais ne meurt, ce qui jamais ne change,
L'entourait. A travers un frisson, on sentait   5
Que ce buccin fatal, qui rêve et qui se tait,
Quelque part, dans l'endroit où l'on crée, où l'on sème,
Avait été forgé par quelqu'un de suprême
Avec de l'équité condensée en airain.
Il était là, lugubre, effroyable, serein.   10
Il gisait sur la brume insondable qui tremble,
Hors du monde, au delà de tout ce qui ressemble
A la forme de quoi que ce soit.
                                        Il vivait.

Il semblait un réveil songeant près d'un chevet.

Oh! quelle nuit! là, rien n'a de contour ni d'âge;   15
Et le nuage est spectre, et le spectre est nuage.

                        *

Et c'était le clairon de l'abîme.

                        Une voix
Un jour en sortira qu'on entendra sept fois.
En attendant, glacé, mais écoutant, il pense;
Couvant le châtiment, couvant la récompense;   20
Et toute l'épouvante éparse au ciel est sœur
De cet impénétrable et morne avertisseur.

Je le considérais dans les vapeurs funèbres
Comme on verrait se taire un coq dans les ténèbres.
Pas un murmure autour du clairon souverain.   25
Et la terre sentait le froid de son airain,
Quoique, là, d'aucun monde on ne vît les frontières.

The Trumpet of Judgement

I saw among the clouds a monstrous trumpet.

On the broad threshold of the skies it seemed
Calmly to wait the vast breath of the archangel.

What never perishes, what never changes,
Surrounded it. You felt—felt with a shudder—
That some almighty being must have forged
This fatal dreaming instrument wherever
Seed is sown and creation is created:
Condensing justice into bronze to make it.

There it was, dismal, fearful, and serene;
It lay on the unfathomable trembling
Mist from outside the world; beyond the semblance
Of any form whatever.
                          It was alive.

Like an alarm-clock dreaming at a bedside.

Such night, too! Nothing there of age or contour:
Clouds, there, are phantoms; phantoms, there, are clouds.
                          *
It was the trumpet of the chasm.
                          One day
A voice will come from it—and be heard sevenfold.
Meanwhile, frozen and yet attentive, it is
Pondering—breeding punishments and rewards;
All terrors strewn in the sky, are sister to
This bleak impenetrable watchman.

It was as silent as a cock at night
Within the dismal mists. I studied it.
No murmur round that sovereign trumpet: none.
And the earth felt its brassy chill—although
The fringes of no world could be discerned there.

Et l'immobilité de tous les cimetières,
Et le sommeil de tous les tombeaux, et la paix
De tous les morts couchés dans la fosse, étaient faits   30
Du silence inouï qu'il avait dans la bouche;
Ce lourd silence était pour l'affreux mort farouche
L'impossibilité de faire faire un pli
Au suaire cousu sur son front par l'oubli.
Ce silence tenait en suspens l'anathème.   35
On comprenait que tant que ce clairon suprême
Se tairait, le sépulcre, obscur, roidi, béant,
Garderait l'attitude horrible du néant,
Que la momie aurait toujours sa bandelette,
Que l'homme irait tombant du cadavre au squelette,   40
Et que ce fier banquet radieux, ce festin
Que les vivants gloutons appellent le destin,
Toute la joie errante en tourbillons de fêtes,
Toutes les passions de la chair satisfaites,
Gloire, orgueil, les héros ivres, les tyrans soûls,   45
Continueraient d'avoir pour but, et pour dessous,
La pourriture, orgie offerte aux vers convives;
Mais qu'à l'heure où soudain, dans l'espace sans rives,
Cette trompette vaste et sombre sonnerait,
On verrait, comme un tas d'oiseaux d'une forêt,   50
Toutes les âmes, cygne, aigle, éperviers, colombes,
Frémissantes, sortir du tremblement des tombes,
Et tous les spectres faire un bruit de grandes eaux,
Et se dresser, et prendre à la hâte leurs os,
Tandis qu'au fond, au fond du gouffre, au fond du rêve,   55
Blanchissant l'absolu, comme un jour qui se lève,
Le front mystérieux du juge apparaîtrait.

                              *

Ce clairon avait l'air de savoir le secret.

On sentait que le râle énorme de ce cuivre
Serait tel qu'il ferait bondir, vibrer, revivre   60
L'ombre, le plomb, le marbre, et qu'à ce fatal glas,

And the tranquillity of all the graveyards,
The sleep of all the sepulchres, the peace
Of all the dead bedded in graves, were drawn
Out of its unknown silence; and that silence was
A ponderous thing—was the impossibility
Of raising even the smallest shroud-fold that oblivion
Had sewn across the brows of the grim dead.
That silence held the anathema suspended.
Clearly, while the last trumpet remained silent,
Graves—dim, stiff, gaping—would retain their dreadful
Nonentity, and mummies their winding-cloths;
Mankind would dwindle still from corpse to skeleton;
And this fine glittering banquet—this festivity
Called 'Fate' by living gluttons—all the joy
Whirling at parties—sated fleshly passions—
Fame, honour—drunken heroes, sozzled tyrants—
Would have their goal and basis in corruption,
In orgies offered to convivial earthworms;
But when that vast and sombre trumpet suddenly
Sounded in boundless space, then you would see,
Like a flock of birds from a forest, all
The souls—swans, eagles, sparrowhawks, and doves—
Rise trembling from their shaken tombs, and all
The ghosts, making a noise of mighty waters,
Stand up and gather up their bones in haste,
While in the depths, in the depths of the pit,
In reverie's depths, and whitening
The Absolute like daybreak, the mysterious
Brow of the Judge would be revealed.

                              *

                                        That trumpet
Appeared to know the secret.

                                        And its metal
Would rattle so—as you could sense—that marble,
Lead, ghost, would leap, vibrate, and live again;
And, at its fatal summons, every dumb thing

Toutes les surdités voleraient en éclats;
Que l'oubli sombre, avec sa perte de mémoire,
Se lèverait au son de la trompette noire;
Que dans cette clameur étrange, en même temps   65
Qu'on entendrait frémir tous les cieux palpitants,
On entendrait crier toutes les consciences;
Que le sceptique au fond de ses insouciances,
Que le voluptueux, l'athée et le douteur,
Et le maître tombé de toute sa hauteur,   70
Sentiraient ce fracas traverser leurs vertèbres;
Que ce déchirement céleste des ténèbres
Ferait dresser quiconque est soumis à l'arrêt;
Que qui n'entendit pas le remords, l'entendrait;
Et qu'il réveillerait, comme un choc à la porte,   75
L'oreille la plus dure et l'âme la plus morte,
Même ceux qui, livrés au rire, aux vains combats,
Aux vils plaisirs, n'ont point tenu compte ici-bas
Des avertissements de l'ombre et du mystère,
Même ceux que n'a point réveillés sur la terre   80
Le tonnerre, ce coup de cloche de la nuit!

Oh! dans l'esprit de l'homme où tout vacille et fuit,
Où le verbe n'a pas un mot qui ne bégaie,
Où l'aurore apparaît, hélas! comme une plaie,
Dans cette esprit, tremblant dès qu'il ose augurer,   85
Oh! comment concevoir, comment se figurer
Cette vibration communiquée aux tombes,
Cette sommation aux blêmes catacombes
Du ciel ouvrant sa porte et du gouffre ayant faim,
Le prodigieux bruit de Dieu disant: Enfin!   90

Oui, c'est vrai,—c'est du moins jusque-là que l'œil plonge,—
C'est l'avenir,—du moins tel qu'on le voit en songe;—
Quand le monde atteindra son but, quand les instants,
Les jours, les mois, les ans, auront rempli le temps,

Would shatter into fragments;
And dark forgetfulness would rise up mindless
At the black trumpet's sound; and, at the same time,
The throbbing heavens would all be heard to shudder,
The consciences all to cry out; and the sceptic
Rapt in his own insouciance, the hedonist,
The atheist, the doubter, and the expert
Fallen from his lofty height, would feel the whole din
Run through their vertebrae; and this celestial
Rending of all the shades, would make whoever
Is subject to condemnation start up suddenly;
Those who had never heard remorse, would hear it;
It would awaken like a battering at the gate
The hardest ear, the deadest spirit—even
Those who had given themselves over to laughter,
To futile squabbles and squalid pleasures, and
Had taken no note of the warnings of
The shadow and the mystery here below—
Yes, even those that never once awakened
To the night's bell-stroke, thunder, here on earth!

Oh, in the human mind, where everything
Wavers and scatters, where language itself
Has no unstammered word, where dawn arises
Like a wound—in this mind, trembling as it
Ventures to prophesy—how can it all
Be pictured, how imagined: the imparted
Quaking of the tombs, the summoning
Of pale catacombs in the opened heavens
And hungry pit—the one colossal sound
Of God saying: 'At last!'

                                  Yes, it is true—
At least, it is as far as the eye penetrates;
Such is the future—as, at least, we see it
In visions: when the world reaches its goal,
When time has filled up—seconds, days, months, years—

Quand tombera du ciel l'heure immense et nocturne,   95
Cette goutte qui doit faire déborder l'urne,
Alors, dans le silence horrible, un rayon blanc,
Long, pâle, glissera, formidable et tremblant,
Sur ces haltes de nuit qu'on nomme cimetières,
Les tentes frémiront, quoiqu'elles soient des pierres,   100
Dans tous ces sombres camps endormis; et, sortant
Tout à coup de la brume où l'univers l'attend,
Ce clairon, au-dessus des êtres et des choses,
Au-dessus des forfaits et des apothéoses,
Des ombres et des os, des esprits et des corps,   105
Sonnera la diane effrayante des morts.

O lever en sursaut des larves pêle-mêle!
Oh! la Nuit réveillant la Mort, sa sœur jumelle!

Pensif, je regardais l'incorruptible airain.

                          *

Les volontés sans loi, les passions sans frein,   110
Toutes les actions de tous les êtres, haines,
Amours, vertus, fureurs, hymnes, cris, plaisirs, peines,
Avaient laissé, dans l'ombre où rien ne remuait,
Leur pâle empreinte autour de ce bronze muet;
Une obscure Babel y tordait sa spirale.   115

Sa dimension vague, ineffable, spectrale,
Sortant de l'éternel, entrait dans l'absolu.
Pour pouvoir mesurer ce tube, il eût fallu
Prendre la toise au fond du rêve, et la coudée
Dans la profondeur trouble et sombre de l'idée;   120
Un de ses bouts touchait le bien, l'autre le mal;
Et sa longueur allait de l'homme à l'animal,
Quoiqu'on ne vît point là d'animal, et point d'homme;
Couché sur terre, il eût joint Éden à Sodome.

Son embouchure, gouffre où plongeait mon regard,   ·   125
Cercle de l'Inconnu ténébreux et hagard,
Pleine de cette horreur que le mystère exhale,
M'apparaissait ainsi qu'une offre colossale

And one nocturnal instant falls from heaven,
The drop that makes the whole vase overflow;
Then, in the dreadful silence, a white gleam
Will slip out, long and pale, fearsome and trembling,
Across night's stopping-points—which we call cemeteries;
The very tents—stone though they are—will shudder,
In all those sombre sleeping camps; and, coming
Suddenly out of the mist where the universe
Is awaiting it, this trumpet, over creatures
And objects, over crimes and apotheoses,
Spirits and bodies, shades and bones, will sound
The terrible reveille of the dead.

One jolt, to raise a jumbled mass of larvae—
Night wakening her own twin sister Death!

I pondered on the incorruptible brass.

*

Such lawless impulses, unbridled passions,
All actions of all creatures, hates and loves,
Virtues and rages, hymns, wails, pains and pleasures,
Had left their pallid imprint in the shadow
Where nothing moved, around this silent metal;
A whole dim Babel wreathed its spiral there.

Obscure in size—ineffable, phantasmic—
It passed from the Eternal to the Absolute.
Only the yard of dreaming's depth could measure it,
The cubit of thought's turbid chasm.
One of its ends touched good, the other evil;
In length it stretched from man to animal,
Though neither animal nor man was there;
On earth, it would have spanned Eden and Sodom.

Its mouth—the gulf in which my gaze was plunged,
A circle of the Unknown, unkempt and tenebrous,
And full of mystery's exhaled horrors—
Appeared to me like one vast invitation

D'entrer dans l'ombre où Dieu même est évanoui.
Cette gueule, avec l'air d'un redoutable ennui,   130
Morne, s'élargissait sur l'homme et la nature,
Et cette épouvantable et muette ouverture
Semblait le bâillement noir de l'éternité.

*

Au fond de l'immanent et de l'illimité,
Parfois, dans les lointains sans nom de l'Invisible,   135
Quelque chose tremblait de vaguement terrible,
Et brillait et passait, inexprimable éclair.
Toutes les profondeurs des mondes avaient l'air
De méditer, dans l'ombre où l'ombre se répète,
L'heure où l'on entendrait de cette âpre trompette   140
Un appel aussi long que l'infini jaillir.
L'immuable semblait d'avance en tressaillir.

Des porches de l'abîme, antres hideux, cavernes
Que nous nommons enfers, puits, gehennams, avernes,
Bouches d'obscurité qui ne prononcent rien,   145
Du vide où ne flottait nul souffle aérien,
Du silence où l'haleine osait à peine éclore,
Ceci se dégageait pour l'âme: Pas encore.

Par instants, dans ce lieu triste comme le soir,
Comme on entend le bruit de quelqu'un qui vient voir,   150
On entendait le pas boiteux de la justice;
Puis cela s'effaçait. Des vermines, le vice,
Le crime, s'approchaient, et, fourmillement noir,
Fuyaient. Le clairon sombre ouvrait son entonnoir.
Un groupe d'ouragans dormait dans ce cratère.   155
Comme cette organum des gouffres doit se taire
Jusqu'au jour monstrueux où nous écarterons
Les clous de notre bière au-dessus de nos fronts,
Nul bras ne le touchait dans l'invisible sphère;
Chaque race avait fait sa couche de poussière   160
Dans l'orbe sépulcral de son évasement;
Sur cette poudre l'œil lisait confusément
Ce mot: Riez, écrit par le doigt d'Épicure;

To join the dark in which God himself vanishes.
Its dismal muzzle, with a dread monotony,
Spread out across humanity and nature;
Its grim and silent aperture was like
The black yawn of eternity.

*

Deep in the immanent and the unlimited,
At times, in the remote unnamed Invisible,
Some vaguely terrible thing was trembling, gleaming,
And passing on—some inexpressible lightning.
The depths of all the worlds, it seemed, were pondering—
In the shadow where shadow multiplies—
The time when that stern trumpet would be heard
To blast a call long as the infinite.
The changeless seemed to quail at it already.

From the vestibules of the abyss—grim chasms,
Caverns that we call hells, Tophets, Gehennas,
Mouths of the darkness, voicing nothing—from
The void where not a wisp of air was floating—
And from the silence where the breath itself
Scarcely dared breathe—the soul was being told:
'Not yet.'

At times, in this realm sad as nightfall,
The limping step of justice could be heard,
Like the sound of a person coming to look;
Then it was gone. Vice, vermin, crime came near
And fled off, black and teeming. The dark trumpet
Was opening its funnel. Swarms of hurricanes
Were sleeping in that crater; but the instrument
Of the abysses must remain in silence
Till the day when we push out the coffin-nails
Above our heads: so, in the unseen regions,
Not a hand touched it. Each race of humanity
Had left a bed of dust in the funereal
Arc of its mouth; across that dirt, your eye
Could vaguely read the word LAUGH, scrawled
By Epicurus' finger; and could see,

Et l'on voyait, au fond de la rondeur obscure,
La toile d'araignée horrible de Satan.   165

Des astres qui passaient murmuraient: «Souviens-t'en!
Prie!» et la nuit portait cette parole à l'ombre.
Et je ne sentais plus ni le temps ni le nombre.

*

Une sinistre main sortait de l'Infini.

Vers la trompette, effroi de tout crime impuni,   170
Qui doit faire à la mort un jour lever la tête,
Elle pendait énorme, ouverte, et comme prête
A saisir ce clairon qui se tait dans la nuit,
Et qu'emplit le sommeil formidable du bruit.
La main, dans la nuée et hors de l'Invisible,   175
S'allongeait. A quel être était-elle? Impossible
De le dire, en ce morne et brumeux firmament.
L'œil dans l'obscurité ne voyait clairement
Que les cinq doigts béants de cette main terrible;
Tant l'être, quel qu'il fût, debout dans l'ombre horrible,   180
—Sans doute quelque archange ou quelque séraphin
Immobile, attendant le signe de la fin,—
Plongeait profondément, sous les ténébreux voiles,
Du pied dans les enfers, du front dans les étoiles!

from *L'Art d'être grand-père*

I.xi. Fenêtres ouvertes

Le matin.—En dormant

J'entends des voix. Lueurs à travers ma paupière.
Une cloche est en branle à l'église Saint-Pierre.
Cris des baigneurs. Plus près! plus loin! non, par ici!
Non, par là! Les oiseaux gazouillent, Jeanne aussi.
Georges l'appelle. Chant des coqs. Une truelle   5

In the depths of the gloomy cavity,
The dreadful spider-web of Satan.

                         Passing
Stars murmured as they went: 'Remember!
Pray!' And night carried off their words to darkness.
And I felt no more time, nor any number.

                     *

A sinister hand came from the Infinite.

Toward the trumpet—that terror of every
Unpunished crime—silent in darkness, full of
The fearful sleep of sound, though it must make death
Lift its head one day—the vast hand was hovering,
Wide open, as if poised to seize the instrument.
It reached out through the cloud, past the Invisible.
Who could say, in that dismal dim expanse,
To what being it might belong?
All that the eye could see with any clarity,
There, were the hand's five gaping fingers;
The creature motionless in that dread gloom—
Whoever he was: seraph or archangel
No doubt, waiting the signal for the end—
Stretched out, behind the shadow-veils, so far;
His foot touched an abyss, his brow a star.

from *The Art of Being a Grandfather*

Open Windows

In the morning—sleeping

I can hear voices. Through my eyelids, light.
There's a bell at St Peter's, in full swing.
Some bathers shouting. Nearer! Further! Right!
No, left! No, right! The birds are twittering,
Jeanne too. Georges calls her. Cock-crows. Horses pass

Racle un toit. Des chevaux passent dans la ruelle.
Grincement d'une faulx qui coupe le gazon.
Chocs. Rumeurs. Des couvreurs marchent sur la maison.
Bruits du port. Sifflement des machines chauffées.
Musique militaire arrivant par bouffées.   10
Brouhaha sur le quai. Voix françaises. Merci.
Bonjour. Adieu. Sans doute il est tard, car voici
Que vient tout près de moi chanter mon rouge-gorge.
Vacarme de marteaux lointains dans une forge.
L'eau clapote. On entend haleter un steamer.   15
Une mouche entre. Souffle immense de la mer.

IV.v. Encore Dieu, mais avec des restrictions

Quel beau lieu! Là le cèdre avec l'orme chuchote,
L'âne est lyrique et semble avoir vu Don Quichotte,
Le tigre en cage a l'air d'un roi dans son palais,
Les pachydermes sont effroyablement laids;
Et puis c'est littéraire, on rêve à des idylles   5
De Viennet en voyant bâiller les crocodiles.
Là, pendant qu'au babouin la singesse se vend,
Pendant que le baudet contemple le savant,
Et que le vautour fait au hibou bon visage,
Certes, c'est un emploi du temps digne d'un sage   10
De s'en aller songer dans cette ombre, parmi
Ces arbres pleins de nids, où tout semble endormi
Et veille, où le refus consent, où l'amour lutte,
Et d'écouter le vent, ce doux joueur de flûte.

Apprenons, laissons faire, aimons, les cieux sont grands; 15
Et devenons savants, et restons ignorants.
Soyons sous l'infini des auditeurs honnêtes;
Rien n'est muet ni sourd; voyons le plus de bêtes
Que nous pouvons; tirons parti de leurs leçons.
Parce qu'autour de nous tout rêve, nous pensons.   20
L'ignorance est un peu semblable à la prière;
L'homme est grand par devant et petit par derrière;
C'est, d'Euclide à Newton, de Job à Réaumur,

Down in the lane. A trowel scraping a tile.
That's the whisk of a scythe-blade cutting grass.
Bangs. Rattles. Roofers on some domicile.
Harbour sounds. Whistlings—engines on the go.
Bits of military music, gust by gust.
French voices; quayside hubbub. Thanks. Hello.
Goodbye. Must be late, surely—because just
Next to me, right here, is my robin singing.
Waves lapping. Steamer, panting audibly.
Far off, in a forge, raucous hammers swinging.
In comes a fly. The vast breath of the sea.

More About God (But With Some Reservations)

Such a splendid place! The cedar and elm are whispering;
The donkey is lyrical, he seems to have seen Don Quixote;
The tiger inside his prison behaves like a king in his palace;
The pachyderms are most dreadfully ugly;
It's all so literary, too: when you see the crocodiles yawning,
It reminds you of Viennet's best *Idylls*.
There, while she-monkey is selling her body to mandrill,
While ass is contemplating sage
And vulture is smiling pleasantly at screech-owl,
It is indeed a pastime worthy of a philosopher
To wander dreamily through this shade,
Among the nest-filled trees, where everything seems asleep
And yet is alert, where refusal consents, where love struggles;
And to hear the wind, that delicate flute-player.

We must learn and be tolerant and love, the heavens are vast;
We must also become learnèd and stay ignorant.
We must be a good honest audience beneath the infinite;
Nothing is dumb or deaf;
We must see every beast we can, and draw lessons from all.
All things are pondering around us, and therefore we ourselves think.
Ignorance is a little like prayer;
Humanity is great from the front, unimposing in rear view;
From Euclid to Newton, from Job to Réaumur,

Un indiscret qui veut voir par-dessus le mur,
Et la nature, au fond très moqueuse, paraphe   25
Notre science avec le cou de la girafe.
Tâchez de voir, c'est bien. Épiez. Notre esprit
Pousse notre science à guetter; Dieu sourit,
Vieux malin.

          Je l'ai dit, Dieu prête à la critique.
Il n'est pas sobre. Il est débordant, frénétique,   30
Inconvenant; ici le nain, là le géant,
Tout à la fois; énorme; il manque de néant.
Il abuse du gouffre, il abuse du prisme.
Tout, c'est trop. Son soleil va jusqu'au gongorisme;
Lumière outrée. Oui, Dieu vraiment est inégal;   35
Ici la Sibérie, et là le Sénégal;
Et partout l'antithèse! il faut qu'on s'y résigne;
S'il fait noir le corbeau, c'est qu'il fit blanc le cygne;
Aujourd'hui Dieu nous gèle, hier il nous chauffait.
Comme à l'académie on lui dirait son fait!   40
Que nous veut la comète? A quoi sert le bolide?
Quand on est un pédant sérieux et solide,
Plus on est ébloui, moins on est satisfait;
La férule à Batteux, le sabre à Galifet
Ne tolèrent pas Dieu sans quelque impatience;   45
Dieu trouble l'ordre; il met sur les dents la science;
A peine a-t-on fini qu'il faut recommencer;
Il semble que l'on sent dans la main vous glisser
On ne sait quel serpent tout écaillé d'aurore.
Dès que vous avez dit: assez! il dit: encore!   50

Ce démagogue donne au pauvre autant de fleurs
Qu'au riche; il ne sait pas se borner; ses couleurs,
Ses rayons, ses éclairs, c'est plus qu'on ne souhaite.
Ah! tout cela fait mal aux yeux! dit la chouette.
Et la chouette, c'est la sagesse.

We are such inquisitive creatures, we want to peek over the wall;
And Nature—a great tease fundamentally, Nature—stamps
Our learning with a giraffe-neck.
Try to look in—an excellent notion. Be spies. Our spirit
Impels our science to watch. God smiles,
The sly old fellow.

                    God—I've said it before—is wide open to
                        criticism.
He knows no restraint. He's wild, unseemly, extravagant:
There giant, here dwarf,
Everything all at the same time; enormous; he doesn't leave out
    things.
He overdoes chasms and prisms.
Everything is too much. His sun goes to the point of Gongorism,
Immoderate light. Yes indeed, God is uneven;
Siberia here, and Senegal there;
Antitheses everywhere, too! you have to accept it:
If he makes the crow black, it's because he made the swan white;
Today God is freezing us, yesterday he was roasting us.
How the Academy would tell him a thing or two!
What is the point of the comet? What is the use of the bolide?
To a sturdy, reliable pedant,
Well, the more one is dazzled, the less one is satisfied;
Polonius's saws and Ockham's razors
Suffer God only with some impatience.
God disturbs law and order, works science to death;
As soon as you finish, you have to start it again;
You seem to feel some kind of serpent all scaly with sunrise
Slipping away through your fingers.
Just when you've said 'Enough!' he says 'In addition!'

A cheap demagogue, too: gives the poor just as many
Flowers as the rich; and he never knows when to stop;
His colours, his light-rays, his lightnings, are more than you'd wish
    for.
'It all hurts the eyes!' hoots the owl.
And the owl is wisdom.

Il est sûr   55
Que Dieu taille à son gré le monde en plein azur;
Il mêle l'ironie à son tonnerre épique;
Si l'on plane il foudroie et si l'on broute il pique.
(Je ne m'étonne pas que Planche eût l'air piqué.)
Le vent, voix sans raison, sorte de bruit manqué,   60
Sans jamais s'expliquer et sans jamais conclure,
Rabâche, et l'océan n'est pas exempt d'enflure.
Quant à moi, je serais, j'en fais ici l'aveu,
Curieux de savoir ce que diraient de Dieu,
Du monde qu'il régit, du ciel qu'il exagère,   65
De l'infini, sinistre et confuse étagère,
De tout ce que ce Dieu prodigue, des amas
D'étoiles de tout genre et de tous les formats,
De sa façon d'emplir d'astres le télescope,
Nonotte et Baculard dans le café Procope.   70

VI.vi. « Jeanne était au pain sec... »

Jeanne était au pain sec dans le cabinet noir,
~~Pour un crime quelconque, et, manquant au devoir,~~
J'allai voir la proscrite en pleine forfaiture,
Et lui glissai dans l'ombre un pot de confiture
Contraire aux lois. Tous ceux sur qui, dans ma cité,   5
Repose le salut de la société,
S'indignèrent, et Jeanne a dit d'une voix douce:
—Je ne toucherai plus mon nez avec mon pouce;
Je ne me ferai plus griffer par le minet.
Mais on s'est récrié:—Cette enfant vous connaît;   10
Elle sait à quel point vous êtes faible et lâche.
Elle vous voit toujours rire quand on se fâche.
Pas de gouvernement possible. A chaque instant
L'ordre est troublé par vous; le pouvoir se détend;
Plus de règle. L'enfant n'a plus rien qui l'arrête.   15
Vous démolissez tout.—Et j'ai baissé la tête,

It's plain

That God moulds the world to his own taste, up there in the blue;
His epic thunderbolts are spiced with irony;
When you soar he strikes you with lightning, he stings you just when
    you bend over.
(No wonder Planche always seemed to be sore about something.)
The wind, an irrational voice, a sort of noise *manqué*,
Never explaining itself, and never concluding,
Simply goes on and on; nor are oceans exempt from redundance.
I myself, I frankly admit,
Would be curious to know what opinion of God,
Of the world he directs, of his overdone sky,
Of his grim muddled shelf of the infinite,
Of everything that God lavishes, such heaps
Of suns, every type, every format,
Of the way he fills the telescope with stars,
Would be held by Nonotte in the Café Procope—and by Baculard,
    too.

'Jeanne was holed up...'

Jeanne was holed up (pitch darkness; bread and water)
For some crime. I, not doing what I ought to,
Went to the exile stealthily, by sham,
And slipped her in the gloom a pot of jam
Against the laws. All those in my society
Who bring the land salvation and propriety
Were angry. Jeanne said very meekly, then:
'Well, I won't ever thumb my nose again;
I won't make Pussy scratch me any more.'
Still they cried out: 'The child just knows the score;
She knows how weak you are, how much you cosset her;
She always sees you laugh when we get cross at her;
What control do we have? You've always blackened
Discipline; our authority is slackened;
It's anarchy. The child will go to rack and
Ruin. You're wrecking things.' I hung my head.

Et j'ai dit:—Je n'ai rien à répondre à cela,
J'ai tort. Oui, c'est avec ces indulgences-là
Qu'on a toujours conduit les peuples à leur perte.
Qu'on me mette au pain sec.—Vous le méritez, certe,   20
On vous y mettra.—Jeanne alors, dans son coin noir,
M'a dit tout bas, levant ses yeux si beaux à voir,
Pleins de l'autorité des douces créatures:
—Eh bien, moi, je t'irai porter des confitures.

VI.viii. Le Pot cassé

O ciel! toute la Chine est par terre en morceaux!
Ce vase pâle et doux comme un reflet des eaux,
Couvert d'oiseaux, de fleurs, de fruits, et des mensonges
De ce vague idéal qui sort du bleu des songes,
Ce vase unique, étrange, impossible, engourdi,   5
Gardant sur lui le clair de lune en plein midi,
Qui paraissait vivant, où luisait une flamme,
Qui semblait presque un monstre et semblait presque une âme,
Mariette, en faisant la chambre, l'a poussé
Du coude par mégarde, et le voilà brisé!   10
Beau vase! Sa rondeur était de rêves pleine,
Des bœufs d'or y broutaient des prés de porcelaine.
Je l'aimais, je l'avais acheté sur les quais,
Et parfois aux marmots pensifs je l'expliquais.
Voici l'yak; voici le singe quadrumane;   15
Ceci c'est un docteur peut-être, ou bien un âne;
Il dit la messe, à moins qu'il ne dise hi-han;
Ça c'est un mandarin qu'on nomme aussi kohan;
Il faut qu'il soit savant, puisqu'il a ce gros ventre.
Attention, ceci, c'est le tigre en son antre,   20
Le hibou dans son trou, le roi dans son palais,
Le diable en son enfer; voyez comme ils sont laids!
Les monstres, c'est charmant, et les enfants le sentent.
Des merveilles qui sont des bêtes les enchantent.
Donc je tenais beaucoup à ce vase. Il est mort.   25

'I can't deny a word of it', I said;
'I've erred. Such laxities *are* what they do in
A country that is being led to ruin.
Put me on bread and water.' 'Let him have it! he
Richly deserves it!' Then from her dark cavity
Jeanne whispered—and within her eyes there swam
All the assurance of a gentle lamb—
                              'I'll bring you jam.'

The Broken Vase

Heavens! all China's on the ground, in pieces!
This vase—covered with birds, flowers, fruit, caprices
Of the ideal that come from dim blue dreams—
Pale-hued and tender like reflected streams,
This unique vase, impossible, strange, fey,
Preserving moonlight in the blaze of day,
Which seemed alive, lit by an aureole,
Almost a monster, or perhaps a soul—
Mariette, when she did the bedroom, dashed
Her elbow at it blindly—and it's smashed!
A lovely vase! a globe of reveries,
Where golden oxen browsed the faience leas.
I loved the thing; I bought it at the quays;
At times I showed our mites its fairylands.
'Here's a yak; there's a monkey with four hands;
This one is a DD, or else an ass,
And if he won't say hee-haw, he'll say mass;
That, that's a bonze or rabbi, very staunch;
He must be learnèd, judging from his paunch.
That's Screech-Owl in his hollow over there,
King in his palace, Tiger in his lair,
And Devil in his hell—ugliness everywhere!'
Monsters are fun; children are keen to sight them;
Wondrous things that are beasts always delight them.
In short, I dearly loved that vase. It's dead.

J'arrivai furieux, terrible, et tout d'abord:
—Qui donc a fait cela? criai-je. Sombre entrée!
Jeanne alors, remarquant Mariette effarée,
Et voyant ma colère et voyant son effroi,
M'a regardé d'un air d'ange, et m'a dit:—C'est moi.   30

from *Le Seuil du gouffre*

« Et je voyais au loin... »

Et je voyais au loin sur ma tête un point noir.

Comme on voit une mouche au plafond se mouvoir.
J'allais, je regardais, et l'ombre était sublime.

Et l'homme, quand il pense, étant ailé, l'abîme
Et la nuit m'attirant toujours de plus en plus,   5
Comme une algue qu'entraîne un ténébreux reflux,
Vers les sombres azurs de la zone suprême,
Tremblant, je me sentais m'envoler de moi-même
Quand dans l'obscurité mon oreille entendit
Une voix qui parlait très bas et qui me dit: 10

—Demeure.—

       Tout en moi tremblait, vie et mémoire.
J'étais déjà très haut dans l'immensité noire.
Je montais, je songeais; peut-être je dormais.
J'entrevoyais d'obscurs et lugubres sommets;
La terre ronde et vague, ainsi qu'un pâle dôme,   15
S'effaçait sous mes pieds comme un globe fantôme;
J'étais dans l'ombre où l'être avec la nuit se fond;
J'apercevais l'horreur de la noirceur sans fond,

In I rushed, furious, fierce; and, roaring, said:
'So! who did that?' Scene set for a disaster!
Then, seeing Mariette in terror—master
Itching to chide, maid dreading to be chid—
With an angelic look, Jeanne said: 'I did.'

from *The Threshold of the Abyss*

'I could see, far above my head...'

I could see, far above my head, a black speck.

Like a fly moving on the ceiling. I
Went to see; and the darkness was sublime.

Man, when he thinks, is winged; night and the chasm were
Drawing me more and more, like seaweed dragged
By some mysterious tide, toward the zenith's
Deep blue. I trembled; I could feel myself
Already soaring off,
But then in the obscurity I heard
A voice, a very quiet voice, that told me:

'Stay.'

My whole being—life and memory—trembled.
I was already high up in the darkness.
I was rising, dreaming—sleeping, possibly.
I could half-see dim and lugubrious summits;
The earth, hazy and round, like a pale dome,
Vanished beneath my feet—a phantom globe;
There I was, in the dark where Night and Being
Are merged, seeing the horror of endless black,

La brume, les lueurs tombant de cime en cime,
Et des blêmissements de roches dans l'abîme.   20

La voix reprit:—Pourquoi sors-tu de ton milieu?
Que demandes-tu? parle.—

                    Et je répondis:—Dieu.—

Tout sembla devant moi se fermer; et l'espèce
De clarté qui tremblait dans la nuée épaisse
Sombra dans l'air plus noir qu'un ciel cimmérien.   25

J'entendis un éclat de rire, et ne vis rien.

Hélas! n'étant qu'un homme, une chair misérable,
Dans cette obscurité fauve, âpre, impénétrable,
Dans ces brumes sans jour, sans bords, sous ce linceul,
Je songeai qu'il était horrible d'être seul.   30
Puis mon esprit revint à son but:—voir, connaître,
Savoir;—pendant que l'ombre informe, louche, traître,
Roulant dans ses échos ce noir rire moqueur,
Grandissait dans l'espace ainsi que dans mon cœur.

Et je criai, ployant mes ailes déjà lasses: 35
—Dites-moi seulement son nom, tristes espaces,
Pour que je le répète à jamais dans la nuit!—

Et je n'entendis rien que la bise qui fuit.

Alors il me sembla qu'en un sombre mirage,
Comme des tourbillons que chasse un vent d'orage,   40
Je voyais devant moi pêle-mêle passer
Et croître et frissonner et fuir et s'effacer
Ces cryptes du vertige et ces villes du rêve,
Rome, sur ses frontons changeant en croix son glaive,
Thèbes, Jérusalem, Mecque, Médine, Hébron;   45
Des figures tenant à la main un clairon,
Et des arbres hagards, des cavernes, des baumes

Luminosities falling from peak to peak,
Fog, and some wan shapes of abysmal rocks.

The voice went on: 'Why have you left your realm?
What do you want? Speak up.'

                              I answered: 'God.'

All seemed to shut before me;
The vague light that was trembling in the cloud
Sank, and the skies grew blacker than Arctic nights.

I heard a burst of laughter, but saw nothing.

Ah! being merely human, wretched flesh,
In the harsh wild imperforable obscurity,
In the dayless boundless mists beneath that shroud,
It was, I felt, dreadful to be alone.
But then my spirit reverted to its purpose,
Wanted to see and know; while the shapeless purblind
Treacherous shade, echoing its sombre
Mockeries, grew in space—and in my heart.

And I cried out, bowing my now-tired wings:
'Simply tell me his name, you comfortless spaces,
So I can say it constantly in the night!'

And I heard nothing but the fleeing winter.

Then, it seemed,
I could see in a dark mirage before me
Cities of dream and crypts of dizziness,
Like whirlwinds driven off by a storm-blast, shuddering
And passing, swelling, fleeing, disappearing:
Rome on its pediments, changing sword for cross,
Hebron, Medina, Mecca, Thebes, Jerusalem;
Shapes holding trumpets in their hands, wild trees,
Caves, solaces where dismal Jeromes prayed

Où priaient, barbe au vent, de ténébreux Jérômes,
Et, parmi des babels, des tours, des temples grecs,
D'horribles fronts d'écueils aux cheveux de varechs;   50
Et tout cela, Ninive, Éphèse, Delphe, Abdère,
Tombeau de saint-Grégoire où veille un lampadaire,
Marches de Bénarès, pagodes de Ceylan,
Monts d'où l'aigle de mer le soir prend son élan,
Minarets, parthénons, wigwams, temple d'Aglaure   55
Où l'on voit l'aube, fleur vertigineuse, éclore,
Et grotte de Calvin, et chambre de Luther,
Passages d'anges bleus dans le liquide éther,
Trépieds où flamboyaient des âmes, yeux de braise
De la chienne Scylla sur la mer calabraise,   60
Dodone, Horeb, rochers effarés, bois troublants,
Couvent d'Eschmiadzin aux quatre clochers blancs,
Noir cromlech de Bretagne, affreux cruach d'Irlande,
Pœstum où les rosiers suspendent leur guirlande,
Temples des fils de Cham, temples des fils de Seth,   65
Tout lentement flottait et s'évanouissait
Dans une sorte d'âpre et vague perspective;
Et ce n'était, devant ma prunelle attentive,
Que de la vision qui ne fait pas de bruit,
Et de la forme obscure éparse dans la nuit.   70

Et, pâle et frissonnant, je fis cet appel sombre,
Sans oser élever la voix, de peur de l'ombre:

—Êtres! lieux! choses! nuit! nuit froide qui te tais!
Cèdres de Salomon, chênes de Teutatès;
O plongeurs de nuée, ô rapporteurs de tables;   75
Devins, mages, voyants, hommes épouvantables;
Thébaïdes, forêts, solitudes; Ombos
Où les docteurs, vivant dans des creux de tombeaux,
S'emplissent d'infini comme d'eau les éponges;
O croisements obscurs des gouffres et des songes,   80
Sommeil, blanc soupirail des apparitions;
Germes, avatars, nuit des incarnations

Beard to the wind; among the various Babels,
Towers, Greek temples, ghastly reef-brows growing
Kelp-tresses; Nineveh, Delphi, Ephesus,
Abdera; Gregory's tomb
Watched by its candelabrum;
Ghats of Benares, Cinghalese pagodas,
Peaks where the osprey launches in the evening,
Minarets, Parthenons, Aglaura's temple
Where the dawn, that vertiginous flower, opens;
Wigwams and Calvin's cave and Luther's chamber;
Thoroughfares of blue wraiths in fluid space,
Braziers where souls are burning, the bitch Scylla's
Glowing eyes on the Calabrian sea,
Dodona, Horeb, startled rocks, unsettling
Forests, Echmiadzin with its four white towers,
Ireland's bleak cruach, Brittany's black cromlech,
Paestum where the rose-bushes hang their garlands,
Temples of Ham's sons, temples of Shem's sons,
All slowly wavering and disappearing
In a rough and indefinite prospect—merely
A noiseless vision, an obscure shape scattered
Throughout the dark, before my eyes.

                              And I,
Faint, tremulously, without venturing
To raise my voice for fear of the shade,
Uttered this dark appeal:

                         'Things! places! creatures!
Night—cold and silent night! Cedars of Solomon,
Oaks of Teutates; you cloud-divers, you
Seance-recorders; magi, seers, sorcerers,
Terrible men; refuges, forests, solitudes;
Ombos where scholars live in hollow tombs
Absorbing the vast as a sponge does water;
Sleep—the dim intersection between dream
And chasm, the white vent of apparitions;
Germs, avatars, nocturnal incarnations

Où l'archange s'envole, où le monstre se vautre;
Mort, noir pont naturel entre une étoile et l'autre,
Communication entre l'homme et le ciel;   85
Colosse de Minerve Aptère, aux pieds duquel
Le vent respectueux fait tomber ceux qui passent;
Flots revenant toujours que les rocs toujours chassent;
Chauve Apollonius, vieux rêveur sidéral;
O scribes, qui, du bout du bâton augural   90
Tracez de l'alphabet les ténébreux jambages;
Époptes grecs, fakirs, voghis, bonzes, eubages,
O tours d'où se jetaient les circumcellions;
Sanctuaires, trépieds, autels, fosse aux lions;
Vous qui voyez suer les fronts pâles des sages,   95
Cimetières, repos, asiles, noirs passages
Où viennent s'essuyer les penseurs, ces vaincus;
Monstrueux caveau peint du roi Psamméticus;
François d'Assises, Scot, Bruno, sainte-Rhipsime;
O marcheurs attirés aux clartés de la cime;   100
Sept sages qui parlez dans l'ombre à Cyrselus;
Du rêve et du désert redoutables reclus
Qui chuchotez avec les bouches invisibles;
Fronts courbés sous les cieux d'où descendent les bibles;
Spectres; effarements de lampe et de flambeau;   105
Toi qui vois Chanaan, montagne de Nébo;
Moines du mont Athos, chantant de sombres proses;
Libellules d'Asie errant dans les jamroses;
Isthme de Suez fermant l'Inde comme un verrou;
O voûtes d'Ellora, croupes du mont Mérou   110
D'où s'échappe le Gange aux grandes eaux sacrées;
Ombre, qui n'as pas l'air de savoir que tu crées;
O vous qui criez: deuil! vous qui criez: espoir!
Spherus qui, toujours seul dans l'antre toujours noir,
Cherches Dieu par les mille ouvertures funèbres,   115
Blanches, tristes, que font à l'âme les ténèbres;
Prêtres qu'en votre nuit suit le doute importun;
Vous, psalmistes, David, Ethan, grave Idithun;
Jean, interlocuteur de l'oiseau Chéroubime;

Where angels fly away but monsters wallow;
Death, nature's black bridge between star and star,
Through which human communicates with heaven;
Colossus of Minerva Apteros,
At whose feet the respectful wind hurls down
The passer-by; incessantly-returning
Waves, by the rocks incessantly repelled;
Old Apollonius, bald sidereal dreamer;
Scribes who set down the dim strokes of the alphabet
With augural wands; Greek epopts, fakirs, yogis,
Bonzes, eubages; towers where Circumcelliones
Flung themselves down; fanes, altars, furnaces,
Lions' dens; cemeteries, resting-places
That see the sweat on the pale brows of sages,
Sanctuaries, collied thoroughfares where conquered
Thinkers come to dry off; huge painted cavern
Of King Psammetichus; Scotus Erigena,
Rhipsima, Bruno, Francis of Assisi,
Climbers drawn to the bright light on the mountaintop;
The Seven Sages, speaking in the dark
With Cypselus; formidable recluses
Of dream and desert, whispering with invisible
Lips; foreheads bent beneath the heavens, from which
Bibles descend; ghosts, fears of lamp and torchlight;
Mount Nebo overlooking Canaan; monks
Chanting the solemn rituals on Mount Athos;
Asiatic dragonflies among the jamrose;
Isthmus of Suez, bolt that shuts off India;
Caves of Ellora, ridges of Mount Meru
Where the vast sacred Ganges has its origin;
You shade, apparently
Ignorant of your own creations;
You that cry "Misery!"—you that cry "Hope!"—
Sphaerus ever-alone in ever-black caverns,
Seeking for God through myriad dismal apertures
Mournful and wan and darkening the soul;
Priests that pursue troublesome doubts nocturnally;
You psalmists, David, Ethan, grave Jeduthun;
John who encountered the winged cherubim;

Et vous, poëtes; Dante, homme effrayant d'abîme,   120
Grand front tragique ombré de feuilles de laurier,
Qui t'en reviens, laissant l'obscurité crier,
Rapportant sous tes cils la lueur des avernes;
Dompteurs qui sans pâlir allez dans les cavernes
Forcer le hurlement jusque dans son chenil;   125
Pilotes nubiens qui remontez le Nil;
O prodigieux cerf aux rameaux noirs qui brames
Dans la forêt des djinns, des pandits et des brames;
Hommes enterrés vifs, songeant dans vos cercueils;
O pâtres accoudés; ô bruyères; écueils   130
Où rêve au crépuscule une forme sinistre;
Pythie assise au front du hideux cap Canistre;
Angles de la syringe où les songeurs entrés
Distinguent vaguement des satrapes mitrés;
Vous que la lune enivre et trouble, sélénites;   135
Vous, bénitiers sanglants des seules eaux bénites,
Yeux en pleurs des martyrs; vous, savants indécis;
Merlin, sous l'escarboucle inexprimable assis;
Job, qui contemples; toi, Jérome, qui médites;
Est-ce qu'on ne peut pas voir un peu de jour, dites?   140

On éclata de rire une seconde fois.

Et ce rire était plus un rictus qu'une voix;
Il remua longtemps l'ombre visionnaire,
Et, s'évanouissant, roula comme un tonnerre
Dans ce prodigieux silence où le néant   145
Semblait vivre, insondable, immobile et béant.

O méditations! oh! comme l'esprit souffre
Sous les porches hagards et difformes du gouffre!
Comme le souffle noir du vide vous poursuit,
Sinistre, en vous jetant du trouble et de la nuit!   150
Comme on sent que le rêve est un être qui vole
Et passe!... —On m'adressait dans l'ombre la parole;
Et de funèbres voix que sur mon front j'avais
Comme les endormis en ont à leurs chevets,
Chuchotaient au-dessus de moi des choses sombres.   155

You poets, Dante of the dread abyss,
Great tragic brow shadowed with laurel-leaves,
Returning—though the obscurity cries out—
With the gleam of Avernus in your eyes;
You conquerors who, without turning pale,
Pursue the howls into their caverned kennels;
Nubian pilots who ascend the Nile;
Black-antlered bellowing stags, with pandits, brahmins,
Djinns, in the forests; men buried alive,
Dreaming in coffins; kneeling shepherds; heaths;
Reefs where ominous shapes reflect at nightfall;
Pythoness fixed on fell Canistro's brow;
Syrinx-nooks where the entering visionaries
Dimly discern some mitred satrap; lunatics
Perturbed, inebriated, by the moon;
You martyrs' weeping eyes—the bleeding stoups
Of the sole blessed waters; hesitant
Savants; Merlin beneath the mystic carbuncle;
Job pondering, Jerome meditating; tell me,
Is there no hope of seeing any daylight?'

A second time there was a burst of laughter.

This laugh was more a rictus than a voice;
Long did it stir the visionary shadow,
And, vanishing, resounded like a thunder
In that mysterious silence where nonentity
Seemed to be living, boundless, still, and gaping.

Ah, meditations! How your spirit suffers
Within the chasm's wild misshapen gateway!
How ominously the void's black breath pursues you
With night and agitation! How you feel
That a dream is a creature,
Flying,
Passing on....
There, in the darkness, words were spoken to me;
Funereal voices, like the things that sleepers
Hear in their beds, were muttering sombre noises

Je sentais la terreur muette des décombres
Et je me demandais:—Qui donc murmure ainsi?—
C'était, dans le ciel morne et de brume épaissi,
Comme un nuage obscur de bouches sur ma tête;
Des faces me parlaient dans un vent de tempête;   160
Puis ces voix s'éteignaient comme le vague son
Qui n'est plus la parole et devient le frisson.
Noirs discours! l'ironie y grinçait dans le râle;
Des plaintes, sanglotant dans l'ombre sépulcrale
Comme entre les roseaux gémit le gavial,   165
S'achevaient en sarcasme amer et trivial;
Je croyais par moments qu'en ces vagues royaumes
J'assistais au concile effrayant des fantômes
Que nous nommons raison, logique, utilité,
Certitude, calcul, sagesse, vérité;   170
Il me semblait, parmi le grand murmure austère
De l'horreur, de la nuit, du tombeau, du mystère,
Entendre Aristophane; et voir, après les pleurs,
Toutes sortes d'éclairs cyniques et railleurs,
Moqueurs, étincelants, percer l'ombre ennemie,   175
Et Diderot passer à travers Jérémie;
J'écoutais frémissant et par moments vaincu.
Était-ce des esprits d'hommes ayant vécu?
Était-ce les conseils qui flottent dans les nues
Pour quiconque s'égare aux routes inconnues?   180
Mon front sous l'infini ployait lugubrement.
L'espace affreux, éther, ténèbres, firmament,
Espèce de taillis sans branches étoilées,
Où les brouillards fuyaient en confuses mêlées,
Semblait d'une forêt le redoutable dais.   185
Qu'était-ce que ces voix? je ne sais. J'entendais.
Et ma raison tremblait en moi, diminuée,
Dans des tressaillements d'orage et de nuée.

Cependant par degrés l'ombre devint visible;
Et l'être qui m'avait parlé précédemment   190
Reparut, mais grandi jusqu'à l'effarement;
Il remplissait du haut en bas le sombre dôme
Comme si l'infini dilatait ce fantôme;

Above me. I could sense the silent terror
Of chaos. Who, I wondered, who was murmuring?
Within the dismal sky and fog
There seemed to be a dim cloud-mass of mouths
Above my head; faces were talking to me
Through storm-winds; then the voices died away
Like vague sounds that are no longer words, but rustlings.
Dark speeches! Irony, there, gnashed its death-rattle;
Wretched complaints in the sepulchral shadows,
Like gavials groaning among the rushes,
Stopped short in derision;
Sometimes, in these vague realms, I thought I was
Watching some terrifying council held
By the ghosts that we call logic, practicality,
Certainty, calculation, sense, truth, wisdom;
Among the stern murmurs of night and horror,
Mystery and tomb, did I hear Aristophanes?
Did I see cynical lightnings of all kinds
After the tears—scoffings and sparks that pierced
The hostile darkness? Was that Diderot
Passing by Jeremiah? Shuddering, now and then
Downcast, I listened. Were these spirits
Of people who had lived? Were they counsellors
Drifting among the clouds, to guide the wanderer
Along these unknown roads? Beneath the infinite
I felt I was a wretched thing. Space, darkness,
The firmament—a branchless starless thicket
Where mists vanished and mingled in confusion—
Seemed the formidable canopy of a forest.
What were these voices? I have no idea.
I listened. And my innermost thoughts all trembled,
Diminished, in the quivering storm and cloud.

Yet gradually the darkness became visible;
The creature that had talked with me before
Reappeared, larger—terrifyingly larger;
It filled the sombre dome from head to foot
As if distended by the infinite;

De sorte que l'esprit effrayant n'offrait plus
Que des visages, flux vivant, vivant reflux,   195
Un sourd fourmillement d'hydres, d'hommes, de bêtes,
Et que le fond du ciel me semblait plein de têtes.

Ces têtes par moments semblaient se quereller.
Je voyais tous ces yeux dans l'ombre étinceler.
Le monstre grandissait et grandissait sans cesse.   200
Et je ne savais plus ce que c'était. Était-ce
Une montagne, une hydre, un gouffre, une cité,
Un nuage, un amas d'ombre, l'immensité?
Je sentais tous ces yeux sur moi fixés ensemble.
Tout à coup, frissonnant comme un arbre qui tremble,   205
Le fantôme géant se répandit en voix
Qui sous ses flancs confus murmuraient à la fois;
Et, comme d'un brasier tombent des étincelles,
Comme on voit des oiseaux épars, pigeons, sarcelles,
D'un grand essaim passant s'écarter quelquefois,   210
Comme un vert tourbillon de feuilles sort d'un bois,
Comme, dans les hauteurs par les vents remuées,
En avant d'un orage il vole des nuées,
Toutes ces voix, mêlant le cri, l'appel, le chant,
De l'immense être informe et noir se détachant,   215
Me montrant vaguement des masques et des bouches,
Vinrent sur moi bruire avec des bruits farouches,
Parfois en même temps et souvent tour à tour,
Comme des monts, à l'heure où se lève le jour,
L'un après l'autre, au fond de l'horizon s'éclairent.   220

Et des formes, sortant du monstre, me parlèrent:

Une Autre Voix

Et d'abord, de quel Dieu veux-tu parler? Précise.
Quel est celui qui tient ta pensée indécise?

Dis, est-ce du Dieu peint en jaune, en rouge, en bleu,
Habitant d'un triangle où flambe un mot hébreu;

The fearsome spirit now presented nothing
But whirling faces—living ebb and flow,
A muffled swarm of dragons, humans, animals,
So that the heavens' depths seemed full of heads.

At times they seemed at odds with one another.
I could see all their eyes glint in the darkness.
The thing grew larger—grew larger incessantly.
No longer could I tell what it might be.
Was it cloud, chasm, monster, mountain, city,
A mass of shadow, the immensity?
And all the eyes seemed fixed on me together.
Suddenly, shuddering like a shaken tree,
The immense phantom broke out into voices,
A confused mutter
On all sides all at once;
As sparks fly from a fire, as scattered birds—
Pigeons or teal—spread out in a great swarm,
As a green whirl of leaves flies from a wood,
Or as, before a storm, driven by gales
In the high places, scuds a flight of clouds,
So all these voices, mingling songs, cries, pleas,
Unleashed from the immense black shapeless being,
Revealed vague mouths and faces; came on me
Roaring with raucous noises, some together
And many separately, like peaks at sunrise
Brightening one by one on the horizon;

Out of the monster
Came shapes that spoke to me:

Another Voice

'Well, first of all, just which God do you mean?
Which is the one that takes your wandering fancy?

Is it a God drawn blue, or red, or yellow,
Inside a triangle in flaming Hebrew,

Face dorée au fond d'une nuée épaisse;   5
Portant couronne, étole, épée, et sceptre, espèce
D'empereur, habillé d'un manteau de soleil,
Ayant au poing le globe et Satan sous l'orteil,
Assis dans une chaire, et dictant la sentence
D'Arius à Nicée et de Huss à Constance;   10
Niant le genre humain, concile universel;
Servant de majuscule aux versets du missel;
Dieu qui met Galilée en prison, et de Maistre
En sentinelle au seuil du paradis terrestre;
Dieu qu'une vieille, en rêve, au bruit qu'en se choquant   15
Font dans l'immensité des foudres de clinquant,
Sous un grand dais d'azur que l'astre damasquine,
Aperçoit lui montrant les numéros d'un quine;
Dieu gothique, irritable, intolérant, tueur,
Noir vitrail effrayant qu'empourpre la lueur   20
Du bûcher qui flamboie et pétille derrière?

Est-ce du Dieu qui veut la chanson pour prière,
Qu'on invoque en trinquant, Dieu bon vivant, qui rit;
Comprend, sait que la chair est faible, a de l'esprit;
Dieu point fâcheux, qui vit en bonne intelligence   25
Avec les passions de votre pauvre engeance,
Excusant le péché, l'expliquant au besoin,
Clignant de l'œil avec le diable dans un coin,
Flânant, regardant l'homme en sa fainéantise,
Mais jamais du côté qui fait une sottise,   30
Et pas très sûr au fond lui-même d'exister?

Est-ce du Dieu qu'on voit à Versailles monter
Aux carrosses du roi, bien né, suivant les modes,
Rendant aux Montespans les Bossuets commodes,
Dieu de cour, Dieu de ville, avec soin expurgé   35
De toute humeur brutale et de tout préjugé,
Complaisant; paternel aux morales mondaines;
Avec les Massillons émoussant les Bridaines;
Dieu que Dubois coudoie avec tranquillité;
Dieu par la politique et le siècle accepté;   40
Lâchant son ciel; disant: Paris vaut une messe;

Deep in thick clouds with gilded face, crowned, sceptred,
Sworded and stoled; a kind of emperor
Garbed in a solar robe, with globe in hand
And Satan underfoot; fixed on a throne,
Imposing Arius' and Huss's sentences
At Constance and Nicaea; a universal
Council denying the whole human race;
A majuscule on the lines of the missal;
God who set Galileo in prison, and
De Maistre at the gates of earthly paradise;
The God old women dream of, to the sound
Of lightning-clashes in the vastness, seated
Beneath a starry azure canopy,
Showing them all the ciphers on a quincunx;
A Gothic God, intolerant, cross, murderous,
A dark dire stained-glass window with the light
Of burning heretics purpling it behind?

Or the good-fellow-and-'twill-all-be-well God
Sensible and fun-loving, who wants love-songs
For prayers and can be called on between drinks,
Who understands, who knows the flesh is weak;
Never a nuisance, excusing or explaining sin,
On good terms with the passions of your puny breed,
Winking at Satan in a corner, idling,
Keeping an ineffective eye on humans,
But never on the side of any silliness,
And not all that sure of his own existence?

Or God as seen at Versailles, well-bred, fashionable,
Travelling in the royal coach, supplying
Comfortable Bossuets for Montespans,
A court-and-city God, meticulously
Bowdlerized of all brutal whims and prejudices,
Complaisant, patronizing worldly morals,
Numbing Bridaine-and-Massillon-style preachers,
A God that louts can comfortably rub shoulders with,
A God up-with-the-times, in-touch-with-politics,
Resilient, flexible, giving up heaven,

Souple et doux, dispensant les rois de leur promesse,
Point janséniste, point pédant, point monacal;
Permettant à Sanchez d'effaroucher Pascal,
Au banquier d'encoffrer cent pour cent, à la femme,⁣   45
Laide, d'être méchante, et, belle, d'être infâme;
Passant l'épice au juge, au marchand le faux poids;
Habile; à Notre-Dame accouplant Quincampoix;
Sévère seulement aux têtes raisonnantes,
Tuant un peu Ramus, biffant l'édit de Nantes,   50
Mais qui, pourvu qu'on soit, dans les grands jours, pilier
A l'église, et qu'on soit cousin d'un marguillier,
Et qu'on veuille que Rome en tout règne et s'accroisse,
Et qu'on rende le pain bénit à sa paroisse,
Vous prend en amitié, vous soutient chaudement,   55
Vous épouse, travaille à votre avancement,
Parle à son excellence, et vous pousse, et procure
Un grade aux fils aînés, aux cadets une cure,
En attendant la mitre ou les canonicats;
Dieu facile, logeable, aimable, utile en-cas   60
Qui se contente, ayant d'indulgence boutique,
D'un peu d'hypocrisie et d'un peu de pratique;
Dogme et religion des dévôts positifs
Qui font de temps en temps des voyages furtifs,
Courts, dans l'éternité, l'abîme, le mystère,   65
Et l'insondable, avec ce Dieu pour pied-à-terre?

Ou parlons-nous du Dieu militaire, sanglant,
Qui s'inquiète peu que vous mangiez du gland
Ou du pain, mais qui veut pour rites et pour cultes
Glaives, piques, corbeaux, scorpions, catapultes,   70
Grappin horrible où pend un vaisseau tout entier,
Tortue avec sa claie enduite du mortier,
Béliers fixes, heurtant les murs comme des proues,
Telenos enlevant des soldats, tours à roues
Recouvertes de mousse et de crin de cheval;   75
Plus tard, pierriers broyant quelque donjon rival
Jusqu'à ce qu'il s'en aille en cendre et se dissoude,
Mangonneaux, fauconneaux, bat-murs, pièces à coude,
Renversant les cités dans leur fossé bourbeux,

Going to masses for the sake of Paris,
Absolving kings of promises, no Jansenist,
Not monkish or pedantic; letting Sanchez
Unsettle Pascal, bankers centuple capital,
Unsightly girls be sour and fair ones infamous;
Mating Notre-Dame and Quincampoix; slipping
Spice to the judges, swindles to the shopkeepers;
Efficient; severe only to philosophers,
Killing off the occasional La Ramée,
And crossing out Edicts of Toleration;
But still (as long as you are some priest's cousin,
Friend to all Rome's expansion and Rome's sovereignty,
Parish distributor of holy wafers,
And pillar of the church on major days)
A God who will befriend you and support you,
Marry you off and work to your advantage,
Speak to His Excellency, push you forward,
Get army posts for older sons and parishes
(Preparatory to canonries or mitres)
For younger ones; an easy, friendly, nice God,
Kind to your trade, handy in an emergency,
A bit pragmatic, a bit hypocritical;
The dogma and religion of blunt zealots
Who venture now and then, briefly and furtively,
Into the realm of mysteries, gulfs, eternities,
Unknown things—with this God as their sure foothold?

Or God the military warrior, bloodthirsty,
Not caring very much whether you eat
Acorns or bread, but keen on certain rituals—
Catapults, pikes, swords, tackling-hooks, and scorpions,
Grapnel enough to hang a whole ship from,
Barricades daubed with mortar, battering-rams
Staving in doors like prows, man-lifting swingbeams,
Movable towers coated with moss and horsehair,
Stone-throwers pulverizing rivals' dungeons
Till they disintegrate and fall to dust,
Falconets, culverins, basilisks, field-piece,
Upturning cities in their miry moats,

Volcans grégeois traînés par trente jougs de bœufs,   80
Canons vénitiens, serpentines lombardes;
Dieu qui dit à Coglione: Attelle les bombardes;
Qui rit, pauvre blessé, du grabat où tu geins,
Que la bataille enivre avec tous ses engins,
Chaudrons à poix bouillante et fours à boulets rouges;   85
Qui chasse les manants éperdus de leurs bouges;
Qui rêve Te-Deum; qui s'endort aux accents
De l'obusier Lancastre et du mortier Paixhans;
Qui prête, quand la mine est faite sous la brèche,
Son tonnerre au besoin pour allumer la mèche,   90
Et, quand la terre s'ouvre avec un large éclair,
S'épanouit de voir les gens sauter en l'air?
Vision du passé par le présent subie!

Ou parles-tu du Dieu jugeur? rare lubie!
Dieu chancelier, portant perruque in-folio,   95
Vidant le procès Homme et l'Être imbroglio!
Dieu président, siégeant dans l'univers grand'chambre,
Jugeant l'âme, et bâillant, sous un ciel de décembre,
Entre l'avocat ange et l'avocat démon?

Dis, est-ce le Dieu guèbre, est-ce le Dieu mormon   100
Qu'il te faut? Ou le Dieu qui fit rouer Labarre?
Vois. Choisis. Ou le Dieu qui donne au turc barbare
Des femmes plein la tombe et plein le firmament?
Ou bien est-ce le Dieu qui fait lugubrement
Chanter, sous les rideaux semés de croix latines,   105
L'homme qui n'est plus homme aux chapelles sixtines,
Et qui, lui créateur, se plaît à l'écouter?

Ou parles-tu du Dieu qu'il faudrait inventer,
Que dans l'ombre la peur concède au phénomène,
Par les sages bâti sur la sagesse humaine,   110
Utile à ton valet, bon pour ton cuisinier,
Modérateur des sauts de l'anse du panier,
Dieu de raison qu'au fond de son spectre solaire
Le bourgeois bienveillant raille, exile et tolère,
Dieu consenti par Locke et que Grimm refusa,   115

Greek fire, volcanoes drawn by twenty oxen,
Venetian cannons, Lombard serpentry;
The God who tells Colleoni: "Yoke the bombards!"
Who laughs when wounded men groan in their pallets;
God who is drunk with war and all its works,
Cauldrons of boiling pitch, red blazing cannonballs,
Hunting the hapless peasants from their hovels;
Who dreams *Te Deums*, drowses to the sound of
Lancaster howitzer and Paixhans mortar;
Who, when a mine is sprung beneath a wall,
Lends his own thunderbolt to light the fuse,
And when the ground blasts with a lightning-flash,
Delights in seeing bodies fly the air?
An ancient sight, but still endured today!

Or God the judge? rare fancy! God the chancellor
In his full-bottomed wig, unravelling
The suit Man versus Being, passing judgement
On souls, in the High Chambers of the universe,
And yawning under a Decembery sky
Between the barristers Angel and Demon?

Perhaps the Gabar God, the Mormon God,
Is the one you require? the God by whom
La Barre was broken on the wheel?
Have a look; take your pick. The God who gives
Barbaric Turks whole heavenfuls of houris?
The God sung glumly, amid cross-strewn curtains,
By a non-man inside some Sistine Chapel
For his listening Creator's delectation?

Or the God it was necessary to invent,
A shadowy concession to phenomena
Constructed by the wise from human wisdom,
Useful for lower classes, good for cooks,
A dampener of underhand skulduggery,
A solar-spectrum rational God, whom
Sane middle-class men mock, exile, and tolerate,
A God allowed by Locke but not by Grimm,

Très-Haut à qui d'Holbach a donné son visa,
Éternel maçonné par le vivant qui passe,
Entre-colonnement du temps et de l'espace,
Pièce d'architecture ajoutée après coup
A la vie, au destin, au bien, au mal, à tout,   120
Tour tremblante du vide et hors-d'œuvre de l'homme?

Tous ces dieux, quel que soit le nom dont on les nomme,
Sont tout, excepté Dieu.

                L'homme abject a besoin,
Étant méchant, d'un juge, et, hideux, d'un témoin;
Il veut un Dieu. C'est bien. L'homme prend de la brique,   125
De la pierre, du plomb, du bois, et le fabrique;
Chaque peuple a le sien; et la religion
A l'Unité pour masque et pour nom Légion.
Un temple voit la nuit où l'autre voit l'aurore;
Chéos adore Ammon que Jagrenat ignore;   130
Pour Delphe Odin n'est pas; la solimanieh
Affirme Mahomet par le dolmen nié.
La terre crée un monstre et se met sous sa garde;
Et c'est avec stupeur que le grand ciel regarde
Croître sur vos fumiers ce misérable Dieu.   135

Nous ne nous mettons pas en peine de si peu,
Nous autres les esprits errant dans l'étendue;
Et, sans nous acharner à la lueur perdue,
Sans poursuivre l'obscur et pâle vision,
Sans exiger de l'ombre une solution,   140
Nous raillons dans la nuit votre Brahma fétiche,
Dieu qui mêle à sa barbe un infini postiche,
Dieu singe pour le nègre et Dieu peste au Thibet,
Bourreau dressant sur l'homme un colossal gibet,
Bœuf à Memphis, dragon à Tyr, hydre en Chaldée,   145
Chimère et non raison, idole et non idée.

Ton globe, vieil enfant, joue avec ce hochet.
Homme, esprit fou qu'en vain Diogène cherchait,
Homme, tu fais pitié même aux êtres du gouffre,

The kind to whom Holbach would give a visa,
The great Eternal masoned by mere mortals,
Set between time and space, an architectural
Afterthought to life, fate, good, evil, everything,
A trembling empty tower, man's masterpiece?

All of these gods, named by whatever name,
Are everything but God.

Degraded humans,
Being vile, need a judge, and being hideous,
Require a witness; so they want a God.
Fine. They take brick and wood, stone, lead, and make him;
Each culture has its own; and so religion
Has Unity for mask, Legion for name.
One temple sees night where the next sees dawn;
Cheops reveres Amon unknown to Juggernaut;
Odin does not exist at Delphi; dolmens
Deny Muhammad of the Suleimaniye.
The world makes monsters, then sets them as its watchdogs;
And heaven sees with some amazement how
These miserable Gods sprout from your dunghills.

We spirits wandering in the infinite
Never trouble about such trivialities;
Hunting no vain gleams, tracking no pale visions,
Insisting on no answers from the shadows,
We laugh in the dark at your fetish Brahma,
Your God bearded with infinite false hairs,
Africa's monkey-God, Tibet's plague-God,
The executioner holding huge gallows
Over humanity, the Memphian ox,
The Tyrian dragon, the Chaldaean hydra,
Mirage, not method; idol, not idea.

That old baby, your globe, toys with such playthings.
Even the creatures of the chasm, even
The shuddering and suffering obscurity,

Même à l'obscurité qui frissonne et qui souffre;   150
Car ton monde étroit rêve un rêve limité;
Il se compose un Dieu de son infirmité,
Et, dans l'abjection de ses passions vaines,
Instinct, science, amour, colère, guerres, haines,
Il se fait de sa fange une divinité!   155
Il pétrit de la terre avec l'éternité!
Et quand dans sa furie, ou bien dans sa débauche,
Inepte, il a forgé cette effroyable ébauche,
Ce géant muet, sourd, aveugle, dur, fatal,
Ce spectre d'ombre ayant l'horreur pour piédestal,   160
Il achève ce Dieu de laideur, d'imposture,
De nuit, avec la peur qu'il a de la nature.
O toi qui passes là, que veux-tu donc?

                         Et moi:
—Je veux le nom du vrai, criai-je plein d'effroi,
Pour que je le redise à la terre inquiète.—   165

Une Autre Voix

Te figures-tu donc être, par aventure,
Autre chose qu'un point dans l'aveugle nature?
Toi, l'homme, cendre et chair, te persuades-tu
Que d'une fonction l'ombre t'a revêtu?
Quel droit te crois-tu donc à chercher, à poursuivre,   5
A saisir ce qui peut exister, durer, vivre,
A surprendre, à connaître, à savoir, toi qui n'es
Qu'une larve, et qui meurs aussitôt que tu nais?
J'admire ton néant inouï s'il suppose
Qu'il est par l'infini compté pour quelque chose!   10
Quelle idée, ô songeur du songe humanité,
As-tu de ton cerveau pour croire, en vérité,
Qu'il peut prendre ou laisser une empreinte à l'abîme?
Ta pensée est abjecte, étroite, folle, infime;
L'homme est de la fumée obscure qui descend.   15
T'imagines-tu donc laisser trace, ô passant?
Rêves-tu l'absolu comme ton fleuve Seine

Take pity on that foolish phantom Man
For whom Diogenes once sought in vain;
Your narrow world is dreaming tiny dreams,
Making a God of its infirmity;
And, sunk in its vain passions—instinct, science,
Love, anger, hatred, war—it makes its filth
Into a god; it kneads earth with eternity!
When, in its madness or debauchery,
It has ineptly forged this fearful botch—
This mute inflexible blind fatal giant,
This ghost of shade with horror for its pedestal—
It finishes off this God of ugliness,
Night, and imposture, with its fear of nature.
So, passer-by, what do you want?'

                      And I
Cried out in awe: 'I want to know the true one,
So I can name him to the troubled earth.'

Another Voice

'You think yourself, perhaps, more than a speck
Within blind Nature? Human—ash and flesh—
You feel the Dark invested you with functions?
What right have you
To seek, hunt, seize on anything
Existing, living or enduring;
To catch or grasp or know—being yourself
The merest larva, dead as soon as born?
What! do you think, you strange nonentity,
The Infinite takes any note of you?
O dreamer of the dream Mankind, what notions
You must have of your brain, if you believe it
Can take or leave some imprint in the chasm!
Your thoughts are squalid, foolish, cramped and flimsy;
Man is a dim diminishing vapour. Why,
You transient thing, what traces will your passing leave?
You think the Absolute is like your Seine—

Coulant entre les quais de ta ville malsaine,
Recueillant les égouts de toutes les maisons,
Doctrines, volontés, illusions, raisons,   20
Ayant dans son courant, si quelqu'un te réclame,
Quelque pont de Saint-Cloud où l'on repêche l'âme?
Crois-tu que cette eau vaste et sourde, Immensité,
Ne t'enveloppe pas d'oubli, de cécité,
De silence, et sanglote à ta chute, et soit triste?   25
Crois-tu que ta chimère en ce gouffre persiste,
Qu'elle y garde sa forme, espoir, rêve, action,
Et qu'on retrouve, après ta disparition,
Quelque chose de toi, ton cadavre ou ton ombre,
Aux noirs filets flottants de l'éternité sombre?   30

Après les voix

Et, sombre, j'attendis; puis je continuai:

—Quoi! l'homme tomberait, hagard, exténué,
Comme le moucheron qui bat la vitre blême!
Quoi! tout aboutirait à du néant suprême!
Tout l'effort des chercheurs frémissants se perdrait!   5
L'homme habiterait l'ombre et serait au secret!
Marchait serait errer! l'aile serait punie!
L'aurore, ô cieux profonds, serait une ironie!—

Alors, tout haut, levant la voix, levant les bras,
Éperdu, je criai:

          —Cela ne se peut pas!   10
Grand Inconnu! méchant ou bon! grand Invisible!
Je te le dis en face, Être! c'est impossible!—

Une troisième fois, dans l'effrayant ciel noir
On éclata de rire.

Flows with your filthy town on either bank,
Accepts the sewage shed from every house—
Doctrines, illusions, wishes, reasonings—
With some Bridge of Saint-Cloud set in its current
To fish your soul back—if anyone wants you?
You think the wide-spread muffled tide Immensity
Will weep and mourn your fall—without engulfing you
In blindness, silence, and oblivion?
You fancy your mirage will linger there,
Keeping its shape, hopes, dreams, deeds, in the chasm—
That, after you have gone, they will retrieve
Some part of you, your shade or your cadaver,
On the dark drifting fish-nets of Eternity?'

After the Voices

I waited, heavy-hearted; then went on:

'What! Then humanity, distraught and wasted,
Would drop like gnats beating the window-pane!
All would result in utter nothingness!
The toil of trembling seekers all would perish!
People would dwell in darkness and confinement,
Stray when they walked, be punished when they flew!
Deep heavens, dawn would be an irony!'

Then, loudly, lifting up my arms,
I cried out desperately:

                    'It can't be so!
Great Unknown—good or evil—great Invisible—
I tell you to your face, it can't be possible!'

A third time, in the terrible black heavens,
There was a burst of laughter.

Et, muet, sans pouvoir
Deviner d'où venait cette gaîté terrible,   15
Je regardai, lutteur frémissant, l'ombre horrible.

—Qui donc a ri? criai-je égaré. Quel qu'il soit,
Qu'il se montre.—

           Alors, blême et se tenant tout droit,
Je vis monter du fond de l'abîme un suaire.
Ses plis vagues jetaient une odeur d'ossuaire;   20
Et sous le drap hideux et livide on sentait
Un de ces êtres noirs sur qui la nuit se tait.
C'était de ce linceul qu'était sorti ce rire.
Sans que la sombre voix s'élevât pour le dire,
Je le compris; ma chair frémit, mon front pâlit.   25
L'être voilé, debout, comme quelqu'un qui lit
En tournant gravement les pages d'un registre,
Se mit à me parler, lent, paisible et sinistre.

—Écoute. Tu n'as vu jusqu'ici que des songes,
Que de vagues lueurs flottant sur des mensonges,   30
Que les aspects confus qui passent dans les vents
Ou tremblent dans la nuit pour vous autres vivants.
Mais maintenant veux-tu d'une volonté forte
Entrer dans l'infini, quelle que soit la porte?
Ce que l'homme endormi peut savoir, tu le sais.   35
Mais, esprit, trouves-tu que ce n'est pas assez?
Ton regard, d'ombre en ombre et d'étage en étage,
A vu plus d'horizon... —en veux-tu davantage?
Veux-tu, perçant le morne et ténébreux réseau,
T'envoler dans le vrai comme un sinistre oiseau?   40
Veux-tu derrière toi laisser tous les décombres,
Temps, espace; et, hagard, sortir des branches sombres?
Veux-tu, réponds, aller plus loin qu'Amos n'alla,
Et plus avant qu'Esdras et qu'Élie, au delà
Des prophètes pensifs et des blancs cénobites,   45
Percer l'ombre, emporté par des ailes subites?
O semeur du sillon nébuleux, laboureur
Perdu dans la fumée horrible de l'erreur,

Silently,
Not knowing where this grim mockery came from,
Trembling but fierce, I watched the dreadful shade.

'Who laughed?' I cried out wildly. 'Whoever it was,
Show yourself.'

Then, pale, upright, there arose,
Out of the depths of the abyss, a shroud.
Its vague folds had a smell of ossuaries;
Under the hideous pallid sheet, you sensed
Some dark thing in whose presence Night is silent.
And from this cloth that laugh had come.
Not that the voice had spoken, or said so;
I knew. My flesh trembled, my forehead paled.
The creature—veiled, erect, like someone reading
Who gravely turns the pages of a register—
Slow, tranquil, sinister, began to speak to me:

'Listen.—Until now, in your present life,
You have seen only dreams, vague lights
Drifting across illusions—flimsy shapes
Trembling at night, or passing in the wind.
Well! Are you willing now, with a strong will,
To enter the infinite—by whatever door?
Oh yes: what sleepers can know, you know. But, spirit,
Would you say that has been enough? Your vision,
From dark to dark, from step to step, has passed
Frontiers beyond frontiers... And would you now
Go further still—piercing the gloomy web—
Flying in Truth, like a sinister bird—
Leaving behind you every form of debris,
Time, space; escaping the dark branches untamed—
Going further than Amos, past the realm
Of Ezra and Elijah, beyond all
The thoughtful prophets and white coenobites—
Sweeping on sudden wings, cleaving the shadows?
You sow your seed in hazy ground; you plough
Lost in the terrifying smoke of error;

Front où s'abat l'essaim tumultueux des rêves,
Doutes, systèmes vains, effrois, luttes sans trêves,   50
Te plaît-il de savoir comment s'évanouit
En adoration toute cette âpre nuit?
Veux-tu, flèche tremblante, atteindre enfin la cible?
Veux-tu toucher le but, regarder l'invisible,
L'innommé, l'idéal, le réel, l'inouï;   55
Comprendre, déchiffrer, lire? être un ébloui?
Veux-tu planer plus haut que la sombre nature?
Veux-tu dans la lumière inconcevable et pure
Ouvrir tes yeux, par l'ombre affreuse appesantis?
Le veux-tu? Réponds.

                    —Oui!—criai-je.

                              Et je sentis   60
Que la création tremblait comme une toile;
Alors, levant un bras et, d'un pan de son voile,
Couvrant tous les objets terrestres disparus,
Il me toucha le front du doigt, et je mourus.

Dans l'obscurité sourde, impalpable, inouïe,   65
Je me retrouvai seul, mais je n'étais plus moi;
Ou du moins, dans ma tête ouverte aux vents d'effroi,
Je sentis, sans pourtant que l'ombre et le mystère
Eussent cassé le fil qui me lie à la terre,
Monter, grossir, entrer, presque au dernier repli,   70
Comme une crue étrange et terrible d'oubli;
Je sentis, dans la forme obscure pour moi-même
Que je suis et qui, brume, erre dans le problème,
Presque s'évanouir tout l'être antérieur;
Si bien que le fantôme et l'effrayant rieur,   75
Et tous les êtres noirs sortis du gouffre énorme
N'étaient plus qu'un nuage en ma mémoire informe,
Et que mon souvenir en un instant perdit
Tout ce que Légion par cent voix m'avait dit.
A peine de ma vie avais-je encor l'idée,   80
Et ce que jusqu'alors, larve aux lueurs guidée,

While a tumultuous swarm of dreams, doubts, fears,
Vain systems, ceaseless struggles, beats your brain.
Well, would you choose to have that bitter night
Vanish in adoration? would you, wavering
Arrow, attain your goal and gain your mark—
See the invisible, ideal, real,
Nameless and unenvisaged—understand,
Decipher, read—and be a dazzled being?
Would you soar high beyond funereal nature?
Would you open your eyes weighed down by shadow
In the pure unimaginable light?
Would you? Tell me.'

I cried out, 'Yes'—

—and felt
The whole creation trembling like a fabric.
Raising an arm then, covering all the vanished
Terrestrial things with the skirts of his veil,
He touched my forehead with his finger; and I died.

In the mute alien impalpable obscurity
I found myself alone again—yet not myself;
At least, in my head swept with winds of terror,
I felt— though neither mystery nor darkness
Had cut the thread that linked me to the earth—
Some strange and terrible flood of oblivion
Rise up, swell, enter almost every cranny;
I felt—in my obscure innermost form,
The fog within that roams the unresolved—
Almost my whole former existence vanish,
So that the phantom and the dreadful mocker
And all the dark things risen from the chasm
Were now mere cloud-shapes in my formless memory;
I, in one moment, lost all recollection
Of what those hundred voices had once told me.
I scarcely retained notions of my life,
And what till then I, as a gleam-led larva,

J'avais nommé mon âme était je ne sais quoi
Dont je n'étais plus sûr et qui flottait en moi.
Il ne restait de moi qu'une soif de connaître,
Une aspiration vers ce qui pouvait être,   85
Une bouche voulant boire un peu d'eau qui fuit,
Fût-ce au creux de la main fatale de la nuit.

—Spectre, tu m'as trompé, je ne sais rien encore.

Had called my soul, was something indescribable
Drifting inside me, of which I felt doubtful.
All that remained of me was a thirst for knowledge,
A yearning for whatever there might be,
A mouth that longed for vanishing drops of water
Even from the fatal hollow of Night's hand.

'Spirit, you cheated me: I still know nothing.'

CHARLES BAUDELAIRE

from *Les Fleurs du mal*

Au Lecteur

La sottise, l'erreur, le péché, la lésine,
Occupent nos esprits et travaillent nos corps,
Et nous alimentons nos aimables remords,
Comme les mendiants nourrissent leur vermine.

Nos péchés sont têtus, nos repentirs sont lâches;   5
Nous nous faisons payer grassement nos aveux,
Et nous rentrons gaiement dans le chemin bourbeux,
Croyant par de vils pleurs laver toutes nos taches.

Sur l'oreiller du mal c'est Satan Trismégiste
Qui berce longuement notre esprit enchanté,   10
Et le riche métal de notre volonté
Est tout vaporisé par ce savant chimiste.

C'est le Diable qui tient les fils qui nous remuent!
Aux objets répugnants nous trouvons des appas;
Chaque jour vers l'Enfer nous descendons d'un pas,   15
Sans horreur, à travers des ténèbres qui puent.

Ainsi qu'un débauché pauvre qui baise et mange
Le sein martyrisé d'une antique catin,
Nous volons au passage un plaisir clandestin
Que nous pressons bien fort comme une vieille orange.   20

Serré, fourmillant, comme un million d'helminthes,
Dans nos cerveaux ribote un peuple de Démons,
Et, quand nous respirons, la Mort dans nos poumons
Descend, fleuve invisible, avec de sourdes plaintes.

TRANSLATED BY JAMES MCGOWAN

from *The Flowers of Evil*

To the Reader

Folly and error, stinginess and sin
Possess our spirits and fatigue our flesh.
And like a pet we feed our tame remorse
As beggars take to nourishing their lice.

Our sins are stubborn, our contrition lax;
We offer lavishly our vows of faith
And turn back gladly to the path of filth,
Thinking mean tears will wash away our stains.

On evil's pillow lies the alchemist
Satan Thrice-Great, who lulls our captive soul,
And all the richest metal of our will
Is vaporized by his hermetic arts.

Truly the Devil pulls on all our strings!
In most repugnant objects we find charms,
Each day we're one step further into Hell,
Content to move across the stinking pit.

As a poor libertine will suck and kiss
The sad, tormented tit of some old whore,
We steal a furtive pleasure as we pass,
A shrivelled orange that we squeeze and press.

Close, swarming, like a million writhing worms,
A demon nation riots in our brains,
And, when we breathe, death flows into our lungs,
A secret stream of dull, lamenting cries.

Si le viol, le poison, le poignard, l'incendie,   25
N'ont pas encor brodé de leurs plaisants dessins
Le canevas banal de nos piteux destins,
C'est que notre âme, hélas! n'est pas assez hardie.

Mais parmi les chacals, les panthères, les lices,
Les singes, les scorpions, les vautours, les serpents,   30
Les monstres glapissants, hurlants, grognants, rampants,
Dans la ménagerie infâme de nos vices,

Il en est un plus laid, plus méchant, plus immonde!
Quoiqu'il ne pousse ni grands gestes ni grands cris,
Il ferait volontiers de la terre un débris   35
Et dans un bâillement avalerait le monde;

C'est l'Ennui!—l'œil chargé d'un pleur involontaire,
Il rêve d'échafauds en fumant son houka.
Tu le connais, lecteur, ce monstre délicat,
—Hypocrite lecteur,—mon semblable,—mon frère!   40

II. L'Albatros

Souvent, pour s'amuser, les hommes d'équipage
Prennent des albatros, vastes oiseaux des mers,
Qui suivent, indolents compagnons de voyage,
Le navire glissant sur les gouffres amers.

A peine les ont-ils déposés sur les planches,   5
Que ces rois de l'azur, maladroits et honteux,
Laissent piteusement leurs grandes ailes blanches
Comme des avirons traîner à côté d'eux.

Ce voyageur ailé, comme il est gauche et veule!
Lui, naguère si beau, qu'il est comique et laid!   10
L'un agace son bec avec un brûle-gueule,
L'autre mime, en boitant, l'infirme qui volait!

If slaughter, or if arson, poison, rape
Have not as yet adorned our fine designs,
The banal canvas of our woeful fates,
It's only that our spirit lacks the nerve.

But there with all the jackals, panthers, hounds,
The monkeys, scorpions, the vultures, snakes,
Those howling, yelping, grunting, crawling brutes,
The infamous menagerie of vice,

One creature only is most foul and false!
Though making no grand gestures, nor great cries,
He willingly would devastate the earth
And in one yawning swallow all the world;

He is Ennui!—with tear-filled eye he dreams
Of scaffolds, as he puffs his water-pipe.
Reader, you know this dainty monster too;
—Hypocrite reader,—fellowman,—my twin!

The Albatross

Often, when bored, the sailors of the crew
Trap albatross, the great birds of the seas,
Mild travellers escorting in the blue
Ships gliding on the ocean's mysteries.

And when the sailors have them on the planks,
Hurt and distraught, these kings of all outdoors
Piteously let trail along their flanks
Their great white wings, dragging like useless oars.

This voyager, how comical and weak!
Once handsome, how unseemly and inept!
One sailor pokes a pipe into his beak,
Another mocks the flier's hobbled step.

Le Poëte est semblable au prince des nuées
Qui hante la tempête et se rit de l'archer;
Exilé sur le sol au milieu des huées,   15
Ses ailes de géant l'empêchent de marcher.

IV. Correspondances

La Nature est un temple où de vivants piliers
Laissent parfois sortir de confuses paroles;
L'homme y passe à travers des forêts de symboles
Qui l'observent avec des regards familiers.

Comme de longs échos qui de loin se confondent   5
Dans une ténébreuse et profonde unité,
Vaste comme la nuit et comme la clarté,
Les parfums, les couleurs et les sons se répondent.

Il est des parfums frais comme des chairs d'enfants,
Doux comme les hautbois, verts comme les prairies,   10
—Et d'autres, corrompus, riches et triomphants,

Ayant l'expansion des choses infinies,
Comme l'ambre, le musc, le benjoin et l'encens,
Qui chantent les transports de l'esprit et des sens.

XXIII. La Chevelure

O toison, moutonnant jusque sur l'encolure!
O boucles! O parfum chargé de nonchaloir!
Extase! Pour peupler ce soir l'alcôve obscure
Des souvenirs dormant dans cette chevelure,
Je la veux agiter dans l'air comme un mouchoir!   5

The Poet is a kinsman in the clouds
Who scoffs at archers, loves a stormy day;
But on the ground, among the hooting crowds,
He cannot walk, his wings are in the way.

Correspondences

Nature is a temple, where the living
Columns sometimes breathe confusing speech;
Man walks within these groves of symbols, each
Of which regards him as a kindred thing.

As the long echoes, shadowy, profound,
Heard from afar, blend in a unity,
Vast as the night, as sunlight's clarity,
So perfumes, colours, sounds may correspond.

Odours there are, fresh as a baby's skin,
Mellow as oboes, green as meadow grass,
— Others corrupted, rich, triumphant, full,

Having dimensions infinitely vast,
Frankincense, musk, ambergris, benjamin,
Singing the senses' rapture, and the soul's.

Head of Hair

O fleece, billowing even down the neck!
O locks! O perfume charged with nonchalance!
What ecstasy! To people our dark room
With memories that sleep within this mane,
I'll shake it like a kerchief in the air!

La langoureuse Asie et la brûlante Afrique,
Tout un monde lointain, absent, presque défunt,
Vit dans tes profondeurs, forêt aromatique!
Comme d'autres esprits voguent sur la musique,
Le mien, ô mon amour! nage sur ton parfum.   10

J'irai là-bas où l'arbre et l'homme, pleins de sève,
Se pâment longuement sous l'ardeur des climats;
Fortes tresses, soyez la houle qui m'enlève!
Tu contiens, mer d'ébène, un éblouissant rêve
De voiles, de rameurs, de flammes et de mâts: 15

Un port retentissant où mon âme peut boire
A grands flots le parfum, le son et la couleur;
Où les vaisseaux, glissant dans l'or et dans la moire,
Ouvrent leurs vastes bras pour embrasser la gloire
D'un ciel pur où frémit l'éternelle chaleur.   20

Je plongerai ma tête amoureuse d'ivresse
Dans ce noir océan où l'autre est enfermé;
Et mon esprit subtil que le roulis caresse
Saura vous retrouver, ô féconde paresse,
Infinis bercements du loisir embaumé!   25

Cheveux bleus, pavillon de ténèbres tendues,
Vous me rendez l'azur du ciel immense et rond;
Sur les bords duvetés de vos mèches tordues
Je m'enivre ardemment des senteurs confondues
De l'huile de coco, du musc et du goudron.   30

Longtemps! toujours! ma main dans ta crinière lourde
Sèmera le rubis, la perle et le saphir,
Afin qu'à mon désir tu ne sois jamais sourde!
N'es-tu pas l'oasis où je rêve, et la gourde
Où je hume à longs traits le vin du souvenir?   35

Languorous Asia, scorching Africa,
A whole world distant, vacant, nearly dead,
Lives in your depths, o forest of perfume!
While other spirits sail on symphonies
Mine, my beloved, swims along your scent.

I will go down there, where the trees and men,
Both full of sap, swoon in the ardent heat;
Strong swelling tresses, carry me away!
Yours, sea of ebony, a dazzling dream
Of sails, of oarsmen, waving pennants, masts:

A sounding harbour where my soul can drink
From great floods subtle tones, perfumes and hues;
Where vessels gliding in the moire and gold
Open their wide arms to the glorious sky
Where purely trembles the eternal warmth.

I'll plunge my drunken head, dizzy with love
In this black sea where that one is confined;
My subtle soul that rolls in its caress
Will bring you back, o fertile indolence!
Infinite lulling, leisure steeped in balm!

Blue head of hair, tent of spread shadows, you
Give me the azure of the open sky;
In downy wisps along your twisted locks
I'll gladly drug myself on mingled scents,
Essence of cocoa-oil, pitch and musk.

For ages! always! in your heavy mane
My hand will scatter ruby, sapphire, pearl
So you will never chill to my desire!
Are you not the oasis where I dream,
My drinking-gourd for memory's fine wine?

XXVI.   *Sed non satiata*

Bizarre déité, brune comme les nuits,
Au parfum mélangé de musc et de havane,
Œuvre de quelque obi, le Faust de la savane,
Sorcière au flanc d'ébène, enfant des noirs minuits,

Je préfère au constance, à l'opium, au nuits,   5
L'élixir de ta bouche où l'amour se pavane;
Quand vers toi mes désirs partent en caravane,
Tes yeux sont la citerne où boivent mes ennuis.

Par ces deux grands yeux noirs, soupiraux de ton âme,
O démon sans pitié! verse-moi moins de flamme;   10
Je ne suis pas le Styx pour t'embrasser neuf fois,

Hélas! et je ne puis, Mégère libertine,
Pour briser ton courage et te mettre aux abois,
Dans l'enfer de ton lit devenir Proserpine!

XXVII.   « Avec ses vêtements... »

Avec ses vêtements ondoyants et nacrés,
Même quand elle marche on croirait qu'elle danse,
Comme ces longs serpents que les jongleurs sacrés
Au bout de leurs bâtons agitent en cadence.

Comme le sable morne et l'azur des déserts,   5
Insensibles tous deux à l'humaine souffrance,
Comme les longs réseaux de la houle des mers,
Elle se développe avec indifférence.

Ses yeux polis sont faits de minéraux charmants,
Et dans cette nature étrange et symbolique   10
Où l'ange inviolé se mêle au sphinx antique,

Sed non satiata

Singular goddess, brown as night, and wild,
Perfumed of fine tobacco smoke and musk,
Work of some Faust, some wizard of the dusk,
Ebony sorceress, black midnight's child,

Rare wines or opium are less a prize
Than your moist lips where love struts its pavane;
When my lusts move toward you in caravan
My ennuis drink from cisterns of your eyes.

From these black orbits where the soul breathes through,
O heartless demon! pour a drink less hot;
I'm not the Styx, nine times embracing you,

Alas! and my Megaera, I can not,
To break your nerve and bring you to your knees,
In your bed's hell become Persephone!

'The way her silky garments...'

The way her silky garments undulate
It seems she's dancing as she walks along,
Like serpents that the sacred charmers make
To move in rhythms of their waving wands.

Like desert sands and skies she is as well,
As unconcerned with human misery,
Like the long networks of the ocean's swells
Unfolding with insensibility.

Her polished eyes are made of charming stones,
And in her essence, where the natures mix
Of holy angel and the ancient sphinx,

Où tout n'est qu'or, acier, lumière et diamants,
Resplendit à jamais, comme un astre inutile,
La froide majesté de la femme stérile.

XXIX. Une Charogne

Rappelez-vous l'objet que nous vîmes, mon âme,
    Ce beau matin d'été si doux:
Au détour d'un sentier une charogne infâme
    Sur un lit semé de cailloux,

Les jambes en l'air, comme une femme lubrique,   5
    Brûlante et suant les poisons,
Ouvrait d'une façon nonchalante et cynique
    Son ventre plein d'exhalaisons.

Le soleil rayonnait sur cette pourriture,
    Comme afin de la cuire à point,   10
Et de rendre au centuple à la grande Nature
    Tout ce qu'ensemble elle avait joint;

Et le ciel regardait la carcasse superbe
    Comme une fleur s'épanouir.
La puanteur était si forte, que sur l'herbe   15
    Vous crûtes vous évanouir.

Les mouches bourdonnaient sur ce ventre putride,
    D'où sortaient de noirs bataillons
De larves, qui coulaient comme un épais liquide
    Le long de ces vivants haillons.   20

Tout cela descendait, montait comme une vague,
    Ou s'élançait en petillant;
On eût dit que le corps, enflé d'un souffle vague,
    Vivait en se multipliant.

Where all is lit with gold, steel, diamonds,
    A useless star, it shines eternally,
The sterile woman's frigid majesty.

A Carcass

Remember, my love, the object we saw
    That beautiful morning in June:
By a bend in the path a carcass reclined
    On a bed sown with pebbles and stones;

Her legs were spread out like a lecherous whore,
    Sweating out poisonous fumes,
Who opened in slick invitational style
    Her stinking and festering womb.

The sun on this rottenness focused its rays
    To cook the cadaver till done,
And render to Nature a hundredfold gift
    Of all she'd united in one.

And the sky cast an eye on this marvellous meat
    As over the flowers in bloom.
The stench was so wretched that there on the grass
    You nearly collapsed in a swoon.

The flies buzzed and droned on these bowels of filth
    Where an army of maggots arose,
Which flowed with a liquid and thickening stream
    On the animate rags of her clothes.

And it rose and it fell, and pulsed like a wave,
    Rushing and bubbling with health.
One could say that this carcass, blown with vague breath,
    Lived in increasing itself.

Et ce monde rendait une étrange musique,   25
    Comme l'eau courante et le vent,
Ou le grain qu'un vanneur d'un mouvement rhythmique
    Agite et tourne dans son van.

Les formes s'effaçaient et n'étaient plus qu'un rêve,
    Une ébauche lente à venir,   30
Sur la toile oubliée, et que l'artiste achève
    Seulement par le souvenir.

Derrière les rochers une chienne inquiète
    Nous regardait d'un œil fâché,
Épiant le moment de reprendre au squelette   35
    Le morceau qu'elle avait lâché.

—Et pourtant vous serez semblable à cette ordure,
    A cette horrible infection,
Étoile de mes yeux, soleil de ma nature,
    Vous, mon ange et ma passion!   40

Oui! telle vous serez, ô la reine des grâces,
    Après les derniers sacrements,
Quand vous irez, sous l'herbe et les floraisons grasses,
    Moisir parmi les ossements.

Alors, ô ma beauté! dites à la vermine   45
    Qui vous mangera de baisers,
Que j'ai gardé la forme et l'essence divine
    De mes amours décomposés!

XLVII. Harmonie du soir

Voici venir les temps où vibrant sur sa tige
Chaque fleur s'évapore ainsi qu'un encensoir;
Les sons et les parfums tournent dans l'air du soir;
Valse mélancolique et langoureux vertige!

And this whole teeming world made a musical sound
    Like babbling brooks and the breeze,
Or the grain that a man with a winnowing-fan
    Turns with a rhythmical ease.

The shapes wore away as if only a dream
    Like a sketch that is left on the page
Which the artist forgot and can only complete
    On the canvas, with memory's aid.

From back in the rocks, a pitiful bitch
    Eyed us with angry distaste,
Awaiting the moment to snatch from the bones
    The morsel she'd dropped in her haste.

— And you, in your turn, will be rotten as this:
    Horrible, filthy, undone,
O sun of my nature and star of my eyes,
    My passion, my angel in one!

Yes, such you will be, o regent of grace,
    After the rites have been read,
Under the weeds, under blossoming grass
    As you moulder with bones of the dead.

Ah then, o my beauty, explain to the worms
    Who cherish your body so fine,
That I am the keeper for corpses of love
    Of the form, and the essence divine!

The Harmony of Evening

Now it is nearly time when, quivering on its stem,
Each flower, like a censer, sprinkles out its scent;
Sounds and perfumes are mingling in the evening air;
Waltz of a mournfulness and languid vertigo!

Chaque fleur s'évapore ainsi qu'un encensoir;   5
Le violon frémit comme un cœur qu'on afflige;
Valse mélancolique et langoureux vertige!
Le ciel est triste et beau comme un grand reposoir.

Le violon frémit comme un cœur qu'on afflige,
Un cœur tendre, qui hait le néant vaste et noir!   10
Le ciel est triste et beau comme un grand reposoir;
Le soleil s'est noyé dans son sang qui se fige.

Un cœur tendre, qui hait le néant vaste et noir,
Du passé lumineux recueille tout vestige!
Le soleil s'est noyé dans son sang qui se fige...   15
Ton souvenir en moi luit comme un ostensoir!

LIII. L'Invitation au voyage

Mon enfant, ma sœur,
Songe à la douceur
D'aller là-bas vivre ensemble!
Aimer à loisir,
Aimer et mourir   5
Au pays qui te ressemble!
Les soleils mouillés
De ces ciels brouillés
Pour mon esprit ont les charmes
Si mystérieux   10
De tes traîtres yeux,
Brillant à travers leurs larmes.

Là, tout n'est qu'ordre et beauté,
Luxe, calme et volupté.

Des meubles luisants,   15
Polis par les ans,
Décoreraient notre chambre;

Each flower, like a censer, sprinkles out its scent,
The violin is trembling like a grieving heart,
Waltz of a mournfulness and languid vertigo!
The sad and lovely sky spreads like an altar-cloth;

The violin is trembling like a grieving heart,
A tender heart, that hates non-being, vast and black!
The sad and lovely sky spreads like an altar-cloth;
The sun is drowning in its dark, congealing blood.

A tender heart that hates non-being, vast and black
Assembles every glowing vestige of the past!
The sun is drowning in its dark, congealing blood...
In me your memory, as in a monstrance, shines!

Invitation to the Voyage

My sister, my child
Imagine how sweet
To live there as lovers do!
To kiss as we choose
To love and to die
In that land resembling you!
The misty suns
Of shifting skies
To my spirit are as dear
As the evasions
Of your eyes
That shine behind their tears.

There, all is order and leisure,
Luxury, beauty, and pleasure.

The tables would glow
With the lustre of years
To ornament our room.

Les plus rares fleurs
Mêlant leurs odeurs
Aux vagues senteurs de l'ambre,   20
Les riches plafonds,
Les miroirs profonds,
La splendeur orientale,
Tout y parlerait
A l'âme en secret   25
Sa douce langue natale.

Là, tout n'est qu'ordre et beauté,
Luxe, calme et volupté.

Vois sur ces canaux
Dormir ces vaisseaux   30
Dont l'humeur est vagabonde;
C'est pour assouvir
Ton moindre désir
Qu'ils viennent du bout du monde.
—Les soleils couchants   35
Revêtent les champs,
Les canaux, la ville entière,
D'hyacinthe et d'or;
Le monde s'endort
Dans une chaude lumière.   40

Là, tout n'est qu'ordre et beauté,
Luxe, calme et volupté.

LVI.   Chant d'automne

I

Bientôt nous plongerons dans les froides ténèbres;
Adieu, vive clarté de nos étés trop courts!
J'entends déjà tomber avec des chocs funèbres
Le bois retentissant sur le pavé des cours.

The rarest of blooms
Would mingle their scents
With amber's vague perfume.
The ceilings, rich
The mirrors, deep—
The splendour of the East—
All whisper there
To the silent soul
Her sweet familiar speech.

There, all is order and leisure,
Luxury, beauty, and pleasure.

And these canals
Bear ships at rest,
Although in a wandering mood;
To gratify
Your least desire
They have sailed around the world.
The setting suns
Enrobe the fields
The canals, the entire town
With hyacinth, gold;
The world falls asleep
In a warmly glowing gown.

There, all is order and leisure,
Luxury, beauty, and pleasure.

Autumn Song

I

Now will we plunge into the frigid dark,
The living light of summer gone too soon!
Already I can hear a distant sound,
The thump of logs on courtyard paving stones.

Tout l'hiver va rentrer dans mon être: colère,   5
Haine, frissons, horreur, labeur dur et forcé,
Et, comme le soleil dans son enfer polaire,
Mon cœur ne sera plus qu'un bloc rouge et glacé.

J'écoute en frémissant chaque bûche qui tombe;
L'échafaud qu'on bâtit n'a pas d'écho plus sourd.   10
Mon esprit est pareil à la tour qui succombe
Sous les coups du bélier infatigable et lourd.

Il me semble, bercé par ce choc monotone,
Qu'on cloue en grande hâte un cercueil quelque part.
Pour qui?—C'était hier l'été; voici l'automne!   15
Ce bruit mystérieux sonne comme un départ.

II

J'aime de vos longs yeux la lumière verdâtre,
Douce beauté, mais tout aujourd'hui m'est amer,
Et rien, ni votre amour, ni le boudoir, ni l'âtre,
Ne me vaut le soleil rayonnant sur la mer.   20

Et pourtant aimez-moi, tendre cœur! soyez mère,
Même pour un ingrat, même pour un méchant;
Amante ou sœur, soyez la douceur éphémère
D'un glorieux automne ou d'un soleil couchant.

Courte tâche! La tombe attend; elle est avide!   25
Ah! laissez-moi, mon front posé sur vos genoux,
Goûter, en regrettant l'été blanc et torride,
De l'arrière-saison le rayon jaune et doux!

LXXIV. La Cloche fêlée

Il est amer et doux, pendant les nuits d'hiver,
D'écouter, près du feu qui palpite et qui fume,
Les souvenirs lointains lentement s'élever
Au bruit des carillons qui chantent dans la brume.

All winter comes into my being: wrath,
Hate, chills and horror, forced and plodding work,
And like the sun in polar underground
My heart will be a red and frozen block.

I shudder as I hear each log that drops;
A gallows being built makes no worse sound.
My mind is like the tower that succumbs,
Under a heavy engine battered down.

It seems to me, dull with this constant thud,
That someone nails a coffin, but for whom?
Yesterday summer, now the fall! something
With all this eerie pounding will be gone.

II

I love the greenish light in your long eyes
My sweet! but all is bitterness to me,
And nothing, not the boudoir nor the hearth,
Today is worth the sunlight on the sea.

But love me anyway, o tender heart!
Be mother of this mean, ungrateful one;
O lover, sister, be the fleeing sweetness
Of the autumn, of the setting sun.

Brief task! The Tomb is waiting in its greed!
Kneeling before you, let me taste and hold,
While I lament the summer, fierce and white,
A ray of the late fall, mellow and gold.

The Cracked Bell

How bittersweet it is on winter nights
To hear old recollections raise themselves
Around the flickering fire's wisps of light
And through the mist, in voices of the bells.

Bienheureuse la cloche au gosier vigoureux   5
Qui, malgré sa vieillesse, alerte et bien portante,
Jette fidèlement son cri religieux,
Ainsi qu'un vieux soldat qui veille sous la tente!

Moi, mon âme est fêlée, et lorsqu'en ses ennuis
Elle veut de ses chants peupler l'air froid des nuits,   10
Il arrive souvent que sa voix affaiblie

Semble le râle épais d'un blessé qu'on oublie
Au bord d'un lac de sang, sous un grand tas de morts,
Et qui meurt, sans bouger, dans d'immenses efforts.

LXXV.   Spleen [I]

Pluviôse, irrité contre la ville entière,
De son urne à grands flots verse un froid ténébreux
Aux pâles habitants du voisin cimetière
Et la mortalité sur les faubourgs brumeux.

Mon chat sur le carreau cherchant une litière   5
Agite sans repos son corps maigre et galeux;
L'âme d'un vieux poëte erre dans la gouttière
Avec la triste voix d'un fantôme frileux.

Le bourdon se lamente, et la bûche enfumée
Accompagne en fausset la pendule enrhumée,   10
Cependant qu'en un jeu plein de sales parfums,

Héritage fatal d'une vieille hydropique,
Le beau valet de cœur et la dame de pique
Causent sinistrement de leurs amours défunts.

Blessed is the bell of clear and virile throat
Alert and dignified despite his rust,
Who faithfully repeats religion's notes
As an old soldier keeps a watchman's trust.

My spirit, though, is cracked; when as she can
She chants to fill the cool night's emptiness,
Too often can her weakening voice be said

To sound the rattle of a wounded man
Beside a bloody pool, stacked with the dead,
Who cannot budge, and dies in fierce distress!

Spleen [1]

Pluvius, this whole city on his nerves,
Spills from his urn great waves of chilling rain
On graveyards' pallid inmates, and he pours
Mortality in gloomy district streets.

My restless cat goes scratching on the tiles
To make a litter for his scabby hide.
Some poet's phantom roams the gutter-spouts,
Moaning and whimpering like a freezing soul.

A great bell wails—within, the smoking log
Pipes in falsetto to a wheezing clock,
And meanwhile, in a reeking deck of cards—

Some dropsied crone's foreboding legacy—
The dandy Jack of Hearts and Queen of Spades
Trade sinister accounts of wasted love.

LXXVI. Spleen [II]

J'ai plus de souvenirs que si j'avais mille ans.

Un gros meuble à tiroirs encombré de bilans,
De vers, de billets doux, de procès, de romances,
Avec de lourds cheveux roulés dans des quittances,
Cache moins de secrets que mon triste cerveau.   5
C'est une pyramide, un immense caveau,
Qui contient plus de morts que la fosse commune.
—Je suis un cimetière abhorré de la lune,
Où comme des remords se traînent de longs vers
Qui s'acharnent toujours sur mes morts les plus chers.   10
Je suis un vieux boudoir plein de roses fanées,
Où gît tout un fouillis de modes surannées,
Où les pastels plaintifs et les pâles Boucher,
Seuls, respirent l'odeur d'un flacon débouché.

Rien n'égale en longueur les boiteuses journées,   15
Quand sous les lourds flocons des neigeuses années
L'ennui, fruit de la morne incuriosité,
Prend les proportions de l'immortalité.
—Désormais tu n'es plus, ô matière vivante!
Qu'un granit entouré d'une vague épouvante,   20
Assoupi dans le fond d'un Saharah brumeux;
Un vieux sphinx ignoré du monde insoucieux,
Oublié sur la carte, et dont l'humeur farouche
Ne chante qu'aux rayons du soleil qui se couche.

LXXVII. Spleen [III]

Je suis comme le roi d'un pays pluvieux,
Riche, mais impuissant, jeune et pourtant très-vieux,
Qui, de ses précepteurs méprisant les courbettes,
S'ennuie avec ses chiens comme avec d'autres bêtes.
Rien ne peut l'égayer, ni gibier, ni faucon,   5
Ni son peuple mourant en face du balcon.

Spleen [II]

More memories than if I'd lived a thousand years!

A giant chest of drawers, stuffed to the full
With balance sheets, love letters, lawsuits, verse
Romances, locks of hair rolled in receipts,
Hides fewer secrets than my sullen skull.
It is a pyramid, a giant vault
Holding more corpses than a common grave.
—I am a graveyard hated by the moon
Where like remorse the long worms crawl, and turn
Attention to the dearest of my dead.
I am a dusty boudoir where are heaped
Yesterday's fashions, and where withered roses,
Pale pastels, and faded old Bouchers,
Alone, breathe perfume from an opened flask.

Nothing is longer than the limping days
When under heavy snowflakes of the years,
Ennui, the fruit of dulling lassitude,
Takes on the size of immortality.
—Henceforth, o living flesh, you are no more!
You are of granite, wrapped in a vague dread,
Slumbering in some Sahara's hazy sands,
An ancient sphinx lost to a careless world,
Forgotten on the map, whose haughty mood
Sings only in the glow of setting sun.

Spleen [III]

I might as well be king of rainy lands—
Wealthy and young, but impotent and old,
Who scorns the troupe of tutors at his feet
And dallies with his dogs and other beasts.
Nothing can cheer him—game or falconry—
Not even subjects dying at his door.

Du bouffon favori la grotesque ballade
Ne distrait plus le front de ce cruel malade;
Son lit fleurdelisé se transforme en tombeau,
Et les dames d'atour, pour qui tout prince est beau,   10
Ne savent plus trouver d'impudique toilette
Pour tirer un souris de ce jeune squelette.
Le savant qui lui fait de l'or n'a jamais pu
De son être extirper l'élément corrompu,
Et dans ces bains de sang qui des Romains nous viennent,   15
Et dont sur leurs vieux jours les puissants se souviennent,
Il n'a su réchauffer ce cadavre hébété
Où coule au lieu du sang l'eau verte du Léthé.

LXXVIII.   Spleen [IV]

Quand le ciel bas et lourd pèse comme un couvercle
Sur l'esprit gémissant en proie aux longs ennuis,
Et que de l'horizon embrassant tout le cercle
Il nous verse un jour noir plus triste que les nuits;

Quand la terre est changée en un cachot humide,   5
Où l'Espérance, comme une chauve-souris,
S'en va battant les murs de son aile timide
Et se cognant la tête à des plafonds pourris;

Quand la pluie étalant ses immenses traînées
D'une vaste prison imite les barreaux,   10
Et qu'un peuple muet d'infâmes araignées
Vient tendre ses filets au fond de nos cerveaux,

Des cloches tout à coup sautent avec furie
Et lancent vers le ciel un affreux hurlement,
Ainsi que des esprits errants et sans patrie   15
Qui se mettent à geindre opiniâtrement.

The comic jingles of the court buffoon
Do not amuse this twisted invalid.
His regal bed is nothing but a tomb,
And courtesans, who dote on any prince,
No longer have the antics or the clothes
To get a smile from this young rack of bones.
The alchemist who made him gold cannot
Amend his soul and extirpate the flaw;
Nor in those baths of blood the Romans claimed
Would bring an old man's body youthful force,
Can scholar's knowledge bring to life a corpse
With Lethe's putrid water in its veins.

Spleen [IV]

When low and heavy sky weighs like a lid
Upon the spirit moaning in ennui,
And when, spanning the circle of the world,
It pours a black day sadder than our nights;

When earth is changed into a sweaty cell,
In which Hope, captured, like a frantic bat,
Batters the walls with her enfeebled wing,
Striking her head against the rotting beams;

When steady rain trailing its giant train
Descends on us like heavy prison bars,
And when a silent multitude of spiders
Spins its disgusting threads deep in our brains,

Bells all at once jump out with all their force,
And hurl about a mad cacophony
As if they were those lost and homeless souls
Who send a dogged whining to the skies.

—Et de longs corbillards, sans tambours ni musique,
Défilent lentement dans mon âme; l'Espoir,
Vaincu, pleure, et l'Angoisse atroce, despotique,
Sur mon crâne incliné plante son drapeau noir.   20

LXXXIX. Le Cygne

I

Andromaque, je pense à vous! Ce petit fleuve,
Pauvre et triste miroir où jadis resplendit
L'immense majesté de vos douleurs de veuve,
Ce Simoïs menteur qui par vos pleurs grandit,

A fécondé soudain ma mémoire fertile,   5
Comme je traversais le nouveau Carrousel.
Le vieux Paris n'est plus (la forme d'une ville
Change plus vite, hélas! que le cœur d'un mortel);

Je ne vois qu'en esprit tout ce camp de baraques,
Ces tas de chapiteaux ébauchés et de fûts,   10
Les herbes, les gros blocs verdis par l'eau des flaques,
Et, brillant aux carreaux, le bric-à-brac confus.

Là s'étalait jadis une ménagerie;
Là je vis, un matin, à l'heure où sous les cieux
Froids et clairs le Travail s'éveille, où la voirie   15
Pousse un sombre ouragan dans l'air silencieux,

Un cygne qui s'était évadé de sa cage,
Et, de ses pieds palmés frottant le pavé sec,
Sur le sol raboteux traînant son blanc plumage.
Près d'un ruisseau sans eau la bête ouvrant le bec   20

Baignait nerveusement ses ailes dans la poudre,
Et disait, le cœur plein de son beau lac natal:
« Eau, quand donc pleuvras-tu? quand tonneras-tu, foudre? »
Je vois ce malheureux, mythe étrange et fatal,

—And long cortèges minus drum or tone
Deploy morosely through my being: Hope,
The conquered, moans, and tyrant Anguish gloats—
In my bowed skull he fixed his black flag.

The Swan

I

Andromache, I think of you—this meagre stream,
This melancholy mirror where had once shone forth
The giant majesty of all your widowhood,
This fraudulent Simois, fed by bitter tears,

Has quickened suddenly my fertile memory
As I was walking through the modern Carrousel.
The old Paris is gone (the form a city takes
More quickly shifts, alas, than does the mortal heart);

I picture in my head the busy camp of huts,
And heaps of rough-hewn columns, capitals and shafts,
The grass, the giant blocks made green by puddle-stain,
Reflected in the glaze, the jumbled bric-à-brac.

Once nearby was displayed a great menagerie,
And there I saw one day—the time when under skies
Cold and newly bright, Labour stirs awake
And sweepers push their storms into the silent air—

A swan, who had escaped from his captivity,
And scuffing his splayed feet along the paving stones,
He trailed his white array of feathers in the dirt.
Close by a dried-out ditch the bird opened his beak,

Flapping excitedly, bathing his wings in dust,
And said, with heart possessed by lakes he once had loved:
'Water, when will you rain? Thunder, when will you roar?'
I see this hapless creature, sad and fatal myth,

Vers le ciel quelquefois, comme l'homme d'Ovide,   25
Vers le ciel ironique et cruellement bleu,
Sur son cou convulsif tendant sa tête avide,
Comme s'il adressait des reproches à Dieu!

II

Paris change! mais rien dans ma mélancholie
N'a bougé! palais neufs, échafaudages, blocs,   30
Vieux faubourgs, tout pour moi devient allégorie,
Et mes chers souvenirs sont plus lourds que des rocs.

Aussi devant ce Louvre une image m'opprime:
Je pense à mon grand cygne, avec ses gestes fous,
Comme les exilés, ridicule et sublime,   35
Et rongé d'un désir sans trêve! et puis à vous,

Andromaque, des bras d'un grand époux tombée,
Vil bétail, sous la main du superbe Pyrrhus,
Auprès d'un tombeau vide en extase courbée;
Veuve d'Hector, hélas! et femme d'Hélénus!   40

Je pense à la négresse, amaigrie et phthisique,
Piétinant dans la boue, et cherchant, l'œil hagard,
Les cocotiers absents de la superbe Afrique
Derrière la muraille immense du brouillard;

A quiconque a perdu ce qui ne se retrouve   45
Jamais, jamais! à ceux qui s'abreuvent de pleurs
Et tettent la Douleur comme une bonne louve!
Aux maigres orphelins séchant comme des fleurs!

Ainsi dans la forêt où mon esprit s'exile
Un vieux Souvenir sonne à plein souffle du cor!   50
Je pense aux matelots oubliés dans une île,
Aux captifs, aux vaincus!... à bien d'autres encor!

Stretching the hungry head on his convulsive neck,
Sometimes towards the sky, like the man in Ovid's book —
Towards the ironic sky, the sky of cruel blue,
As if he were a soul contesting with his God!

II

Paris may change, but in my melancholy mood
Nothing has budged! New palaces, blocks, scaffoldings,
Old neighbourhoods, are allegorical for me,
And my dear memories are heavier than stone.

And so outside the Louvre an image gives me pause:
I think of my great swan, his gestures pained and mad,
Like other exiles, both ridiculous and sublime,
Gnawed by his endless longing! Then I think of you,

Fallen Andromache, torn from a husband's arms,
Vile property beneath the haughty Pyrrhus' hand,
Next to an empty tomb, head bowed in ecstasy,
Widow of Hector! O! and wife of Helenus!

I think of a negress, thin and tubercular,
Treading in the mire, searching with haggard eye
For palm trees she recalls from splendid Africa,
Somewhere behind a giant barrier of fog;

Of all those who have lost something they may not find
Ever, ever again! who steep themselves in tears
And suck a bitter milk from that good she-wolf, grief!
Of orphans, skin and bones, dry and wasted blooms!

And likewise in the forest of my exiled soul
Old Memory sings out a full note of the horn!
I think of sailors left forgotten on an isle,
Of captives, the defeated... many others more!

xc. Les Sept Vieillards

Fourmillante cité, cité pleine de rêves,
Où le spectre en plein jour raccroche le passant!
Les mystères partout coulent comme des séves
Dans les canaux étroits du colosse puissant.

Un matin, cependant que dans la triste rue   5
Les maisons, dont la brume allongeait la hauteur,
Simulaient les deux quais d'une rivière accrue,
Et que, décor semblable à l'âme de l'acteur,

Un brouillard sale et jaune inondait tout l'espace,
Je suivais, roidissant mes nerfs comme un héros   10
Et discutant avec mon âme déjà lasse,
Le faubourg secoué par les lourds tombereaux.

Tout à coup, un vieillard dont les guenilles jaunes
Imitaient la couleur de ce ciel pluvieux,
Et dont l'aspect aurait fait pleuvoir les aumônes,   15
Sans la méchanceté qui luisait dans ses yeux,

M'apparut. On eût dit sa prunelle trempée
Dans le fiel; son regard aiguisait les frimas,
Et sa barbe à longs poils, roide comme une épée,
Se projetait, pareille à celle de Judas.   20

Il n'était pas voûté, mais cassé, son échine
Faisant avec sa jambe un parfait angle droit,
Si bien que son bâton, parachevant sa mine,
Lui donnait la tournure et le pas maladroit

D'un quadrupède infirme ou d'un juif à trois pattes.   25
Dans la neige et la boue il allait s'empêtrant,
Comme s'il écrasait des morts sous ses savates,
Hostile à l'univers plutôt qu'indifférent.

The Seven Old Men

City of swarming, city full of dreams
Where ghosts in daylight tug the stroller's sleeve!
Mysteries everywhere run like the sap
That fills this great colossus' conduits.

One morning, while along the sombre street
The houses, rendered taller by the mist,
Seemed to be towering wharves at riverside,
And while (our stage-set like the actor's soul)

A dirty yellow stream filled all the space,
I followed, with a hero's iron nerve
To set against my spirit's lassitude,
The district streets shaken by rumbling carts.

Then, an old man whose yellowed rags
Were imitations of the rainy sky,
At whose sight charity might have poured down,
Without the evil glitter in his eyes,

Appeared quite suddenly to me. I'd say
His eye was steeped in gall; his glance was sharp
As frost, his shaggy beard, stiff as a sword,
Stood out, and Judas came into my mind.

You would not call him bent, but cut in two—
His spine made a right angle with his legs
So neatly that his cane, that final touch,
Gave him the figure and the clumsy step

Of some sick beast, or a three-legged Jew.
In snow and filth he made his heavy way,
As if his old shoes trampled on the dead
In hatred, not indifference to life.

Son pareil le suivait: barbe, œil, dos, bâton, loques,
Nul trait ne distinguait, du même enfer venu,   30
Ce jumeau centenaire, et ces spectres baroques
Marchaient du même pas vers un but inconnu.

A quel complot infâme étais-je donc en butte,
Ou quel méchant hasard ainsi m'humiliait?
Car je comptai sept fois, de minute en minute,   35
Ce sinistre vieillard qui se multipliait!

Que celui-là qui rit de mon inquiétude,
Et qui n'est pas saisi d'un frisson fraternel,
Songe bien que malgré tant de décrépitude
Ces sept monstres hideux avaient l'air éternel!   40

Aurais-je, sans mourir, contemplé le huitième,
Sosie inexorable, ironique et fatal,
Dégoûtant Phénix, fils et père de lui-même?
—Mais je tournai le dos au cortège infernal.

Exaspéré comme un ivrogne qui voit double,   45
Je rentrai, je fermai ma porte, épouvanté,
Malade et morfondu, l'esprit fiévreux et trouble,
Blessé par le mystère et par l'absurdité!

Vainement ma raison voulait prendre la barre;
La tempête en jouant déroutait ses efforts,   50
Et mon âme dansait, dansait, vieille gabarrre
Sans mâts, sur une mer monstrueuse et sans bords!

xcii. Les Aveugles

Contemple-les, mon âme; ils sont vraiment affreux!
Pareils aux mannequins; vaguement ridicules;
Terribles, singuliers comme les somnambules;
Dardant on ne sait où leurs globes ténébreux.

His double followed: beard, eye, back, stick, rags,
No separate traits, and come from the same hell.
This second ancient man, baroque, grotesque,
Trod with the same step towards their unknown goal.

To what conspiracy was I exposed,
What wicked chance humiliated me?
For one by one I counted seven times
Multiples of this sinister old man!

Those who would laugh at my frenetic state,
Who are not seized by a fraternal chill,
Must ponder that, despite their feebleness,
These monsters smacked of all eternity!

Could I still live and look upon the eighth
Relentless twin, fatal, disgusting freak,
Trick Phoenix, son and father of himself?
—I turned my back on this parade from Hell.

Bedazzled, like a double-visioned drunk,
I staggered home and shut the door, aghast,
Shaking and sick, the spirit feverous,
Struck by this mystery, this absurdity!

Vainly my reason reached to clutch the helm;
The giddy tempest baffled every grasp,
And my soul danced in circles like a hull
Dismasted, on a monstrous shoreless sea!

The Blind

Consider them, my soul, they are a fright!
Like mannequins, vaguely ridiculous,
Peculiar, terrible somnambulists,
Beaming—who can say where—their eyes of night.

Leurs yeux, d'où la divine étincelle est partie,   5
Comme s'ils regardaient au loin, restent levés
Au ciel; on ne les voit jamais vers les pavés
Pencher rêveusement leur tête appesantie.

Ils traversent ainsi le noir illimité,
Ce frère du silence éternel. O cité!   10
Pendant qu'autour de nous tu chantes, ris et beugles,

Éprise du plaisir jusqu'à l'atrocité,
Vois! je me traîne aussi! mais, plus qu'eux hébété,
Je dis: Que cherchent-ils au Ciel, tous ces aveugles?

CXVI. Un Voyage à Cythère

Mon cœur, comme un oiseau, voltigeait tout joyeux
Et planait librement à l'entour des cordages;
Le navire roulait sous un ciel sans nuages,
Comme un ange enivré d'un soleil radieux.

Quelle est cette île triste et noire?—C'est Cythère,   5
Nous dit-on, un pays fameux dans les chansons,
Eldorado banal de tous les vieux garçons.
Regardez, après tout, c'est un pauvre terre.

—Ile des doux secrets et des fêtes du cœur!
De l'antique Vénus le superbe fantôme   10
Au-dessus de tes mers plane comme un arome,
Et charge les esprits d'amour et de langueur.

Belle île aux myrtes verts, pleine de fleurs écloses,
Vénérée à jamais par toute nation,
Où les soupirs des cœurs en adoration   15
Roulent comme l'encens sur un jardin de roses

These orbs, in which a spark is never seen,
As if in looking far and wide stay raised
On high; they never seem to cast their gaze
Down to the street, head hung, as in a dream.

Thus they traverse the blackness of their days,
Kin to the silence of eternity,
O city! while you laugh and roar and play,

Mad with your lusts to point of cruelty,
Look at me! dragging, dazed more than their kind.
What in the Skies can these men hope to find?

A Voyage to Cythera

My heart was like a bird that fluttered joyously
And glided free among the tackle and the lines!
The vessel rolled along under a cloudless sky—
An angel, tipsy, gay, full of the radiant sun.

What is that sad black isle? I asked as we approached—
They call it Cythera, land to write songs about,
Banal Utopia of veterans of love;
But look, it seems to be a poor land after all.

—Island of sweet intrigues, and feastings of the heart!
The ghost of ancient Venus the magnificent
Glides like a haunting scent above your swelling seas,
Enrapturing the soul in languishing and love.

Sweet isle of greenery, myrtle and blooming flowers,
Perpetual delight of those in every land,
Where sighs of adoration from the hearts of lovers
Roll as incense does over a rosy bower,

Ou le roucoulement éternel d'un ramier!
—Cythère n'était plus qu'un terrain des plus maigres,
Un désert rocailleux troublé par des cris aigres.
J'entrevoyais pourtant un objet singulier!   20

Ce n'était pas un temple aux ombres bocagères,
Où la jeune prêtresse, amoureuse des fleurs,
Allait, le corps brûlé de secrètes chaleurs,
Entre-bâillant sa robe aux brises passagères;

Mais voilà qu'en rasant la côte d'assez près   25
Pour troubler les oiseaux avec nos voiles blanches,
Nous vîmes que c'était un gibet à trois branches,
Du ciel se détachant en noir, comme un cyprès.

De féroces oiseaux perchés sur leur pâture
Détruisaient avec rage un pendu déjà mûr,   30
Chacun plantant, comme un outil, son bec impur
Dans tous les coins saignants de cette pourriture;

Les yeux étaient deux trous, et du ventre effondré
Les intestins pesants lui coulaient sur les cuisses,
Et ses bourreaux, gorgés de hideuses délices,   35
L'avaient à coups de bec absolument châtré.

Sous les pieds, un troupeau de jaloux quadrupèdes,
Le museau relevé, tournoyait et rôdait;
Une plus grande bête au milieu s'agitait
Comme un exécuteur entouré de ses aides.   40

Habitant de Cythère, enfant d'un ciel si beau,
Silencieusement tu souffrais ces insultes
En expiation de tes infâmes cultes
Et des péchés qui t'ont interdit le tombeau.

Ridicule pendu, tes douleurs sont les miennes!   45
Je sentis, à l'aspect de tes membres flottants,
Comme un vomissement, remonter vers mes dents
Le long fleuve de fiel des douleurs anciennes;

Or like the constant crooning of a turtle-dove!
—Cythera was an island barren in terrain,
A mere deserted rock, disturbed by piercing cries.
But on it I could glimpse a curious device!

No temple was this thing, among the woodland shades,
Where the young worshipper, the flowers' devotee,
Would tarry, body burning, hot with secret lusts,
Her robe half-open to the fleeting wisps of breeze;

But as we skimmed the shore, fairly near enough
To agitate the birds with swelling of our sails,
What we saw was a gibbet, made of three great stakes.
It reared against the sky, black, as a cypress stands.

Ferocious birds were gathered, snatching at their food,
Raging around a hanging shape already ripe;
Each creature worked his tool, his dripping filthy beak,
Into the bleeding corners of this rottenness.

The eyes were two blank gaps, and from the hollow paunch
Its tangled guts let loose, spilling over the thighs,
And those tormentors, gorged with hideous delights,
Had castrated the corpse with snapping of their beaks.

Under the feet, a troupe of jealous quadrupeds,
The muzzle lifted high, eddied and prowled about;
One larger, bolder beast was restless all the more,
The leader of the pack, surrounded by his aides.

Dweller in Cythera, child of a sky so clear,
In silence you endure these desecrations—
In expiation for your infamous beliefs
And crimes which have denied you proper burial.

Hanged man, ridiculous, your sorrows are my own!
I feel, in blinding view of your loose-hanging limbs,
A rising to the teeth, a building in my throat
Of a choking spew of gall, and all my ancient griefs;

Devant toi, pauvre diable au souvenir si cher,
J'ai senti tous les becs et toutes les mâchoires   50
Des corbeaux lancinants et des panthères noires
Qui jadis aimaient tant à triturer ma chair.

—Le ciel était charmant, la mer était unie;
Pour moi tout était noir et sanglant désormais,
Hélas! et j'avais, comme en un suaire épais,   55
Le cœur enseveli dans cette allégorie.

Dans ton île, ô Vénus! je n'ai trouvé debout
Qu'un gibet symbolique où pendait mon image...
—Ah! Seigneur! donnez-moi la force et le courage
De contempler mon cœur et mon corps sans dégoût!   60

CXXVI. Le Voyage

I

Pour l'enfant, amoureux de cartes et d'estampes,
L'univers est égal à son vaste appétit.
Ah! que le monde est grande à la clarté des lampes!
Aux yeux du souvenir que le monde est petit!

Un matin nous partons, le cerveau plein de flamme   5
Le cœur gros de rancune et de désirs amers,
Et nous allons, suivant le rhythme de la lame,
Berçant notre infini sur le fini des mers:

Les uns, joyeux de fuir une patrie infâme;
D'autres, l'horreur de leurs berceaux, et quelques-uns,   10
Astrologues noyés dans les yeux d'une femme,
La Circé tyrannique aux dangereux parfums.

Pour n'être pas changés en bêtes, ils s'enivrent
D'espace et de lumière et de cieux embrasés;
La glace qui les mord, les soleils qui les cuivrent,   15
Effacent lentement la marque des baisers.

Along with you, poor devil, dear to memory,
I suffered all the stabs of all the killer crows
And felt the grinding jaws of panthers, cruel and black,
Who once took such delight in feasting on my flesh.

—The sky was ravishing, the sea a very glass;
For me the world was black, and bloody it would be.
Alas! And as within a heavy shroud, I have
Entombed my heart in this perverse allegory!

Venus, in your black isle not one thing was erect
But the symbolic tree whereon my image hung.
Ah, Lord! I beg of you the courage and the strength
To take without disgust my body and my heart!

Voyaging

I

The wide-eyed child in love with maps and plans
Finds the world equal to his appetite.
How grand the universe by light of lamps,
How petty in the memory's clear sight.

One day we leave, with fire in the brain,
Heart great with rancour, bitter in its mood;
Outward we travel on the rolling main,
Lulling infinity in finitude:

Some gladly flee their homelands gripped in vice,
Some, horrors of their childhood, others still—
Astrologers lost in a woman's eyes—
Some perfumed Circe with a tyrant's will.

Not to become a beast, each desperate one
Makes himself drunk on space and burning skies;
The gnawing ice, the copper-burning sun
Efface the scars of kisses and of lies.

Mais les vrais voyageurs sont ceux-là seuls qui partent
Pour partir; cœurs légers, semblables aux ballons,
De leur fatalité jamais ils ne s'écartent,
Et, sans savoir pourquoi, disent toujours: Allons!   20

Ceux-là dont les désirs ont la forme des nues,
Et qui rêvent, ainsi qu'un conscrit le canon,
De vastes voluptés, changeantes, inconnues,
Et dont l'esprit humain n'a jamais su le nom!

II

Nous imitons, horreur! la toupie et la boule   25
Dans leur valse et leurs bonds; même dans nos sommeils
La Curiosité nous tormente et nous roule,
Comme un Ange cruel qui fouette des soleils.

Singulière fortune où le but se déplace,
Et, n'étant nulle part, peut être n'importe où!   30
Où l'Homme, dont jamais l'espérance n'est lasse,
Pour trouver le repos court toujours comme un fou!

Notre âme est un trois-mâts cherchant son Icarie;
Une voix retentit sur le pont: « Ouvre l'œil! »
Une voix de la hune, ardente et folle, crie: 35
« Amour... gloire... bonheur! » Enfer! c'est un écueil!

Chaque îlot signalé par l'homme de vigie
Est un Eldorado promis par le Destin;
L'Imagination qui dresse son orgie
Ne trouve qu'un récif aux clartés du matin.   40

O le pauvre amoureux des pays chimériques!
Faut-il le mettre aux fers, le jeter à la mer,
Ce matelot ivrogne, inventeur d'Ameriques
Dont le mirage rend le gouffre plus amer?

But the true voyagers set out to sea
Just for the leaving's sake; hearts lift aloft,
Nothing dissuades them from their destiny,
Something beyond their knowing cries, 'We're off!'

These, then, whose ecstasies are wide as air
As conscripts dream of cannons, have their dreams
Of luxuries beyond what man can bear,
Such as the soul has neither named nor seen.

II

Our actions are grotesque—in leaps and bounds
We waltz like balls or tops; when day is done
Our curiosity rolls us around
As if a cruel Angel lashed the sun.

Strange thing it is, to chase a shifting fake—
A goal that's nowhere, anywhere at all!
Man, whose anticipation stays awake,
To find his rest goes racing like a fool!

Our soul's three-master seeks the blessed isle:
A voice on deck shouts: 'Ho there, have a look!'
Some crow's-nest spy cries in romantic style
'Love... glory... happiness!' Damn, just a rock!

Each isle is named the long-awaited sight,
The Eldorado of our Destiny;
Fancy, that grows us orgies in the night,
Breaks on a reef in morning's clarity.

Oh, the inebriate of distant lands,
This sot who sees Americas at will,
Must he be chained, abandoned on the sands,
Whose visions make the gulf more bitter still?

Tel le vieux vagabond, piétinant dans la boue,   45
Rêve, le nez dans l'air, de brillants paradis;
Son œil ensorcelé découvre une Capoue
Partout où la chandelle illumine un taudis.

III

Étonnants voyageurs! quelles nobles histoires
Nous lisons dans vos yeux profonds comme les mers!   50
Montrez-nous les écrins de vos riches mémoires,
Ces bijoux merveilleux, faits d'astres et d'éthers.

Nous voulons voyager sans vapeur et sans voile!
Faites, pour égayer l'ennui de nos prisons,
Passer sur nos esprits, tendus comme une toile,   55
Vos souvenirs avec leurs cadres d'horizons.

Dites, qu'avez-vous vu?

IV

              « Nous avons vu des astres
Et des flots; nous avons vu des sables aussi;
Et, malgré bien des chocs et d'imprévus désastres,
Nous nous sommes souvent ennuyés, comme ici.   60

La gloire du soleil sur la mer violette,
La gloire des cités dans le soleil couchant,
Allumaient dans nos cœurs une ardeur inquiète
De plonger dans un ciel au reflet alléchant.

Les plus riches cités, les plus grands paysages,   65
Jamais ne contenaient l'attrait mystérieux
De ceux que le hasard fait avec les nuages.
Et toujours le désir nous rendait soucieux!

—La jouissance ajoute au désir de la force.
Désir, vieil arbre à qui le plaisir sert d'engrais,   70
Cependant que grossit et durcit ton écorce,
Tes branches veulent voir le soleil de plus près!

So the old tramp who shuffles in the filth
Dreams of a paradise and lifts his head—
In his wild eyes, Capua and her wealth
Wherever candle glow lights up a shed.

III

Fabulous voyagers! What histories
Are there behind your deep and distant stare!
Show us the treasures of your memories,
Those jewels and riches made of stars and air.

We're travellers afraid of steam and sail!
Here in our prison every day's the same.
Oh, paint across the canvas of our souls
Your memoirs, with horizon as their frame.

Tell us, what have you seen?

IV

'We've seen the stars
And waves, and we have seen the sandy shores;
Despite disasters, all our jolts and jars,
On sea, on land we find that we are bored.

The glorious sun across the violet sea,
Great sunlit cities dreaming as they lie,
Made our heart yearn with fierce intensity
To plunge towards those reflections in the sky.

Rich cities, and the grandest mountain spires
Somehow could never hold the same allure
As shifting clouds, the shape of our desires,
Which left us unfulfilled and insecure.

—Surely enjoyment quickens passion's spark.
Desire, old tree, that fattens on delight,
As you grow older, toughening your bark,
You want to see the sun from nearer height!

Grandiras-tu toujours, grand arbre plus vivace
Que le cyprès?—Pourtant nous avons, avec soin,
Cueilli quelques croquis pour votre album vorace,　　　75
Frères qui trouvez beau tout ce qui vient de loin!

Nous avons salué des idoles à la trompe;
Des trônes constellés de joyaux lumineux;
Des palais ouvragés dont la féerique pompe
Serait pour vos banquiers un rêve ruineux;　　　80

Des costumes qui sont pour les yeux une ivresse;
Des femmes dont les dents et les ongles sont teints,
Et des jongleurs savants que le serpent caresse. »

V

Et puis, et puis encore?

VI

« O cervaux enfantins!

Pour ne pas oublier la chose capitale,　　　85
Nous avons vu partout, et sans l'avoir cherché,
Du haut jusques en bas de l'échelle fatale,
Le spectacle ennuyeux de l'immortel péché:

La femme, esclave vile, orgueilleuse et stupide,
Sans rire s'adorant et s'aimant sans dégoût;　　　90
L'homme, tyran goulu, paillard, dur et cupide,
Esclave de l'esclave et ruisseau dans l'égout;

Le bourreau qui jouit, le martyr qui sanglote;
La fête qu'assaisonne et parfume le sang;
Le poison du pouvoir énervant le despote,　　　95
Et le peuple amoureux du fouet abrutissant;

Do you grow always taller, grandest tree,
Older than cypress?—Still, we have with care
Brought sketch-book pieces from across the sea
For brothers who love all that's strange and rare!

Idols with trunks we've greeted in our time;
Great palaces enwrought with filigree
And jewelled thrones in luminous design,
To send your brokers dreams of bankruptcy;

Scant costumes that can stupefy the gaze
On painted women, every nail and tooth,
And subtle jugglers, wise in serpents' ways.'

V

And then, and then what more?

VI

'O childish dupes!

You want the truth? We'll tell you without fail—
We never thought to search it out, but saw
From heights to depths, through all the mortal scale
The numbing spectacle of human flaw.

Woman, vile slave, proud in stupidity,
Tasteless and humourless in self-conceit;
Man, greedy tyrant, lustful, slovenly,
Slave of the slave, a sewer in the street;

The hangman jokes, the martyr sobs and faints,
The feast of blood is seasoned perfectly;
Poison of power drains a tyrant's strength,
Whose subjects love the whip's brutality.

Plusieurs religions semblables à la nôtre,
Toutes escaladant le ciel; la Sainteté,
Comme en un lit de plume un délicat se vautre,
Dans les clous et le crin cherchant la volupté;   100

L'Humanité bavarde, ivre de son génie,
Et, folle maintenant comme elle était jadis,
Criant à Dieu, dans sa furibonde agonie:
« O mon semblable, ô mon maître, je te maudis! »

Et les moins sots, hardis amants de la Démence,   105
Fuyant le grand troupeau parqué par le Destin,
Et se réfugiant dans l'opium immense!
—Tel est du globe entier l'éternel bulletin. »

VII

Amer savoir, celui qu'on tire du voyage!
Le monde, monotone et petit, aujourd'hui,   110
Hier, demain, toujours, nous fait voir votre image:
Une oasis d'horreur dans un désert d'ennui!

Faut-il partir? rester? Si tu peux rester, reste;
Pars, s'il le faut. L'un court, et l'autre se tapit
Pour tromper l'ennemi vigilant et funeste,   115
Le Temps! Il est, hélas! des coureurs sans répit,

Comme le Juif errant et comme les apôtres,
A qui rien ne suffit, ni wagon ni vaisseau,
Pour fuir ce rétiaire infâme; il en est d'autres
Qui savent le tuer sans quitter leur berceau.   120

Lorsque enfin il mettra le pied sur notre échine,
Nous pourrons espérer et crier: En avant!
De même qu'autrefois nous partions pour la Chine,
Les yeux fixés au large et les cheveux au vent,

Religions like our own in most details
Climb skyward on their saints, who it is said
Indulge their lusts with hairshirts, or with nails,
As dainty fops sprawl on a feather bed.

Drunk on her genius, Humanity,
Mad now as she has always been, or worse,
Cries to her God in raging agony:
"Master, my image, damn you with this curse!"

Not quite so foolish, bold demented ones
Flee from the feeding lot that holds the herd;
Their boundless shelter is in opium.
—From all the world, such always is the word.'

VII

How bitter, what we learn from voyaging!
The small and tedious world gives us to see
Now, always, the real horror of the thing,
Ourselves—that sad oasis in ennui!

Must one depart? or stay? Stand it and stay,
Leave if you must. One runs, one finds a space
To hide and cheat the deadly enemy
Called Time. Alas, some run a constant race—

The twelve apostles, or the Wandering Jew—
For them no ship avails, no ways or means
To flee that gladiator; others know
From infancy how to defeat the fiend.

Finally, though, his boot is on our chest;
Then we may hope, and call out 'Onward ho!'
Even as once we set out for the East,
Our eyes fixed widely, hair blown to and fro,

Nous nous embarquerons sur la mer des Ténèbres   125
Avec le cœur joyeux d'un jeune passager.
Entendez-vous ces voix, charmantes et funèbres,
Qui chantent: « Par ici! vous qui voulez manger

Le Lotus parfumé! c'est ici qu'on vendange
Les fruits miraculeux dont votre cœur a faim;   130
Venez vous enivrer de la douceur étrange
De cette après-midi qui n'a jamais de fin? »

A l'accent familier nous devinons le spectre;
Nos Pylades là-bas tendent leurs bras vers nous.
« Pour rafraîchir ton cœur nage vers ton Électre! »   135
Dit celle dont jadis nous baisions les genoux.

VIII

O Mort, vieux capitaine, il est temps! levons l'ancre!
Ce pays nous ennuie, ô Mort! Appareillons!
Si le ciel te la mer sont noirs comme de l'encre,
Nos cœurs que tu connais sont remplis de rayons!   140

Verse-nous poison pour qu'il nous reconforte!
Mous voulons, tant ce feu nous brûle le cerveau,
Plonger au fond du gouffre, Enfer ou Ciel, qu'importe?
Au fond de Inconnu pour trouver du *nouveau!*

Now sailing on the sea of shades we go,
With all the plans of passengers well-pleased
To hear the voice, funereal and low,
That sings: 'This way! Come here and take your ease

And eat the Lotus! Here we gather in
These fruits for hearts that yearn for strange delights;
Intoxicate yourselves on alien
Enjoyment through these days without a night.'

We understand the phantom's friendly part,
That Pylades who reaches out to tease:
'Swim towards Electra now, to ease your heart!'
She cries, and long ago we kissed her knees.

VIII

O Death, old captain, time to make our trip!
This country bores us, Death! Let's get away!
Even if sky and sea are black as pitch
You know our hearts are full of sunny rays!

Serve us your poison, sir, to treat us well!
Minds burning, we know what we have to do,
And plunge to depths of Heaven or of Hell,
To fathom the Unknown, and find the *new!*

PAUL VERLAINE

from *Poèmes saturniens*

Chanson d'automne

Les sanglots longs
Des violons
  De l'automne
Blessent mon cœur
D'une langueur   5
  Monotone.

Tout suffocant
Et blême, quand
  Sonne l'heure,
Je me souviens   10
Des jours anciens
  Et je pleure;

Et je m'en vais
Au vent mauvais
  Qui m'emporte   15
Deçà, delà,
Pareil à la
  Feuille morte.

TRANSLATED BY MARTIN SORRELL

from *Saturnian Poems*

Autumn Song

The long sobs of
The violins
    Of autumn
Lay waste my heart
With monotones
    Of boredom.

Quite colourless
And choking when
    The hour strikes
I think again
Of vanished days
    And cry.

And so I leave
On cruel winds
    Squalling
And gusting me
Like a dead leaf
    Falling.

from *Fêtes galantes*

Sur l'herbe

L'abbé divague.—Et toi, marquis,
Tu mets de travers ta perruque.
—Ce vieux vin de Chypre est exquis
Moins, Camargo, que votre nuque.

—Ma flamme... —Do, mi, sol, la, si.   5
—L'abbé, ta noirceur se dévoile!
—Que je meure, Mesdames, si
Je ne vous décroche une étoile!

—Je voudrais être petit chien!
—Embrassons nos bergères l'une   10
Après l'autre.—Messieurs, eh bien?
—Do, mi, sol.—Hé! bonsoir, la Lune!

Les Ingénus

Les hauts talons luttaient avec les longues jupes,
En sorte que, selon le terrain et le vent,
Parfois luisaient des bas de jambes, trop souvent
Interceptés!—et nous aimions ce jeu de dupes.

Parfois aussi le dard d'un insecte jaloux   5
Inquiétait le col des belles sous les branches,
Et c'étaient des éclairs soudains de nuques blanches,
Et ce régal comblait nos jeunes yeux de fous.

Le soir tombait, un soir équivoque d'automne:
Les belles, se pendant rêveuses à nos bras,   10
Dirent alors des mots si spécieux, tout bas,
Que notre âme, depuis ce temps, tremble et s'étonne.

from *Fun and Games*

On the Grass

The abbé rambles—Marquis, I think you'll find
You've got your wig on all askew.
—This Cyprus wine's not so divine,
Camargo of the lovely neck, as you.

—I burn... —Do re mi fa sol la.
—Your black soul's showing under your black cloak,
Abbé.—Sweet ladies, may I choke
If I don't reach you down a star!

—I'd love to be your little doggie!
—Let's kiss these shepherdesses, one by
One, good gentlemen. So, who's with me?
—Do re mi.—Oh look, there's a moon in the sky!

Without Guile

High heels fought a battle with long skirts
So that, subject to terrain and strength of wind,
An ankle sometimes was glimpsed, too often
Caught!—we loved to work out who was fooling whom.

And sometimes too a darting jealous insect swooped
And irritated lovely necks beneath the trees.
Flashing glimpses of pale napes were seen,
A sight for young besotted eyes.

Evening fell, autumnal, indeterminate.
The lovely girls in a dream on our arms
Murmured such empty words so low
That ever since we've trembled with delight.

Fantoches

Scaramouche et Pulcinella
Qu'un mauvais dessein rassembla
Gesticulent, noirs sur la lune.

Cependant l'excellent docteur
Bolonais cueille avec lenteur   5
Des simples parmi l'herbe brune.

Lors sa fille, piquant minois,
Sous la charmille, en tapinois,
Se glisse, demi-nue, en quête

De son beau pirate espagnol,   10
Dont un langoureux rossignol
Clame la détresse à tue-tête.

Colombine

Léandre le sot,
Pierrot qui d'un saut
     De puce
Franchit le buisson,
Cassandre sous son   5
     Capuce,

Arlequin aussi,
Cet aigrefin si
     Fantasque
Aux costumes fous,   10
Ses yeux luisant sous
     Son masque,

—Do, mi, sol, mi, fa,—
Tout ce monde va,
     Rit, chante   15

Weird as Puppets

Scaramouche and Pulcinella
Making evil plans together
Wave their arms, moon-silhouettes.

But the excellent Bolognese
Doctor's picking some of these
Special herbs among the grass.

His daughter with the pretty eyes,
In the arbour, on the sly's
Looking—semi-naked—for

Her handsome Spanish buccaneer
Whose sad affliction she can hear
Well noted by a nightingale.

Colombine

Stupid Leander,
Pierrot who with a
   Flea-hop
Clears the espalier,
Pantaloon under
   His cloak,

Harlequin also,
That reprobate so
   Bizarre
In his crazy clothes
With his glowing eyes
   Disguised,

—Do re mi fa sol,
Round and round they go,
   Laugh, sing

Et danse devant
Une belle enfant
 Méchante

Dont les yeux pervers
Comme les yeux verts   20
 Des chattes
Gardent ses appas
Et disent: « A bas
 Les pattes! »

—Eux ils vont toujours!   25
Fatidique cours
 Des astres,
Oh! dis-moi vers quels
Mornes ou cruels
 Désastres   30

L'implacable enfant,
Preste et relevant
 Ses jupes,
La rose au chapeau,
Conduit son troupeau   35
 De dupes?

En sourdine

Calmes dans le demi-jour
Que les branches hautes font,
Pénétrons bien notre amour
De ce silence profond.

Fondons nos âmes, nos cœurs   5
Et nos sens extasiés,
Parmi les vagues langueurs
Des pins et des arbousiers.

And dance before a
Sweet improper
   Young thing

Whose eyes say beware,
The way the green stare
   Of cats
Entices and draws
In and says: 'Keep your
   Hands off!'

The others dance on
Like fated astron-
   Omers...
Tell me, towards which
Ghastly or savage
   Wreckage

The determined child
With lifted hem, wild
   And loose,
A flower in her hat,
Is leading her lamb-
   Like fools?

Muted Tones

Calm in the half-light
Cast by the high branches
Let the deep quiet
Reach into our love.

Melt as one soul
One heart one charm
Of senses under soft swaying
Pines and arbuti.

Ferme tes yeux à demi,
Croise tes bras sur ton sein,　　　　　　10
Et de ton cœur endormi
Chasse à jamais tout dessein.

Laissons-nous persuader
Au souffle berceur et doux
Qui vient à tes pieds rider　　　　　　15
Les ondes de gazon roux.

Et quand, solennel, le soir
Des chênes noirs tombera,
Voix de notre désespoir,
Le rossignol chantera.　　　　　　20

Colloque sentimental

Dans le vieux parc solitaire et glacé,
Deux formes ont tout à l'heure passé.

Leurs yeux sont morts et leurs lèvres sont molles,
Et l'on entend à peine leurs paroles.

Dans le vieux parc solitaire et glacé,　　　　　　5
Deux spectres ont évoqué le passé.

— Te souvient-il de notre extase ancienne?
—Pourquoi voulez-vous qu'il me souvienne?

—Ton cœur bat-il toujours à mon seul nom?
Toujours vois-tu mon âme en rêve?—Non.　　　　　　10

—Ah! les beaux jours de bonheur indicible
Où nous joignions nos bouches!—C'est possible.

— Qu'il était bleu, le ciel, et grand, l'espoir!
—L'espoir a fui, vaincu, vers le ciel noir.

Half-close your eyes
Fold your arms
Empty for good your sleeping heart
Of all its concerns.

Be captivated by
Air's lullaby
Whispering over
The russet lawn where you stand.

And when solemn evening
Falls dark with oak
That voice of our despair
The nightingale will start to sing.

Exchange of Feelings

In the old park frozen and alone
Two shapes passed by a while ago.

Their eyes were dead, their lips weak,
And the words they spoke were barely heard.

In the old park frozen and alone
Two ghosts recalled a vanished time.

'Do you recall how much we were in love?'
'Why should I want to think of that?'

'Does your heart still beat to my name alone?
When you dream, is it me you dream about?' 'No.'

'Sweet days of happiness beyond words,
Days that passed in a kiss!' 'And why not.'

'Such blue skies, then, such great hopes!'
'Hope's done for, a black hole in space.'

Tels ils marchaient dans les avoines folles,   15
Et la nuit seule entendit leurs paroles.

from *Romances sans paroles*

« C'est l'extase langoureuse... »

> Le vent dans la plaine
> Suspend son haleine.
>   **(Favart)**

C'est l'extase langoureuse,
C'est la fatigue amoureuse,
C'est tous les frissons des bois
Parmi l'étreinte des brises,
C'est, vers les ramures grises,   5
Le chœur des petites voix.

O le frêle et frais murmure!
Cela gazouille et susurre,
Cela ressemble au cri doux
Que l'herbe agitée expire...   10
Tu dirais, sous l'eau qui vire,
Le roulis sourd des cailloux.

Cette âme qui se lamente
En cette plainte dormante
C'est la nôtre, n'est-ce pas?   15
La mienne, dis, et la tienne,
Dont s'exhale l'humble antienne
Par ce tiède soir, tout bas?

And so they went on among the rough grass
With only the night to hear what they said.

from *Songs Without Words*

'It's languor and ecstasy'

> The wind on the plain
> Ceases its flight.
>
> (Favart)

It's languor and ecstasy,
It's the sleep of love,
Woods trembling
In the bite of the wind,
It's small voices chorusing
Over by the trees.

Fresh, frail murmur!
Whispers and warbles
Like the sigh
Of grass disturbed...
Like the muffled roll
Of pebbles under moving water.

This soul lost
In sleep-filled lamentation
Surely is ours?
Mine, surely, and yours,
Softly breathing
Low anthems on a warm evening?

« Il pleure dans mon cœur... »

Il pleut doucement sur la ville.

(Arthur Rimbaud)

Il pleure dans mon cœur
Comme il pleut sur la ville;
Quelle est ce langueur
Qui pénètre mon cœur?

O bruit doux de la pluie   5
Par terre et sur les toits!
Pour un cœur qui s'ennuie
O le chant de la pluie!

Il pleure sans raison
Dans ce cœur qui s'écœure.   10
Quoi! nulle trahison?...
Ce deuil est sans raison.

C'est bien la pire peine
De ne savoir pourquoi
Sans amour et sans haine   15
Mon cœur a tant de peine!

« Il faut, voyez-vous... »

Il faut, voyez-vous, nous pardonner les choses.
De cette façon nous serons bien heureuses,
Et si notre vie a des instants moroses,
Du moins nous serons, n'est-ce pas? deux pleureuses.

O que nous mêlions, âmes sœurs que nous sommes,   5
A nos vœux confus la douceur puérile
De cheminer loin des femmes et des hommes,
Dans le frais oubli de ce qui nous exile!

'Falling tears...'

Soft rain falling on the town.
                    (Rimbaud)

Falling tears in my heart,
Falling rain on the town.
Why this long ache,
A knife in my heart?

Oh, soft sound of rain
On ground and roof!
For hearts full of ennui
The song of the rain!

Tearfall without reason
In my sickened heart.
Really, no treason?
This grief has no reason.

By far the worst pain
Is not to understand
Why without love or hate
My heart's full of pain.

'You see, we have to be forgiven...'

You see, we have to be forgiven things;
This way happiness lies,
And if our life goes through gloomy times,
Why then, we'll be a pair of snivellers.

How good if our twin souls could blend
Vague desires with the infantile joy
Of walking free of women and men,
Backs turned on persecutors.

Soyons deux enfants, soyons deux jeunes filles
Éprises de rien et de tout étonnées,   10
Qui s'en vont pâlir sous les chastes charmilles
Sans même savoir qu'elles sont pardonnées.

« Le piano que baise... »

> Son joyeux, importun, d'un clavecin sonore.
>   (Pétrus Borel)

Le piano que baise une main frêle
Luit dans le soir rose et gris vaguement,
Tandis qu'avec un très léger bruit d'aile
Un air bien vieux, bien faible et bien charmant
Rôde discret, épeuré quasiment,   5
Par le boudoir longtemps parfumé d'Elle.

Qu'est-ce que c'est que ce berceau soudain
Qui lentement dorlote mon pauvre être?
Que voudrais-tu de moi, doux Chant badin?
Qu'as-tu voulu, fin refrain incertain   10
Qui vas tantôt mourir vers la fenêtre
Ouverte un peu sur le petit jardin?

« Dans l'interminable... »

Dans l'interminable
Ennui de la plaine
La neige incertaine
Luit comme du sable.

Le ciel est de cuivre   5
Sans lueur aucune.
On croirait voir vivre
Et mourir la lune.

Let's be children, let's be two young girls
Free as air and full of wonder,
Who grow pale in simple groves of trees,
Not knowing that they've been forgiven.

'The piano kissed...'

Unbidden, happy sound of a melodious harpsichord.

(Pétrus Borel)

The piano kissed by a slender hand
Has vague sheens in the grey-pink light
Of evening, while on almost silent wings
A slight and very old and charming air
Roams discreetly as if scared
Of that inner sanctum full of Her.

Tell me, why suddenly this cradle
Rocking my poor bones to gentle rhythms?
Why this soft song playing games with me?
What did you want, you fine wisps
Of music dying at the window
Half-opened on the little garden?

'Endless sameness...'

Endless sameness
Of the plain.
Uncertain snow
Gleams like sand.

A dull matt
Copper sky where
The moon appears
To live and die.

Comme des nuées
Flottent gris les chênes   10
Des forêts prochaines
Parmi les buées.

Le ciel est de cuivre
Sans lueur aucune.
On croirait voir vivre   15
Et mourir la lune.

Corneille poussive
Et vous, les loups maigres,
Par ces bises aigres
Quoi donc vous arrive?   20

Dans l'interminable
Ennui de la plaine
La neige incertaine
Luit comme du sable.

Bruxelles: simples fresques I

La fuite est verdâtre et rose
Des collines et des rampes
Dans un demi-jour de lampes
Qui vient brouiller toute chose.

L'or, sur les humbles abîmes,   5
Tout doucement s'ensanglante,
Des petites arbres sans cimes
Où quelque oiseau faible chante.

Triste à peine tant s'effacent
Ces apparences d'automne,   10
Toutes mes langueurs rêvassent,
Que berce l'air monotone.

Like large clouds
Mist-shrouded
Oaks in woods
Nearby float grey.

A dull matt
Copper sky where
The moon appears
To live and die.

Asthmatic crow
Famished wolves
What's happening to you
In these sharp winds?

Endless sameness
Of the plain.
Uncertain snow
Gleams like sand.

Brussels: Simple Frescos I

Green-tinged pink tones fade
Up slopes and away up hills
In the half-light of lamps which casts
Question-marks on everything.

In simple hollows gold
Gently turns blood-red.
In unseen tops of trees, somewhere
A bird sings a faint song.

I drift in languor of dreams,
Becalmed in monotone air
And hardly even sad, so much
Does this early autumn picture fade.

Bruxelles: simples fresques II

L'allée est sans fin
Sous le ciel, divin
D'être pâle ainsi:
Sais-tu qu'on serait
Bien sous le secret   5
De ces arbres-ci?

Des messieurs bien mis,
Sans nul doute amis
Des Royers-Collards,
Vont vers le château: 10
J'estimerais beau
D'être ces vieillards.

Le château, tout blanc
Avec, à son flanc,
Le soleil couché,   15
Les champs à l'entour:
Oh! que notre amour
N'est-il là niché!

Malines

Vers les prés le vent cherche noise
Aux girouettes, détail fin
Du château de quelque échevin,
Rouge de brique et bleu d'ardoise,
Vers les prés clairs, les prés sans fin...   5

Comme les arbres des féeries,
Des frênes, vagues frondaisons,
Échelonnent mille horizons
A ce Sahara de prairies,
Trèfle, luzerne et blancs gazons.   10

Brussels: Simple Frescos II

The path goes on and on
Beneath the sky, sacred
Because pallid.
You know, we'd feel so good
Here beneath the secret
Of these trees.

Some well-groomed gentlemen,
Friends surely
Of the Royers-Collards,
Head towards the château.
I'd find it good
To be these old men.

On the white château
Ending sun declines
Down one elevation;
Fields on every side.
Why can't our love hide
In there somewhere?

Malines

Over in the fields the wind provokes
The weathervanes, refinements
On some worthy burgher's country house,
Red of brick and blue of tile,
In the bright and endless fields...

In a kind of make-believe,
Vague leaf-sprouting ashes stand
In line around the thousand
Edges of the desert meadowland,
Clover, lucerne, white lawns.

Les wagons filent en silence
Parmi ces sites apaisés.
Dormez, les vaches! Reposez,
Doux taureaux de la plaine immense,
Sous vos cieux à peine irisés!   15

Le train glisse sans un murmure,
Chaque wagon est un salon
Où l'on cause bas et d'où l'on
Aime à loisir cette nature
Faite à souhait pour Fénelon.   20

Green

Voici des fruits, des fleurs, des feuilles et des branches
Et puis voici mon cœur qui ne bat que pour vous.
Ne le déchirez pas avec vos deux mains blanches
Et qu'à vos yeux si beaux l'humble présent soit doux.

J'arrive tout couvert encore de rosée   5
Que le vent du matin vient glacer à mon front.
Souffrez que ma fatigue à vos pieds reposée
Rêve des chers instants qui la délasseront.

Sur votre jeune sein laissez rouler ma tête
Toute sonore encor de vos derniers baisers;   10
Laissez-la s'apaiser de la bonne tempête,
Et que je dorme un peu puisque vous reposez.

Spleen

Les roses étaient toutes rouges
Et les lierres étaient tout noirs.

Chère, pour peu que tu te bouges,
Renaissent tous mes désespoirs.

Silently the train moves
Through a landscape deep in peace.
Sleep, cows! Lie down and rest,
Sweet bulls of this immensity
Below the sky's dull uniformity.

The train slides without a sound,
Each coach a saloon
Full of quiet talk, easy vantage-point
To admire this Nature
Tailor-made for Fénelon.

Green

Take this fruit, these flowers, these branches and leaves,
Then take my heart, which beats only for you.
Don't tear it apart with those two white hands;
It's my humble gift to your lovely eyes.

I stand before you, my face still frozen
By the sharpness of the morning dew.
Let me recover at your feet
And dream the perfect moments of new life.

Let me rest my head on your young breast,
My head still swirling with your last embrace;
Let it find refuge from the storm
And let me sleep since now you've found some rest.

Spleen

The roses were bright red
The ivy deepest black.

My love, your slightest movement
Rekindles my despair.

Le ciel était trop bleu, trop tendre,
La mer trop verte et l'air trop doux.

Je crains toujours,—ce qu'est d'attendre!—
Quelque fuite atroce de vous.

Du houx à la feuille vernie
Et du luisant buis je suis las,   10

Et de la campagne infinie
Et de tout, fors de vous, hélas!

Streets I

Dansons la gigue!

J'aimais surtout ses jolis yeux,
Plus clairs que l'étoile des cieux,
J'aimais ses yeux malicieux.

Dansons la gigue!   5

Elle avait des façons vraiment
De désoler un pauvre amant,
Que c'en était vraiment charmant!

Dansons la gigue!

Mais je trouve encore meilleur   10
Le baiser de sa bouche en fleur
Depuis qu'elle est morte à mon cœur.

Dansons la gigue!

Je me souviens, je me souviens
Des heures et des entretiens,   15
Et c'est le meilleur de mes biens.

Dansons la gigue!

Too blue, the sky, too soft,
The sea too green, too sweet the air.

And still I fear you'll vanish—
Such torture, waiting!

I'm tired of waxy-leaf holly,
Of gleaming box-tree,

I'm tired of this endless countryside,
Of all, in fact, save you.

Streets I

A jig! Let's dance!

What I loved most were her fine eyes
Firmament-bright.
Those eyes, malice personified.

A jig! Let's dance!

She had such charming ways and means
Of ruining her men
She'd be forgiven everything.

A jig! Let's dance!

But now that I no longer care
What I much prefer's
The brush of her lovely lips.

A jig! Let's dance!

I remember—oh and how—
Those times those conversations
My greatest consolations.

A jig! Let's dance!

Streets II

O la rivière dans la rue!
Fantastiquement apparue
Derrière un mur haut de cinq pieds,
Elle roule sans un murmure
Son onde opaque et pourtant pure   5
Par les faubourgs pacifiés.

La chaussée est très large, en sorte
Que l'eau jaune comme une morte
Dévale ample et sans nuls espoirs
De rien refléter que la brume,   10
Même alors que l'aurore allume
Les cottages jaunes et noirs.

Beams

Elle voulut aller sur les flots de la mer,
Et comme un vent bénin soufflait une embellie,
Nous nous prêtâmes tous à sa belle folie,
Et nous voilà marchant par le chemin amer.

Le soleil luisait haut dans le ciel calme et lisse,   5
Et dans ses cheveux blonds c'étaient des rayons d'or,
Si bien que nous suivions son pas plus calme encor
Que le déroulement des vagues, ô délice!

Des oiseaux blancs volaient alentour mollement,
Et des voiles au loin s'inclinaient toutes blanches.   10
Parfois de grands varechs filaient en longues branches,
Nos pieds glissaient d'un pur et large mouvement.

Elle se retourna, doucement inquiète
De ne nous croire pas pleinement rassurés,
Mais nous voyant joyeux d'être ses préférés,   15
Elle reprit sa route et portait haut la tête.

Streets II

A river in the street!
Dream apparition
Flowing soundless
Behind a five-foot wall.
Dark yet still pure tide
Threading the quiet town.

The road's so wide
That death-yellow water spreads
Unable to reflect
More than fog
Though dawn lights
Black and yellow houses up.

Beams

She wanted to tread the surge of the sea,
And as pleasant breezes cleared the skies
We fell in with her little whim
And started on the tricky walk.

The sun stood tall in a quiet smooth sky;
Her light hair was touched with gold.
Enchanted, we followed her calm steps,
Calmer than the sigh of waves.

White sea-birds circled aimlessly.
In the distance clean white sails were leaning.
Great hanks of seaweed drifted past.
Bravely, our feet slithered on.

She turned around, sweetly anxious
To reassure us.
But seeing we were thrilled to be her chosen ones,
Off she went again, her head held high.

from *Sagesse*

I.V. « Beauté des femmes... »

Beauté des femmes, leur faiblesse, et ces mains pâles
Qui font souvent le bien et peuvent tout le mal,
Et ces yeux, où plus rien ne reste d'animal
Que juste assez pour dire: « assez » au fureurs mâles!

Et toujours, maternelle endormeuse des râles,   5
Même quand elle ment, cette voix! Matinal
Appel, ou chant bien doux à vêpre, ou frais signal,
Ou beau sanglot qui va mourir au pli des châles!...

Hommes durs! Vie atroce et laide d'ici-bas!
Ah! que du moins, loin des baisers et des combats,   10
Quelque chose demeure un peu sur la montagne,

Quelque chose du cœur enfantin et subtil,
Bonté, respect! Car, qu'est-ce qui nous accompagne,
Et vraiment, quand la mort viendra, que reste-t-il?

I.viii. « La vie humble aux travaux... »

La vie humble aux travaux ennuyeux et faciles
Est une œuvre de choix qui veut beaucoup d'amour:
Rester gai quand le jour, triste, succède au jour,
Être fort, et s'user en circonstances viles,

N'entendre, n'écouter aux bruits des grandes villes   5
Que l'appel, ô mon Dieu, des cloches dans la tour,
Et faire un de ces bruits soi-même, cela pour
L'accomplissement vil des tâches puériles,

from *Wisdom*

'Beauty of women...'

Beauty of women, their weakness, those pale hands
Which often do good and can do every harm,
And those eyes, just animal enough
To say 'Enough!' to the rampant male.

Always that voice, rage-calming lullaby,
Even when it's lying. Morning call
Or soft sunset song or bright sign
Or beautiful sob lost in the folds of a shawl...

Hard men! Ugly, awful life on this earth!
Far from fights and caresses,
Let something at least remain on the mountain,

Something of the subtle childlike heart,
Goodness, respect. For what accompanies us,
And when death comes, what is left which lasts?

'The humble life...'

The humble life of dull and easy work
Is choice labour requiring great love.
Lifting spirits day after dismal day,
Keeping us strong, worn down by vile conditions,

Hearing, listening only in the city's noise,
Great God, to the church-tower's ring of bells,
Joining in the noise oneself
To put an awful end to childish tasks,

Dormir chez les pécheurs étant un pénitent,
N'aimer que le silence et converser pourtant;   10
Le temps si grand dans la patience si grande,

Le scrupule naïf aux repentirs têtus,
Et tous ces soins autour de ces pauvres vertus!
—Fi, dit l'Ange gardien, de l'orgueil qui marchande!

I.xix. « Voix de l'Orgueil... »

Voix de l'Orgueil: un cri puissant comme d'un cor,
Des étoiles de sang sur des cuirasses d'or.
On trébuche à travers des chaleurs d'incendie...
Mais en somme la voix s'en va, comme d'un cor.

Voix de la Haine: cloche en mer, fausse, assourdie   5
De neige lente. Il fait si froid! Lourde, affadie,
La vie a peur et court follement sur le quai
Loin de la cloche qui devient plus assourdie.

Voix de la Chair: un gros tapage fatigué.
Des gens ont bu. L'endroit fait semblant d'être gai.   10
Des yeux, des noms, et l'air plein de parfums atroces
Où vient mourir le gros tapage fatigué.

Voix d'Autrui: des lointains dans des brouillards. Des noces
Vont et viennent. Des tas d'embarras. Des négoces,
Et tout le cirque des civilisations   15
Au son trotte-menu du violon des noces.

Colères, soupirs noirs, regrets, tentations
Qu'il a fallu pourtant que nous entendissions
Pour l'assourdissement des silences honnêtes,
Colères, soupirs noirs, regrets, tentations,   20

Asleep, a penitent among sinners,
Liking only silence but chattering still...
Time stretching out in fields of patience,

Naïve scruples with their stubborn remorse
And all that fuss about feeble virtues!
—Don't accept, my angel says, deals proposed by pride.

'Voice of Pride...'

Voice of Pride: shout of blaring trumpets,
Stars of blood on golden breast-plates,
A stumble through heat as intense as fire...
But then the sound's dispelled like trumpets.

Voice of Hate: bell on the sea, flat note muffled
By dogged snow. Such cold! Drab and heavy,
Life takes fright and flees down quays
Away from the bell, getting more muffled.

Voice of Flesh: huge, weary commotion,
The tipsy and drunk, a pretence of fun.
Eyes, names, air heavy with awful scent
Smothering the huge and weary commotion.

Voice of Others: space in mist, wedding-parties
Leaving, arriving. Difficulties, dealings,
The whole circus of civilizations
To the skipping violins of wedding-parties.

Anger, black sighs, regrets, temptations
Which we had to hear so that mute-damped
Honest silence might be heard,
Anger, black sighs, regrets, temptations,

Ah, les Voix, mourez donc, mourantes que vous êtes,
Sentences, mots en vain, métaphores mal faites,
Toute la rhétorique en fuite des péchés,
Ah, les Voix, mourez donc, mourantes que vous êtes!

Nous ne sommes plus ceux que vous auriez cherchés.   25
Mourez à nous, mourez aux humbles vœux cachés
Que nourrit la douceur de la Parole forte,
Car notre cœur n'est plus de ceux que vous cherchez!

Mourez parmi la voix que la Prière emporte
Au ciel, dont elle seule ouvre et ferme la porte   30
Et dont elle tiendra les sceaux au dernier jour,
Mourez parmi la voix que la Prière apporte,

Mourez parmi la voix terrible de l'Amour!

III.iii. « L'espoir luit comme un brin de paille... »

L'espoir luit comme un brin de paille dans l'étable.
Que crains-tu de la guêpe ivre de son vol fou?
Vois, le soleil toujours poudroie à quelque trou.
Que ne t'endormais-tu, le coude sur la table?

Pauvre âme pale, au moins cette eau du puits glacé,   5
Bois-la. Puis dors après. Allons, tu vois, je reste,
Et je dorloterai les rêves de ta sieste,
Et tu chantonneras comme un enfant bercé.

Midi sonne. De grâce, éloignez-vous, madame.
Il dort. C'est étonnant comme les pas de femme   10
Résonnent au cerveau des pauvres malheureux.

Midi sonne. J'ai fait arroser dans la chambre.
Va, dors! L'espoir luit comme un caillou dans un creux.
Ah, quand refleuriront les roses de septembre!

Voices, die then, since you're dying
Away, maxims, vain words, ill-turned metaphors,
Rhetoric of sin in flight,
Die then, Voices, since you're dying.

We're no longer those you'd want to find.
Be dead in us, dead to humble hidden prayers
Nourished by the strong Word's gentleness,
Because our heart's no longer what you'd want to find.

Die in the voice which Prayer
Lifts to Heaven, whose gate it alone can work,
Whose seal it will set on Judgement Day,
Die in the voice brought by Prayer,

Die in the awesome voice of Love!

'Hope like a wisp of straw...'

Hope like a wisp of straw shines in the stable.
Why do you fear the crazed flight of the drunken wasp?
See, still the powdered sunlight shows in some recess.
Why didn't you sleep, your elbow on the table?

Poor soul, drink at least this freezing water
From the well. Then sleep. There, see, I'll stay
And cradle the dreams in your sleep,
And you'll coo like a cradled child.

Midday strikes. I beg of you madame, go.
He's asleep. It's startling how women's feet
Send echoes through the heads of poor unhappy men.

Midday strikes. I've had water sprinkled round the room.
Go on, sleep. Hope shines like a stone in a hollow.
Ah, when will September roses flower again?

III.iv. « Je suis venu, calme orphelin... »

Gaspard Hauser chante:

Je suis venu, calme orphelin,
Riche de mes seuls yeux tranquilles,
Vers les hommes des grandes villes:
Ils ne m'ont pas trouvé malin.

A vingt ans un trouble nouveau,   5
Sous le nom d'amoureuses flammes,
M'a fait trouver belles les femmes:
Elles ne m'ont pas trouvé beau.

Bien que sans patrie et sans roi
Et très brave ne l'étant guère,   10
J'ai voulu mourir à la guerre:
La mort n'a pas voulu de moi.

Suis-je né trop tôt ou trop tard?
Qu'est-ce que je fais en ce monde?
O vous tous, ma peine est profonde: 15
Priez pour le pauvre Gaspard!

III.vi. « Le ciel est, par-dessus le toit... »

Le ciel est, par-dessus le toit,
   Si bleu, si calme!
Un arbre, par-dessus le toit,
   Berce sa palme.

La cloche, dans le ciel qu'on voit,   5
   Doucement tinte.
Un oiseau sur l'arbre qu'on voit
   Chante sa plainte.

'Peaceful eyes my only wealth'

Kaspar Hauser sings:

Peaceful eyes my only wealth
Calm orphan I arrived
Innocent
In the cities of men.

At twenty new stirrings—
Love's fever so-called—
Made women lovely
Me unlovely to them.

Stateless un-kinged
Brave coward
I went to war to die.
Death turned me down.

Was I born too early
Or too late? Or why at all?
People, I'm a pit of pain.
Say prayers for poor Kaspar.

'The sky above the roof...'

The sky above the roof's
   So blue so calm.
A branch above the roof's
   Fanning the air.

The bell up there in the sky
   Makes little sounds.
A bird up there in the tree
   Sings its lament.

Mon Dieu, mon Dieu, la vie est là,
   Simple et tranquille.   10
Cette paisible rumeur-là
   Vient de la ville.

—Qu'as-tu fait, ô toi que voilà
   Pleurant sans cesse,
Dis, qu'as-tu fait, toi que voilà,   15
   De ta jeunesse?

III.x. « La tristesse, la langueur... »

La tristesse, la langueur du corps humain
M'attendrissent, me fléchissent, m'apitoient.
Ah! surtout quand des sommeils noirs le foudroient,
Quand les draps zèbrent la peau, foulent la main!

Et que mièvre dans la fièvre du demain,   5
Tiède encor du bain de sueur qui décroît,
Comme un oiseau qui grelotte sur un toit!
Et les pieds, toujours douloureux du chemin!

Et le sein, marqué d'un double coup de poing!
Et la bouche, une blessure rouge encor,   10
Et la chair frémissante, frêle décor!

Et les yeux, les pauvres yeux si beaux où point
La douleur de voir encore du fini!...
Triste corps! Combien faible et combien puni!

III.xi. « La bise se rue... »

La bise se rue à travers
Les buissons tout noirs et tout verts,
Glaçant la neige éparpillée
Dans la campagne ensoleillée.

Dear God dear God life's there
   Simple and quiet.
Those soft and distant sounds
   Come from the town.

What have you done, you standing there
   In floods of tears?
Tell me what have you done
   With your young life?

'The sadness, the languor...'

The sadness, the languor of the human body
Move me to pity, melt and weaken me—
Most of all when dark sleep strikes it down,
When sheets stripe skin, press down on hands.

How frail it is in the fever of tomorrow,
Still warm from evaporating sweat,
Like a bird shivering on a roof!
And then the feet, painful still from walking,

And the breast, double-marked by fists,
The mouth, a still-red wound,
And trembling flesh, a fragile arrangement.

And the eyes, poor eyes, so beautiful, pricked
With the pain of seeing nothing but this world...
Sad body, so sad, and punished so much!

'A cold wind...'

A cold wind hurls itself at
Dark green and black bushes
Turning bits of snow to ice
In the sunlit countryside.

L'odeur est aigre près des bois,   5
L'horizon chante avec des voix,
Les coqs des clochers des villages
Luisent crûment sur les nuages.
C'est délicieux de marcher
A travers ce brouillard léger   10
Qu'un vent taquin parfois retrousse.
Ah! fi de mon vieux feu qui tousse!
J'ai des fourmis pleins les talons.
Debout, mon âme, vite, allons!
C'est le printemps sévère encore,   15
Mais qui par instant s'édulcore
D'un souffle tiède juste assez
Pour mieux sentir les froids passés
Et penser au Dieu de clémence...
Va, mon âme, à l'espoir immense!   20

III.xiii. « L'échelonnement des haies... »

L'échelonnement des haies
Moutonne à l'infini, mer
Claire dans le brouillard clair
Qui sent bon les jeunes baies.

Des arbres et des moulins   5
Sont légers sur le vert tendre
Où vient s'ébattre et s'étendre
L'agilité des poulains.

Dans ce vague d'un Dimanche
Voici se jouer aussi   10
De grandes brebis aussi
Douces que leur laine blanche.

Tout à l'heure déferlait
L'onde, roulée en volutes,
De cloches comme des flûtes   15
Dans le ciel comme du lait.

Over by the woods the air's sharp.
Voices wake horizons up.
And village weathervanes
Cast raw bright light onto the clouds.
It's wonderful to walk
Through this thin mist lifted
Sometimes by a teasing wind.
Enough of my old fire coughing in its grate.
I'm itching to make a move now.
Up up, my soul, no more delays.
Severe Spring's still with us,
But growing gentler by the hour
In breaths of air just warm enough
To make the past cold keener
And recall God's mercy...
Soul, give yourself up to the greatness of hope.

'Uneven rows...'

. Uneven rows of hedges
Unfold forever like clear
Waves billowing under clear
Haze scented with young berries.

There are trees there are mills
Standing light on tender green
Where frolicking gambolling
Colts play and stretch out.

In this Sunday haze
See as well big ewes at play,
Ewes as soft as
Their coats of white wool.

A short while ago
Leaping fluting sound
Spiralled from the belfry
Up into a milky sky.

from *Jadis et naguère*

Art poétique

De la musique avant toute chose,
Et pour cela préfère l'Impair
Plus vague et plus soluble dans l'air,
Sans rien en lui qui pèse ou qui pose.

Il faut aussi que tu n'ailles point   5
Choisir tes mots sans quelque méprise:
Rien de plus cher que la chanson grise
Où l'Indécis au Précis se joint.

C'est des beaux yeux derrière des voiles,
C'est le grand jour tremblant de midi,   10
C'est, par un ciel d'automne attiédi,
Le bleu fouillis des claires étoiles!

Car nous voulons la Nuance encor,
Pas la Couleur, rien que la nuance!
Oh! la nuance seul fiance   15
Le rêve au rêve et la flûte au cor!

Fuis du plus loin la Pointe assassine,
L'Esprit cruel et le Rire impur,
Qui font pleurer les yeux de l'Azur,
Et tout cet ail de basse cuisine!   20

Prends l'éloquence et tords-lui son cou!
Tu feras bien, en train d'énergie,
De rendre un peu la Rime assagie.
Si l'on n'y veille, elle ira jusqu'où?

from *Once Upon a Time*

The Art of Poetry

Let's hear the music first and foremost,
And that means no more one-two-one-twos...
Something more vague instead, something lighter
Dissolving in air, weightless as air.

When you choose your words, no need to search
In strict dictionaries for pinpoint
Definitions. Better the subtle
And heady Songs of Imprecision.

Imagine fine eyes behind a veil,
Imagine the shimmer of high noon,
Imagine, in skies cooled for autumn,
Blue entanglements of lucent stars.

No, what we must have is more Nuance,
Colour's forbidden, only Nuance!
Nuance alone writes the harmonies
Of dream and dream, of woodwind and brass.

Clever-clever phrases are deadly,
So too are rapier Wit and cheap Laughs,
Ubiquitous garlic of bad cooks,
Only fit to fill blue air with tears.

Grip eloquence by the throat and squeeze
It to death. And while you're about it
You might corral that runaway, Rhyme,
Or you'll get Rhyme Without End, Amen.

O qui dira les torts de la Rime? 25
Quel enfant sourd ou quel nègre fou
Nous a forgé ce bijou d'un sou
Qui sonne creux et faux sous la lime?

De la musique encore et toujours!
Que ton vers soit la chose envolée 30
Qu'on sent qui fuit d'une âme en allée
Vers d'autres cieux à d'autres amours.

Que ton vers soit la bonne aventure
Éparse au vent crispé du matin
Qui va fleurant la menthe et le thym... 35
Et tout le reste est littérature.

from *Amour*

Parsifal

Parsifal a vaincu les Filles, leur gentil
Babil et la luxure amusante—et sa pente
Vers la Chair de garçon vierge que cela tente
D'aimer les seins légers et ce gentil babil;

Il a vaincu la Femme belle, au cœur subtil, 5
Étalant ses bras frais et sa gorge excitante;
Il a vaincu l'Enfer et rentre sous sa tente
Avec un lourd trophée à son bras puéril,

Avec la lance qui perça le Flanc suprême!
Il a guéri le roi, le voici roi lui-même, 10
Et prêtre du très saint Trésor essentiel.

En robe d'or il adore, gloire et symbole,
Le vase pur où resplendit le Sang réel.
—Et, ô ces voix d'enfants chantant dans la coupole!

Who will denounce that criminal, Rhyme?
Tone-deaf children or crazed foreigners
No doubt fashioned its paste jewellery,
Tinplate on top, hollow underneath.

Music, more music, always music!
Create verse which lifts and flies away,
Verse of a soul that has taken off
Into other stratospheres of love.

You must let your poems ride their luck
On the back of the sharp morning air
Touched with the fragrance of mint and thyme...
And everything else is LIT-RIT-CHER.

from *Love*

Parsifal

Parsifal has conquered the Maidens, their sweet
Talk, their seductions. He's sidestepped
Flesh, soft murmurs and high breasts,
Traps for virgin boys.

He's turned away from subtle beautiful Woman
Open-armed and thrilling-breasted.
He's seen off the Devil. The young man returns
To his tent, in his arms a heavy prize—

The lance which pierced the supreme body's side.
He's cured the King, now he himself is king,
Priest of the holiest of Holy Treasures.

He venerates in golden robes that symbol,
That glory, that pure vessel where real Blood gleams.
—And then, those children's voices singing in the dome!

ARTHUR RIMBAUD

Le Dormeur du val

C'est un trou de verdure où chante une rivière
Accrochant follement aux herbes des haillons
D'argent; où le soleil, de la montagne fière,
Luit: c'est un petit val qui mousse de rayons.

Un soldat jeune, bouche ouverte, tête nue,   5
Et la nuque baignant dans le frais cresson bleu,
Dort; il est étendu dans l'herbe, sous la nue,
Pâle dans son lit vert où la lumière pleut.

Les pieds dans les glaïeuls, il dort. Souriant comme
Sourirait un enfant malade, il fait un somme: 10
Nature, berce-le chaudement: il a froid.

Les parfums ne font pas frissonner sa narine;
Il dort dans le soleil, la main sur sa poitrine
Tranquille. Il a deux trous rouges au côté droit.

Ma Bohème (Fantaisie)

Je m'en allais, les poings dans mes poches crevées;
Mon paletot aussi devenait idéal;
J'allais sous le ciel, Muse! et j'étais ton féal;
Oh! là là! que d'amours splendides j'ai rêvées!

Mon unique culotte avait un large trou.   5
—Petit Poucet rêveur, j'égrenais dans ma course
Des rimes. Mon auberge était à la Grande-Ourse.
—Mes étoiles au ciel avaient un doux frou-frou

TRANSLATED BY MARTIN SORRELL

Asleep in the Valley

A gully of green, a laughing river
Where silver tatters snag
Madly in grasses; where, from the proud
Mountain the sun shines; foaming trough of light.

A young soldier, mouth open, head bare,
Neck on a pillow of cool cress,
Sleeps, stretched out in the grass, sky above,
Pale on his green bed where light teems down.

Feet among the flags, he sleeps, smiling how
A sick child might; he takes a nap.
Gather him close, Nature, rock him. He's cold.

No scent makes his nostril quiver.
He sleeps in the sun, one hand on his still
Chest. In his right side, two red holes.

My Bohemia

And so I went, hands thrust in torn pockets.
My coat was more idea than fact.
Beneath the sky —my Muse, my liege — I went;
Oh my! what dreams of splendid loves I had!

My one and only trousers were hugely holed.
Starry-eyed Tom Thumb, I strewed my path
With verse. I laid my head at Great Bear Inn.
— My stars swished softly in the sky

Et je les écoutais, assis au bord des routes,
Ces bons soirs de septembre où je sentais des gouttes   10
De rosée à mon front, comme un vin de vigueur;

Où, rimant au milieu des ombres fantastiques,
Comme des lyres, je tirais les élastiques
De mes souliers blessés, un pied près de mon cœur!

Les Chercheuses de poux

Quand le front de l'enfant, plein de rouges tourmentes,
Implore l'essaim blanc des rêves indistincts,
Il vient près de son lit deux grandes sœurs charmantes
Avec de frêles doigts aux ongles argentins.

Elles assoient l'enfant devant une croisée   5
Grande ouverte où l'air bleu baigne un fouillis de fleurs.
Et dans ses lourds cheveux où tombe la rosée
Promènent leurs doigts fins, terribles et charmeurs.

Il écoute chanter leurs haleines craintives
Qui fleurent de longs miels végétaux et rosés,   10
Et qu'interrompt parfois un sifflement, salives
Reprises sur la lèvre ou désirs de baisers.

Il entend leurs cils noirs battant sous les silences
Parfumés; et leurs doigts électriques et doux
Font crépiter parmi ses grises indolences   15
Sous leurs ongles royaux la mort des petits poux.

Voilà que monte en lui le vin de la Paresse,
Soupir d'harmonica qui pourrait délirer;
L'enfant se sent, selon la lenteur des caresses,
Sourdre et mourir sans cesse un désir de pleurer.   20

And, seated on roadsides, I heard them
On lovely evenings in September, feeling dew
Drops on my face, like invigorating wine;

Rhyming verse among the phantom shadows,
I harped on the laces of my wounded boots,
One foot by my heart.

Lice-Seekers

When the boy's head, full of red torment,
Pleads for white swarms of cloudy dreams,
Two charming big sisters approach his bed,
All dainty fingers and silver nails.

They sit the child by an open window
Where blue air bathes a tumult of flowers,
And run enchanting, slender, awful
Fingers through his dew-moist heavy hair.

He listens to the music of their nervy breath
Scented with the long rose-honey of plants,
Music broken sometimes by a hiss, saliva
Salvaged from lips, longing for more lips;

Hears the dark beat of eyelashes in the scented
Silence; and in his grey, narcotic letting-go,
The royal nails of their electric fingers
Softly make the small lice crackle as they die.

The wine of Indolence wells up in him,
Delirium of a harmonica sigh; on slow
Tides of caresses, the child feels his need to cry
Ebb and flow, and ebb and flow.

Le Cœur volé

Mon triste cœur bave à la poupe,
Mon cœur couvert de caporal:
Ils y lancent des jets de soupe,
Mon triste cœur bave à la poupe:
Sous les quolibets de la troupe   5
Qui pousse un rire général,
Mon triste cœur bave à la poupe
Mon cœur couvert de caporal!

Ithyphalliques et pioupiesques
Leurs quolibets l'ont dépravé!   10
Au gouvernail on voit des fresques
Ithyphalliques et pioupiesques
Ô flots abracadabrantesques
Prenez mon cœur, qu'il soit lavé
Ithyphalliques et pioupiesques,   15
Leurs quolibets l'ont dépravé!

Quand ils auront tari leurs chiques
Comment agir, ô cœur volé?
Ce seront des hoquets bachiques
Quand ils auront tari leurs chiques   20
J'aurai des sursauts stomachiques
Moi, si mon cœur est ravalé:
Quand ils auront tari leurs chiques
Comment agir, ô cœur volé?

Le Bateau ivre

Comme je descendais des Fleuves impassibles,
Je ne me sentis plus guidé par les haleurs:
Des Peaux-Rouges criards les avaient pris pour cibles
Les ayant cloués nus aux poteaux de couleurs.

Cheated Heart

On the poop-deck my sad heart drips,
My heart covered in tobacco:
They squirt at it their jets of soup,
On the poop-deck my sad heart drips:
Lashed by the soldiers' jeering tongues,
Amid the general laughter,
On the poop-deck my sad heart drips,
My heart covered in tobacco.

Priapic privates parading,
Their jeering has corrupted it!
The wheel-house has been defaced by
Priapic privates parading.
Oh, you abracadabra waves,
Take my heart, wash it clean again.
Priapic privates parading,
Their jeering has corrupted it!

Once the lads have had a good chew,
What's to be done, my cheated heart?
An orgy of belching and booze
Once the lads have had a good chew;
Me, I'll seize up with stomach-cramps
If my heart's swallowed down again:
Once the lads have had a good chew
What's to be done, my cheated heart?

Drunken Boat

I followed deadpan rivers down and down,
And knew my haulers had let go the ropes.
Whooping redskins took my men as targets
And nailed them nude to technicolour posts.

J'étais insoucieux de tous les équipages,   5
Porteur de blés flamands ou de cotons anglais.
Quand avec mes haleurs ont fini ces tapages
Les Fleuves m'ont laissé descendre où je voulais.

Dans les clapotements furieux de marées
Moi l'autre hiver plus sourd que les cerveaux d'enfants,   10
Je courus! Et les Péninsules démarrées
N'ont pas subi tohu-bohus plus triomphants.

Le tempête a béni mes éveils maritimes.
Plus léger qu'un bouchon j'ai dansé sur les flots
Qu'on appelle rouleurs éternels de victimes,   15
Dix nuits, sans regretter l'œil niais des falots!

Plus douce qu'aux enfants la chair des pommes sures
L'eau verte pénétra ma coque de sapin
Et des taches de vins bleus et des vomissures
Me lava, dispersant gouvernail et grappin.   20

Et dès lors, je me suis baigné dans le Poème
De la Mer, infusé d'astres, et lactescent,
Dévorant les azurs verts; où, flottaison blême
Et ravie, un noyé pensif parfois descend;

Où, teignant tout à coup les bleuités, délires   25
Et rhythmes lents sous les rutilements du jour,
Plus fortes que l'alcool, plus vastes que nos lyres,
Fermentent les rousseurs amères de l'amour!

Je sais les cieux crevant en éclairs, et les trombes
Et les ressacs et les courants: je sais le soir,   30
L'Aube exaltée ainsi qu'un peuple de colombes
Et j'ai vu quelquefois ce que l'homme a cru voir!

J'ai vu le soleil bas, taché d'horreurs mystiques,
Illuminant de longs figements violets,
Pareils à des acteurs de drames très-antiques   35
Les flots roulant au loin leurs frissons de volets!

I didn't give a damn about the crews,
Or the Flemish wheat and English cotton.
Once the shindig with my haulers finished
I had the current take me where I willed.

In the furious riptides last winter,
With ears as tightly shut as any child's,
I ran, and unanchored Peninsulas
Have never known such carnivals of triumph.

The storm blessed my maritime wakefulness.
Lighter than a cork I danced on the waves
Which some call eternal victim-breakers —
Ten blind nights free of idiot guiding flares.

Sweeter than sour apple-flesh to children
Green water slid inside my pine-clad hull
And washed me clean of vomit and cheap wine,
Sweeping away rudder-post and grapnel.

From that time on, I bathed in the Poem
Of the Sea, lactescent and steeped in stars,
Devouring green azures; where a drowned man
Like bleached flotsam sometimes sinks in a trance;

Where suddenly tinting the bluities,
Slow deliriums in shimmering light,
Fiercer than alcohol, vaster than lyres,
The bitter rednesses of love ferment.

I know skies splintered by lightning, breakers,
Waterspouts, undertows; I know the dusk,
And dawn, exalted like a host of doves—
And then I've seen what men believe they've seen.

I've seen low suns smeared with mystic horrors
Set fire to monster scars of violet;
Like actors in the very oldest plays
Slatted light shimmered, away on the waves.

J'ai rêvé la nuit verte aux neiges éblouies
Baiser montant aux yeux des mers avec lenteurs,
La circulation des sèves inouïes,
Et l'éveil jaune et bleu des phosphores chanteurs!   40

J'ai suivi, des mois pleins, pareille aux vacheries
Hystériques, la houle à l'assaut des récifs,
Sans songer que les pieds lumineux des Maries
Pussent forcer le mufle aux Océans poussifs!

J'ai heurté, savez-vous, d'incroyables Florides   45
Mêlant aux fleurs des yeux de panthères à peaux
D'hommes! Des arcs-en-ciel tendus comme des brides
Sous l'horizon des mers, à de glauques troupeaux!

J'ai vu fermenter les marais énormes, nasses
Où pourrit dans les joncs tout un Léviathan!   50
Des écroulements d'eaux au milieu des bonaces
Et les lointains vers les gouffres cataractant!

Glaciers, soleils d'argent, flots nacreux, cieux de braises!
Échouages hideux au fond des golfes bruns
Où les serpents géants dévorés des punaises   55
Choient, des arbres tordus, avec de noirs parfums!

J'aurais voulu montrer aux enfants ces dorades
Du flot bleu, ces poissons d'or, ces poissons chantants.
—Des écumes de fleurs ont bercé mes dérades
Et d'ineffables vents m'ont ailé par instants.   60

Parfois, martyr lassé des pôles et des zones,
La mer dont le sanglot faisait mon roulis doux
Montait vers moi ses fleurs d'ombre aux ventouses jaunes
Et je restais, ainsi qu'une femme à genoux...

Presque île, ballottant sur mes bords les querelles   65
Et les fientes d'oiseaux clabaudeurs aux yeux blonds
Et je voguais, lorsqu'à travers mes liens frêles
Des noyés descendaient dormir, à reculons!

Green nights I dreamed bedazzlements of snow,
A kiss rising to the sea's eyes slowly,
Circulation of undiscovered saps,
Blue-yellow wakefulness of phosphorsongs.

For whole months on end I followed the swell
Charging the reefs like hysterical beasts,
Not thinking that luminous Maryfeet
Could force a muzzle on to breathy seas.

I struck, you know, amazing Floridas
Where flowers twine with panther eyes inside
Men's skins! Rainbows flung like bridles under
Sea horizons harnessed the glaucous herds.

I saw great swamps seethe like nets laid in reeds
Where a whole Leviathan lay rotting,
Collapse of water in the midst of calm
And distances tumbling into nothing.

Glaciers, silver suns, pearl seas, firecoal skies!
Hideous wreckages down in brown depths
Where enormous insect-tormented snakes
Crash from twisted trees, reeking with blackness.

I'd like to have shown children blue-water
Dorados, golden fish and fish that sing.
Foam-sprays of flowers cradled my drifting;
At times I flew on ineffable winds.

Sometimes, martyr tired of poles and wastelands,
My pitching was stilled by the sobbing sea
Which raised to me its yellow-sucker
Shadow-flowers — and I, like a woman, knelt.

Jutting outcrop where the brawls and guano
Of fierce albino birds bounced off my sides,
I sailed, while down among my fraying ropes
Drowned men descended backwards into sleep.

Or moi, bateau perdu sous les cheveux des anses,
Jeté par l'ouragan dans l'éther sans oiseau   70
Moi dont les Monitors et les voiliers des Hanses
N'auraient pas repêché la carcasse ivre d'eau;

Libre, fumant, monté de brumes violettes,
Moi qui trouais le ciel rougeoyant comme un mur,
Qui porte, confiture exquise aux bons poètes,   75
Des lichens de soleil et des morves d'azur;

Qui courais, taché de lunules électriques,
Planche folle, escorté des hippocampes noirs,
Quand les juillets faisaient crouler à coups de triques
Les cieux ultramarins aux ardents entonnoirs;   80

Moi qui tremblais, sentant geindre à cinquante lieues
Le rut des Béhémots et les Maelstroms épais
Fileur éternel des immobilités bleues
Je regrette l'Europe aux anciens parapets!

J'ai vu des archipels sidéraux! et des îles   85
Dont les cieux délirants sont ouverts au vogueur:
—Est-ce en ces nuits sans fonds que tu dors et t'exiles,
Million d'oiseaux d'or, ô future Vigueur?—

Mais, vrai, j'ai trop pleuré! Les aubes sont navrantes,
Toute lune est atroce et tout soleil amer: 90
L'âcre amour m'a gonflé de torpeurs enivrantes.
Ô que ma quille éclate! O que j'aille à la mer!

Si je désire un eau d'Europe, c'est la flache
Noire et froide où vers le crépuscule embaumé
Un enfant accroupi plein de tristesses, lâche   95
Un bateau frêle comme un papillon de mai.

Je ne puis plus, baigné de vos langueurs, ô lames,
Enlever leur sillage aux porteurs de cotons,
Ni traverser l'orgueil des drapeaux et des flammes,
Ni nager sous les yeux horribles des pontons.   100

Now, I, boat tangled in the hair of bights,
Hurled high by hurricanes through birdless space,
Whom no protection vessel in the world
Would fish up from the drink, half-drowned, half-crazed;

Free, smoking, got up in violet spume,
I, who holed the sky like a wall in flames
Which bears, good poet's exquisite preserve,
Lichen of sun and cerulean snot;

Mad plank streaked with electric crescents, flanked
By dark formations of speeding sea-horse,
When Julys bludgeoned ultramarine skies
And pulverized them into scorching winds;

Trembling as I heard the far-away groans
Of rutting Behemoths and swirling storms;
Eternal spinner of blue stillnesses,
I long for Europe's ancient parapets.

I've seen star-sown islands cluster; others
Whose delirious skies summon sailors.
Do you sleep banished in the pit of night,
You myriad golden birds, the Strength to come?

I've wept too much, it's true. Dawn breaks my heart.
All moons are atrocious, all suns bitter.
Acrid love has pumped me with drugged torpor.
Let my keel burst, let me go to the sea!

If I want Europe, it's a dark cold pond
Where a small child plunged in sadness crouches
One fragrant evening at dusk, and launches
A boat, frail as a butterfly in May.

Steeped in your slow wine, waves, no more can I
Cadge rides in the cotton-freighters' slipstream,
Nor brave proud lines of ensigns and streamers,
Nor face the prison-ships' terrible eyes!

Voyelles

A noir, E blanc, I rouge, U vert, O bleu: voyelles,
Je dirai quelque jour vos naissances latentes:
A, noir corset velu des mouches éclatantes
Qui bombinent autour des puanteurs cruelles,

Golfes d'ombre; E, candeurs des vapeurs et des tentes,   5
Lances des glaciers fiers, rois blancs, frissons d'ombelles;
I, pourpres, sang craché, rire des lèvres belles
Dans la colère ou les ivresses pénitentes;

U, cycles, vibrements divins des mers virides,
Paix des pâtis semés d'animaux, paix des rides   10
Que l'alchimie imprime aux grands fronts studieux;

Ô, Suprême Clairon plein des strideurs étranges,
Silences traversés des Mondes et des Anges:
—Ô l'Omêga, rayon violet de Ses Yeux!—

La Rivière de Cassis

La Rivière de Cassis roule ignorée
      En des vaux étranges:
La voix de cent corbeaux l'accompagne vraie
      Et bonne voix d'anges:
Avec les grands mouvements des sapinaies   5
      Quand plusieurs vents plongent.

Tout roule avec des mystères révoltants
      De campagnes d'anciens temps;
De donjons visités, de parcs importants:
      C'est en ces bords qu'on entend   10
Les passions mortes de chevaliers errants:
      Mais que salubre est le vent!

Vowels

A black, E white, I red, U green, O blue: vowels.
One day I'll tell your embryonic births:
A, black fur-clad brilliant flies
Cluster-bombing every cruel stench,

Defiles of darkness; E, blank spread of mists and tents,
Proud glacier spears, white kings, a sigh of umbel;
I, purples, blood spat, beautiful lips laughing
In anger or penitential ecstasies;

U, cycles, divine shudder of viridian seas,
Peace of pastures grazed by cattle, peace of high
Pensive foreheads rucked by alchemy;

O, the last trumpet, strange crescendo blast,
Navigated silences of Worlds and Angels,
— O Omega, the violet radiance of Those Eyes.

Blackcurrant River

Unsuspected Blackcurrant river rolls
    Through strange valleys.
To the sound of a hundred crows, true
    Good voice of angels,
And sweeping forest pines lean
    When several winds swoop.

Everything rolls with the sickening mysteries
    Of olden day lands;
Dungeons inspected, substantial parks;
    On these banks you hear
The dead passions of knights-errant—
    But how the wind restores!

Que le piéton regarde à ces clairevoies:
    Il ira plus courageux.
Soldats des forêts que le Seigneur envoie,   15
    Chers corbeaux délicieux!
Faites fuir d'ici le paysan matois
    Qui trinque d'un moignon vieux.

Bonne pensée du matin

A quatre heures du matin, l'été,
Le sommeil d'amour dure encore.
Sous les bosquets l'aube évapore
    L'odeur du soir fêté.

Mais là-bas dans l'immense chantier   5
Vers le soleil des Hesperides,
En bras de chemise, les charpentiers
    Déjà s'agitent.

Dans leur désert de mousse, tranquilles,
Ils préparent les lambris précieux   10
Où la richesse de la ville
    Rira sous de faux cieux.

Ah! pour ces Ouvriers charmants
Sujets d'un roi de Babylone,
Vénus! laisse un peu les Amants,   15
    Dont l'âme est en couronne.

    O Reine des Bergers!
    Porte aux travailleurs l'eau-de-vie,
    Pour que leurs forces soient en paix
En attendant le bain dans la mer, à midi.   20

Let the walker look through this lattice-work;
   He'll proceed with more courage.
You soldiers of the forest, sent by Heaven,
   Dear delicious crows,
See off the cunning peasant, raising
   A glass in his old stump!

Lovely Morning Thought

Four a.m. in summertime
Love stays fast asleep
In gardens dawn dispels last
   Evening's headiness.

But on the vast site stretching up
Towards the golden apple sun
The shirt-sleeved carpenters
   Already work.

Calm in their deserts of moss
They panel fine ceilings
For the town's wealth to laugh
   Under false skies.

For these charming Workers,
These Babylon King's men,
Venus, leave the lovers be
   In aureoles of bliss.

   O Queen of Shepherds!
  Bring the workers eau-de-vie
  And flood their strength with calm
Until they can bathe at noon in the sea.

« O saisons, ô chateaux... »

O saisons, ô chateaux,
Quelle âme est sans défauts?

O saisons, ô chateaux,

J'ai fait la magique étude
Du bonheur, que nul n'élude.   5

O vive lui, chaque fois
Que chante le coq gaulois.

Mais je n'aurai plus d'envie,
Il s'est chargé de ma vie.

Ce charme! il prit âme et corps,   10
Et dispersa tous efforts.

Que comprendre à ma parole?
Il fait qu'elle fuie et vole!

O saisons, ô chateaux!

from *Les Illuminations*

Après le Déluge

Aussitôt que l'idée du Déluge se fût rassise,
    Un lièvre s'arrêta dans les sainfoins et les clochettes mouvantes et dit sa prière à l'arc-en-ciel à travers la toile de l'araignée.
    Oh! les pierres précieuses qui se cachaient,—les fleurs qui regardaient déjà.
    Dans la grande rue sale les étals se dressèrent, et l'on tira les barques vers la mer étagée là haut comme sur les gravures.

'O seasons, o châteaux...'

O seasons, o châteaux,
Which soul has no flaw?

O seasons, o châteaux,

I've made the magic study
Of happiness, that none evades.

Long may it live, each time
The Gallic cockerel crows.

No, I'll not want again:
It's taken over my life.

That spell! took soul and body,
And scattered all effort.

What to make of what I say?
It would have my words take flight.

O seasons, o châteaux.

from *Illuminations*

After the Flood

As soon as the idea of the Flood had subsided,
   A hare stopped among the clover and the moving flower-bells
and said its prayer to the rainbow through the spider's web.
   Oh! the precious stones hiding themselves—the flowers looking
around already.
   In the dirty main street the stalls were set up, and the boats
were dragged towards the sea moving up in shelves, as in old prints.

Le sang coula, chez Barbe-Bleue,—aux abattoirs,—dans les cirques, où le sceau de Dieu blêmit les fenêtres. Le sang et le lait coulèrent.

Les castors bâtirent. Les «mazagrans» fumèrent dans les estaminets. Dans la grande maison de vitres encore ruisselante les enfants en deuil regardèrent les merveilleuses images.

Une porte claqua, et sur la place du hameau, l'enfant tourna ses bras compris des girouettes et des coqs des clochers de partout, sous l'éclatante giboulée.

Madame *** établit un piano dans les Alpes. La messe et les premières communions se célèbrèrent aux cent mille autels de la cathédrale.

Les caravanes partirent. Et le Splendide Hôtel fut bâti dans le chaos de glaces et de nuit du pôle.

Depuis lors, la Lune entendit les chacals piaulant par les déserts de thym,—et les eglogues en sabots grognant dans le verger. Puis, dans la futaie violette, bourgeonnante, Eucharis me dit que c'était le printemps.

Sourds, étang,—Ecume, roule sur le pont, et par-dessus les bois;—draps noirs et orgues,—éclairs et tonnerres,—montez et roulez;—Eaux et tristesses, montez et relevez les Déluges.

Car depuis qu'ils se sont dissipés,—oh les pierres précieuses s'enfouissant, et les fleurs ouvertes,!—c'est un ennui! et la Reine, la Sorcière qui allume sa braise dans le pot de terre, ne voudra jamais nous raconter ce qu'elle sait, et que nous ignorons.

Being Beauteous

Devant une neige un Être de Beauté de haute taille. Des sifflements de mort et des cercles de musique sourde font monter, s'élargir et trembler comme un spectre ce corps adoré, des blessures écarlates et noires éclatent dans les chairs superbes. Les couleurs propres de la vie se foncent, dansent, et se dégagent autour de la Vision, sur le chantier. Et les frissons s'élèvent et grondent et la saveur forcenée de ces effets se chargeant avec les sifflements mortels et les rauques musiques que le monde, loin derrière nous, lance sur notre mère de beauté,—elle recule, elle se dresse. Oh! nos os sont revêtus d'un nouveau corps amoureux.

***

At Bluebeard's, blood flowed—in abattoirs—in circuses, where the seal of God blanched the windows. Blood and milk flowed.

Beavers built. In bars and cafés, fierce coffees steamed.

In the great house of window-panes still running with water, the children in mourning looked at the marvellous pictures.

A door slammed shut, and, on the village square, the child whirled his arms, recognized by weathervanes and steeplecocks everywhere, under the brilliant sudden shower.

Madame *** installed a piano in the Alps. Mass and first communions were celebrated at the cathedral's hundred thousand altars.

Caravans departed. And the Hotel Splendide was built in the chaos of ice and polar night.

From then on, the Moon heard jackals howling across the deserts of thyme—and eclogues in their wooden shoes grumbling in the orchard. Then, in the violet, budding grove, Eucharis told me it was Spring.

Surge up, pond,—Foam, roll across the bridge, over the woods;—black drapes and organs,—lightnings, thunder,—rise and roll;—Waters and sorrows, rise and heighten the Floods.

For since they have dispersed,—oh the precious stones burying themselves, and the opened flowers!—all the excitement has gone! and the Queen, the Witch who lights her charcoal fire in the earthen pot, will never deign to tell us what she knows, and we do not.

Being Beauteous

Against the snow a tall Being of Beauty. Hisses of death and circles of muffled music make this worshipped body rise, expand and tremble like a ghost; black and scarlet wounds burst in splendid flesh. The colours, clearly those of life, grow dark, dance, stand out against the Vision taking shape. And the shudders rise and rumble and the frenzied flavour of these effects as they load deadly hisses and raucous music which the world, far behind us, hurls at our mother of beauty—she moves back, makes herself tall. Oh! our bones now wear a new and loving body.

* * *

O la face cendrée, l'écusson de crin, les bras de cristal! Le canon
sur lequel je dois m'abattre à travers la mêlée des arbres et de l'air
léger!

Départ

Assez vu. La vision s'est rencontrée à tous les airs.
Assez eu. Rumeurs des villes, le soir, et au soleil, et toujours.
Assez connu. Les arrêts de la vie.—O Rumeurs et Visions!
Départ dans l'affection et le bruit neufs!

Matinée d'ivresse

O *mon* Bien! o *mon* Beau! Fanfare atroce où je ne trébuche point!
chevalet féerique! Hourra pour l'œuvre inouïe et pour le corps
merveilleux, pour la première fois! Cela commença sous les rires des
enfants, cela finira par eux. Ce poison va rester dans toutes nos
veines même quand, la fanfare tournant, nous serons rendu à l'anci-
enne inharmonie. Ô maintenant nous si digne de ces tortures!
rassemblons fervemment cette promesse surhumaine faite à notre
corps et à notre âme créés: cette promesse, cette démence!
L'élégance, la science, la violence! On nous a promis d'enterrer dans
l'ombre l'arbre du bien et du mal, de déporter les honnêtetés tyran-
niques, afin que nous amenions notre très pur amour. Cela com-
mença par quelques dégoûts et cela finit,—ne pouvant nous saisir sur
le champ de cette éternité,—cela finit par une débandade de
parfums.
    Rire des enfants, discrétion des esclaves, austérité des vierges,
horreur des figures et des objets d'ici, sacrés soyez vous par le sou-
venir de cette veille. Cela commençait par toute la rustrerie, voici que
cela finit par des anges de flamme et de glace.
    Petite veille d'ivresse, sainte! quand ce ne serait que pour le
masque dont tu nous as gratifié. Nous t'affirmons, méthode! Nous
n'oublions pas que tu as glorifié hier chacun de nos âges. Nous avons
foi au poison. Nous savons donner notre vie tout entière tous les jours.
    Voici le temps des *Assassins*.

O the ashen face, the horsehair escutcheon, the crystal arms! the cannon on which I must fall through the fray of trees and buoyant air!

Departure

Enough seen. The vision has been met in every air.
Enough had. Distant sounds of cities, in the evening, and in the sun, and always.
Enough known. Life's injunctions. O Sounds and Visions!
Departure in new affection and new noise.

Morning of Drunkenness

Oh *my* Good, *my* Beauty! Atrocious fanfare in which I do not waver! magical torture-rack! Salute the unheard-of work and the marvellous body, for the first time! It began amid the laughter of the children, it will finish there. The poison will stay in all our veins when the fanfare changes and brings us back to old disharmony. O now, let us who so deserve these tortures fervently gather that superhuman promise made to our created bodies, that promise, that madness! Elegance, knowledge, violence! We have the promise that the tree of good and evil shall be buried in darkness, that tyrannical decencies shall be exiled, so that we may introduce our love of utmost purity. It began with some disgust and it finished—unable as we are to seize this eternity here and now—it finished in a riot of perfumes.

Laughter of the children, discretion of the slaves, the virgins' austerity, the horror of the faces and objects which belong here, may you be hallowed by the memory of this wake. It began in utter boorishness, here it is ending in angels of fire and ice.

Small drunken wake, holy! if only for the mask you have bestowed on us. Method, we confirm you! We do not forget that yesterday you glorified each part of our lives. We have faith in the poison. We know how to give our life whole, every day.

This is the time of ASSASSINS.

Ville

Je suis un éphémère et point trop mécontent citoyen d'une métropole crue moderne parce que tout goût connu a été éludé dans les ameublements et l'extérieur des maisons aussi bien que dans le plan de la ville. Ici vous ne signaleriez les traces d'aucun monument de superstition. La morale et la langue sont réduites à leur plus simple expression, enfin! Ces millions de gens qui n'ont pas besoin de se connaître amènent si pareillement l'éducation, le métier et la vieillesse, que ce cours de vie doit être plusieurs fois moins long que ce qu'une statistique folle trouve pour les peuples du continent. Aussi comme, de ma fenêtre, je vois des spectres nouveaux roulant à travers l'épaisse et éternelle fumée de charbon,—notre ombre des bois, notre nuit d'été!—des Erynnies nouvelles, devant mon cottage qui est ma patrie et tout mon cœur puisque tout ici ressemble à ceci,—la Mort sans pleurs, notre active fille et servante, un Amour désespéré, et un joli Crime piaulant dans la boue de la rue.

Aube

J'ai embrassé l'aube d'été.

Rien ne bougeait encore au front des palais. L'eau était morte. Les camps d'ombres ne quittaient pas la route du bois. J'ai marché, réveillant les haleines vives et tièdes, et les pierreries regardèrent, et les ailes se levèrent sans bruit.

La première entreprise fut, dans le sentier déjà empli de frais et blêmes éclats, une fleur qui me dit son nom.

Je ris au wasserfall blond qui s'échevela à travers les sapins: à la cime argentée, je reconnus la déesse.

Alors je levai un à un les voiles. Dans l'allée, en agitant les bras. Par la plaine, où je l'ai dénoncée au coq. À la grand'ville elle fuyait parmi les clochers et les dômes, et courant comme un mendiant sur les quais de marbre, je la chassais.

En haut de la route, près d'un bois de lauriers, je l'ai entourée avec ses voiles amassés, et j'ai senti un peu son immense corps. L'aube et l'enfant tombèrent au bas du bois.

Au réveil il était midi.

City

I am an ephemeral and none too discontented citizen of a metropolis thought to be modern because all established taste has been avoided in the furnishings and on the outsides of houses as well as in the city plan. Here you will find no trace of any monument to superstition. So, morals and language finally have been reduced to their simplest expression! These myriad people who have no need to know one another carry on in such similar ways their education, their work and their old age that their life-span must be many times shorter than what certain mad statistics show about the people of the continent. And so I see from my window new spectres rolling through the thick, eternal coal-smoke—our woodland shade, our summer night!—new Erinyes, in front of the cottage which is my country and all my heart as everything here looks like this,—dry-eyed Death, our busy daughter and servant, a desperate Love and a nice Crime whimpering in the muck of the street.

Dawn

I have embraced the summer dawn.

Nothing yet stirred on the palace fronts. The water was lifeless. The shadow-camps on the woodland road had not yet been struck. I walked awakening warm and living breaths, and the precious stones looked, and the wings lifted without a sound.

The first enterprise was, on the path already live with shards of clean, cool light, a flower which told me its name.

I laughed at the waterfall which tossed its blond cascade down through the pines: at the silver summit I recognized the goddess.

Then one by one I raised the veils. Down the path, my arms flailing. Across the levels, where I denounced her to the cock. In the city she flitted from belfry to dome, and running like a beggar across the marble quays, I kept up the chase.

At the top of the road, by a laurel grove, her veils gathered, I enfolded her and managed to sense her enormous body. In the depths of the wood, dawn and the child fell.

On waking, it was noon.

Marine

Les chars d'argent et de cuivre—
Les proues d'acier et d'argent—
Battent l'écume,—
Soulèvent les souches des ronces—
   Les courants de la lande,   5
Et les ornières immenses du reflux
Filent circulairement vers l'est,
Vers les piliers de la forêt—
Vers les fûts de la jetée,
Dont l'angle est heurté par des tourbillons de lumière.   10

Promontoire

L'aube d'or et la soirée frissonnante trouvent notre brick en large en face de cette Villa et ses dépendances qui forment un promontoire aussi étendu que l'Épire et le Péloponnèse ou que la grande île du Japon, ou que l'Arabie! Des fanums qu'éclaire la rentrée des théories, d'immenses vues de la défense des côtes modernes; des dunes illustrées de chaudes fleurs et de bacchanales; de grands canaux de Carthage et des Embankments d'une Venise louche, de molles éruptions d'Etnas et des crevasses de fleurs et d'eaux des glaciers, des lavoirs entourés de peupliers d'Allemagne; des talus de parcs singuliers penchant des têtes d'Arbre du Japon; et les façades circulaires des «Royal» ou des «Grand» de Scarbro' ou de Brooklyn; et leurs railways flanquent, creusent, surplombent les dispositions de cet Hôtel, choisies dans l'histoire des plus élegantes et des plus colossales constructions de l'Italie, de l'Amérique et de l'Asie, dont les fenêtres et les terrasses à présent pleines d'éclairages, de boissons et de brises riches, sont ouvertes à l'esprit des voyageurs et des nobles,—qui permettent, aux heures du jour, à toutes les tarentelles des côtes,—et même aux ritournelles des vallées illustres de l'art, de décorer merveilleusement les façades du Palais. Promontoire.

Seascape

Silver chariots, and copper—
Steel prows, and silver—
Smack the foam—
Heave the thorn-stumps out.
    The currents of the great expanse
Huge lines scored by back-tracking tides
Circle away to the East
Towards the limbs of the forest—
Towards the piers of the jetty,
A salient lashed by gale-force light.

Promontory

Golden dawn and trembling dusk find our brig lying off the coast opposite that villa and its outbuildings, a promontory as long as Epirus and the Peloponnese or the great island of Japan, or Arabia! Temples lit by returning processions; huge views of modern coastal defences; dunes coloured by incandescent flowers and bacchanals; great Carthaginian waterworks, embankments of a shitty Venice; feeble eruptions of Etnas; crevasses filled with flowers and glacier water; wash-houses ringed with German poplars; slopes of strange parks where Trees of Japan hang their heads; the curving frontage of *Royals* and *Grands* in Scarborough and Brooklyn; their railways run beside and under and over the planes and surfaces of this Hotel, chosen from the history of the most elegant, most colossal buildings of Italy, America, Asia; its windows and terraces, bathed now in precious lights, drinks, sweet air, are open to the spirit of the travellers and the nobility—and they permit, in daylight hours, every tarantella of the coasts, and even the ritornelli of art's illustrious valleys, to cover in splendour the façades of the Palace. Promontory.

Solde—

A vendre ce que les Juifs n'ont pas vendu, ce que noblesse ni crime n'ont goûté, ce qu'ignorent l'amour maudit et la probité infernale des masses: ce que le temps ni la science n'ont pas à reconnaître:

Les Voix reconstituées; l'éveil fraternel de toutes les énergies chorales et orchestrales et leurs applications instantanées; l'occasion, unique, de dégager nos sens!

A vendre les Corps sans prix, hors de toute race, de tout monde, de toute sexe, de toute descendance! Les richesses jaillissant à chaque démarche! Solde de diamants sans contrôle!

A vendre l'anarchie pour les masses; la satisfaction irrépressible pour les amateurs supérieurs; la mort atroce pour les fidèles et les amants!

A vendre les habitations et les migrations, sports, féeries et comforts parfaits, et le bruit, le mouvement et l'avenir qu'ils font!

A vendre les applications de calcul et les sauts d'harmonie inouis. Les trouvailles et les termes non soupçonnés, possession immédiate,

Elan insensé et infini aux splendeurs invisibles aux délices insensibles,—et ses secrets affolants pour chaque vice—et sa gaîté effrayante pour la foule—.

—A vendre les Corps, les voix, l'immense opulence inquestionable, ce qu'on ne vendra jamais. Les vendeurs ne sont pas à bout de solde! Les voyageurs n'ont pas à rendre leur commission de si tôt!

from *Une Saison en enfer*

Nuit de l'enfer

J'ai avalé une fameuse gorgée de poison.—Trois fois béni soit le conseil qui m'est arrivé!—Les entrailles me brûlent. La violence du venin tord mes membres, me rend difforme, me terrasse. Je meurs de soif, j'étouffe, je ne puis crier. C'est l'enfer, l'éternelle peine! Voyez comme le feu se relève! Je brûle comme il faut. Va, démon!

Sales

For sale what the Jews have not sold, what neither nobility nor crime has tasted, what cursed love and the damnable integrity of the masses do not know; what neither time nor knowledge needs to recognize:

The Voices reconstituted; the brotherly awakening of every choral and orchestral energy and their instantaneous application; the opportunity, the only one, to free our senses!

For sale the priceless bodies, belonging to no race, no world, no sex, no lineage! Riches gushing forth at every step! Unrestricted sale of diamonds!

For sale anarchy for the masses; irrepressible satisfaction for true connoisseurs; atrocious death for the faithful and for lovers!

For sale dwelling-places and migrations, sports, perfect magic, perfect comforts, and the noise, the movement and the future they create!

For sale applications of calculus and harmonic ranges never heard before. Unsuspected finds and terms, immediate possession,

A senseless and infinite impetus towards invisible splendours, imperceptible delights,—and its hair-raising secrets for every vice— and its frightening gaiety for the crowd —

For sale the Bodies, the voices, the huge unquestionable opulence; what will never be sold. The vendors still have goods to clear! Travellers will not have to settle up just yet!

from *A Season in Hell*

Night in Hell

I have swallowed a mighty gulp of poison.—Thrice blessed be the counsel I was given!—My insides burn. The violence of the poison racks my limbs, renders me deformed, lays me out. I die of thirst, I choke, I cannot cry out. This is hell, the eternal torment! See how the fire burns more fiercely! I am roasting to a tee. So there, demon!

J'avais entrevu la conversion au bien et au bonheur, le salut. Puis-je décrire la vision, l'air de l'enfer ne souffre pas les hymnes! C'était des millions de créatures charmantes, un suave concert spirituel, la force et la paix, les nobles ambitions, que sais-je?

Les nobles ambitions!

Et c'est encore la vie!—Si la damnation est éternelle! Un homme qui veut se mutiler est bien damné, n'est-ce pas? Je me crois en enfer, donc j'y suis. C'est l'exécution du catéchisme. Je suis esclave de mon baptême. Parents, vous avez fait mon malheur et vous avez fait le vôtre. Pauvre innocent!—L'enfer ne peut attaquer les païens.—C'est la vie encore! Plus tard, les délices de la damnation seront plus profondes. Un crime, vite, que je tombe au néant, de par la loi humaine.

Tais-toi, mais tais-toi!... C'est la honte, le reproche, ici: Satan qui dit que le feu est ignoble, que ma colère est affreusement sotte.— Assez!... Des erreurs qu'on me souffle, magies, parfums faux, musiques puériles.—Et dire que je tiens la vérité, que je vois la just-ice: j'ai un jugement sain et arrêté, je suis prêt pour la perfection... Orgueil.—La peau de ma tête se dessèche. Pitié! Seigneur, j'ai peur. J'ai soif, si soif! Ah! l'enfance, l'herbe, la pluie, le lac sur les pierres, *le clair de lune quand le clocher sonnait douze*... le diable est au clocher, à cette heure. Marie! Sainte-Vierge!... —Horreur de ma bêtise.

Là-bas, ne sont-ce pas des âmes honnêtes, qui me veulent du bien... Venez... J'ai un oreiller sur la bouche, elles ne m'entendent pas, ce sont des fantômes. Puis, jamais personne ne pense à autrui. Qu'on n'approche pas. Je sens le roussi, c'est certain.

Les hallucinations sont innombrables. C'est bien ce que j'ai toujo-urs eu: plus de foi en l'histoire, l'oubli des principes. Je m'en tairai: poëtes et visionnaires seraient jaloux. Je suis mille fois le plus riche, soyons avare comme la mer.

Ah çà! l'horloge de la vie s'est arrêtée tout à l'heure. Je ne suis plus au monde.—La théologie est sérieuse, l'enfer est certainement *en bas*—et le ciel en haut.—Extase, cauchemar, sommeil dans un nid de flammes.

Que de malices dans l'attention dans la campagne... Satan, Fer-dinand, court avec les grains sauvages... Jésus marche sur les ronces purpurines, sans les courber... Jésus marchait sur les eaux irritées. La lanterne nous le montra debout, blanc et des tresses brunes, au flanc d'une vague d'émeraude...

I had glimpsed, once, the conversion to goodness and happiness, salvation. I might want to describe the vision, but the air of hell does not suffer hymns! There were a myriad charming creatures, a soothing spiritual concert, strength and peace, noble ambitions, and more, no doubt.

Noble ambitions!

And still I am here, alive! Could damnation be eternal? A man who wants to mutilate himself is truly damned, no? I think I am in hell, therefore I am. That is the catechism in action. I am the slave of my baptism. Parents, you have caused my unhappiness, created your own. Poor innocent!—Hell cannot touch the heathen.—Still I am alive! Later, the delights of damnation will get deeper. Quick, a crime, so that I may plunge into nothingness, according to human law.

Shut up, shut up! Satan who tells me that hellfire is unworthy, that my anger is impossibly stupid.—Enough!... Untruths whispered to me, magic, false scents, puerile music.—And to think I have the truth, and see justice: my judgement is sane and sound, I am ready for perfection... Pride. The skin on my head is drying up. Mercy, Lord, I am afraid! I am thirsty, so thirsty! Ah, childhood, the grass, the rain, the lake on the stones, *the moonlight as the church clock struck twelve...* the devil is in the belfry, at this very moment.—Mary! Holy Virgin!... —Horror of my stupidity.

Over there, are they not honest souls, who wish me well?... Come... A pillow stops my mouth, they cannot hear me, they are ghosts. And then, no one ever thinks of others. Do not come near. I stink of burnt flesh, for sure.

The hallucinations cannot be counted. That is who I have always been: no more faith in history, principles forgotten. I shall be silent on this matter: poets and visionaries would be jealous. I am a thousand times richer than they, I shall store it away like the sea.

And see this, the clock of life stopped a while ago. I am no longer of the world.—Theology means it, hell is certainly *down below*—and heaven is above—Ecstasy, nightmare, sleep in a nest of flames.

How the mind plays up in the country... Satan, Old Nick, runs with the wild seed... Jesus walks on crimson tangles of thorn and does not bend them... Jesus walked on troubled waters once. In the lantern-light we saw him, robed in white, his hair brown and lank, standing on an emerald wave...

Je vais dévoiler tous les mystères: mystères réligieux ou naturels, mort, naissance, avenir, passé, cosmogonie, néant. Je suis maître en fantasmagories.

Écoutez!...

J'ai tous les talents!—Il n'y a personne ici et il y a quelqu'un: je ne voudrais pas répandre mon trésor.—Veut-on des chants nègres, des danses de houris? Veut-on que je disparaisse, que je plonge à la recherche de l'*anneau*? Veut-on? Je ferai de l'or, des remèdes.

Fiez-vous donc à moi, la foi soulage, guide, guérit. Tous, venez,— même les petits enfants,—que je vous console, qu'on répande pour vous son cœur,—le cœur merveilleux!—Pauvres hommes, travailleurs! Je ne demande pas de prières; avec votre confiance seulement, je serai heureux.

—Et pensons à moi. Ceci me fait peu regretter le monde. J'ai de la chance de ne pas souffrir plus. Ma vie ne fut que folies douces, c'est regrettable.

Bah! faisons toutes les grimaces imaginables.

Décidément, nous sommes hors du monde. Plus aucun son. Mon tact a disparu. Ah! mon château, ma Saxe, mon bois de saules. Les soirs, les matins, les nuits, les jours... Suis-je las!

Je devrais avoir mon enfer pour la colère, mon enfer pour l'orgueil,—et l'enfer de la caresse; un concert d'enfers.

Je meurs de lassitude. C'est le tombeau, je m'en vais aux vers, horreur de l'horreur! Satan, farceur, tu veux me dissoudre, avec tes charmes. Je réclame. Je réclame! un coup de fourche, une goutte de feu.

Ah! remonter à la vie! Jeter les yeux sur nos difformités. Et ce poison, ce baiser mille fois maudit! Ma faiblesse, la cruauté du monde! Mon Dieu, pitié, cachez-moi, je me tiens trop mal!—Je suis caché et je ne le suis pas.

C'est le feu qui se relève avec son damné.

Matin

N'eus-je pas *une fois* une jeunesse aimable, héroïque, fabuleuse, à écrire sur des feuilles d'or,—trop de chance! Par quel crime, par quelle erreur, ai-je mérité ma faiblesse actuelle? Vous qui prétendez que des bêtes poussent des sanglots de chagrin, que des malades

I shall unveil every mystery: religious or natural mysteries, death, birth, future, past, cosmogony, the void. I am the master of phantasmagoria.

Listen!...

I have all the talents!—There is no one here and there is someone: I do not want to spill my treasure.—What would you like, negro songs, Eastern dancing-girls? Or shall I disappear, or dive in search of the *ring*? Ask, and I shall make gold, cures.

Trust me, then, faith relieves, guides, heals. Come, everyone,— even the little children—let me console you, let someone give his heart for you—the marvellous heart!—Poor men, workers! I do not ask for prayers, with your trust alone I shall be happy.

—And let us think of me. All this scarcely makes me regret the world. I am lucky not to suffer more. My life was only sweet madness, and that is a shame.

Bah! why not pull every conceivable face.

There can be no doubt, we have left the world. Not a sound anywhere. My sense of touch has gone. Ah, my château, my Saxony, my willow wood. Evenings, mornings, nights, days... Such fatigue!

I should have a hell for my anger, a hell for my pride—there should be a hell for sex; a symphony of hells.

I am dying of fatigue. This is the grave, I am headed for the worms, horror of horrors! Satan, you joker, you want to undo me with your spells. I beg, I demand you spike me with your pitchfork, drop fire on me.

Ah, to return to life! Cast eyes on our deformities. And that poison, that kiss damned a thousand times! My weakness, the cruelty of the world! Mercy, my God, hide me, I cannot look out for myself!—I am hidden and not hidden.

And there, the flames rise up again with the damned soul.

Morning

Did I not *once* have a pleasant childhood, heroic and fabulous, to be written on leaves of gold,—too much to ask! What crime, what error has led me to my present weakness? You who claim that beasts can weep with grief, the sick abandon hope, the dead have bad

désespèrent, que des morts rêvent mal, tâchez de raconter ma chute et mon sommeil. Moi, je ne puis pas plus m'expliquer que le mendiant avec ses continuels *Pater* et *Ave Maria*. *Je ne sais plus parler!*

Pourtant, aujourd'hui, je crois avoir fini la relation de mon enfer. C'était bien l'enfer; l'ancien, celui dont le fils de l'homme ouvrit les portes.

Du même désert, à la même nuit, toujours mes yeux las se réveillent à l'étoile d'argent, toujours, sans que s'émeuvent les Rois de la vie, les trois mages, le cœur, l'âme, l'esprit. Quand irons-nous, par delà les grèves et les monts, saluer la naissance du travail nouveau, la sagesse nouvelle, la fuite des tyrans et des démons, la fin de la superstition, adorer—les premiers!—Noël sur la terre!

Le chant des cieux, la marche des peuples! Esclaves, ne maudissons pas la vie.

Adieu

L'automne déjà!—Mais pourquoi regretter un éternel soleil, si nous sommes engagés à la découverte de la clarté divine,—loin des gens qui meurent sur les saisons.

L'automne. Notre barque élevée dans les brumes immobiles tourne vers le port de la misère, la cité énorme au ciel taché de feu et de boue. Ah! les haillons pourris, le pain trempé de pluie, l'ivresse, les mille amours qui m'ont crucifié! Elle ne finira donc point cette goule reine de millions d'âmes et de corps morts *et qui seront jugés!* Je me revois la peau rongée par la boue et la peste, des vers plein les cheveux et les aisselles et encore de plus gros vers dans le cœur, étendu parmi les inconnus sans âge, sans sentiment... J'aurais pu y mourir... L'affreuse évocation! J'exècre la misère.

Et je redoute l'hiver parce que c'est la saison du comfort!

—Quelquefois je vois au ciel des plages sans fin couvertes de blanches nations en joie. Un grand vaisseau d'or, au-dessus de moi, agite ses pavillons multicolores sous les brises du matin. J'ai créé toutes les fêtes, tous les triomphes, tous les drames. J'ai essayé d'inventer de nouvelles fleurs, de nouveaux astres, de nouvelles chairs, de nouvelles langues. J'ai cru acquérir des pouvoirs surnaturels. Eh bien! je dois enterrer mon imagination et mes souvenirs! Une belle gloire d'artiste et de conteur emportée!

dreams, try to tell the story of my fall and my sleeping. For my part, I can no more explain myself than can a beggar with his endless *Pater Nosters* and *Ave Marias*. *I no longer know how to speak!*

And yet, today, I think I have completed the account of my hell. It was hell indeed; the ancient one whose gates were opened by the Son of Man.

Out of the same desert, on the same night, my weary eyes awaken always to the silver star, always, without a flicker from the Kings of life, the three wise men, the heart, the soul, the mind. When, beyond the shores and mountains, shall we go to greet the birth of the new work, the new wisdom, the flight of tyrants and demons, the end of superstition, and—the very first!—worship Christmas on earth!

The song of the heavens, nations on the march! We are slaves, but let us not curse life.

Farewell

Autumn this soon! But why hanker after an eternal sun if our quest is divine light, far away from those who die with the seasons.

Autumn. Our boat, high in the still mists, turns towards the harbour of poverty, the huge city, its filth-stained fire-streaked sky. Ah, the rotted rags, the rain soaked bread, the drunkenness, the thousand loves that crucified me! Will she never have done, this Queen of the Night, monarch of a million dead *who will now be judged!* I see once more my filthy pestilential skin, my hair and armpits rank with worms, and bigger worms still in my heart, me, stretched out among ageless unknown people who feel nothing... I could have died there... Nightmare thought! I hate poverty.

How I fear winter, season of slippers!

Sometimes I see in the sky beaches without end, swarming with enraptured white nations. Above me a great golden ship flutters flags of every colour in the morning breezes. I have created every carnival, every triumph, every drama. I have sought to invent new flowers, new stars, new bodies, new tongues. I thought I could acquire supernatural powers. Well no, I must lay my memories and imaginings in the ground! No fame, no glory, artist and storyteller manqué!

Moi! moi qui me suis dit mage ou ange, dispensé de toute morale, je suis rendu au sol, avec un devoir à chercher, et la réalité rugueuse à étreindre! Paysan!

Suis-je trompé? la charité serait-elle sœur de la mort, pour moi?

Enfin, je demanderai pardon pour m'être nourri de mensonge. Et allons.

Mais pas une main amie! et où puisser le secours?

*

Oui l'heure nouvelle est au moins très-sévère.

Car je puis dire que la victoire m'est acquise: les grincements de dents, les sifflements de feu, les soupirs empestés se modèrent. Tous les souvenirs immondes s'effacent. Mes derniers regrets détalent,—des jalousies pour les mendiants, les brigands, les amis de la mort, les arriérés de toutes sortes.—Damnés, si je me vengeais!

Il faut être absolument moderne.

Point de cantiques: tenir le pas gagné. Dure nuit! le sang séché fume sur ma face, et je n'ai rien derrière moi, que cet horrible arbrisseau!... Le combat spirituel est aussi brutal que la bataille d'hommes; mais la vision de la justice est le plaisir de Dieu seul.

Cependant c'est la veille. Recevons tous les influx de vigueur et de tendresse réelle. Et à l'aurore, armés d'une ardente patience, nous entrerons aux splendides villes.

Que parlais-je de main amie! Une bel avantage, c'est que je puis rire des vieilles amours mensongères, et frapper de honte ces couples menteurs,—j'ai vu l'enfer des femmes là-bas;—et il me sera loisible de *posséder la vérité dans une âme et un corps.*

Me,—ha!—who thought myself a magus, an angel, above morality. I am restored to the earth, looking out a task, with raw reality to embrace. Peasant!

Have I been wrong? Could charity be for me the sister of death? Ah well, I shall seek forgiveness for a life of lies. Onwards. But no helping hand! and where to search for help?

*

Yes, the new era is certainly hard.

For I can say that victory is mine: grinding teeth, hissing fire, pestilential sighs are on the wane. All vile memories dissolve. My last regrets make themselves scarce; let beggars, brigands, those in love with death, the retarded of every kind, squabble over them—And they would know damnation, should I take revenge.

It is necessary to be absolutely modern.

No hymns of thanksgiving; yield not one inch. A hard night. Dried blood smokes on my face and there is nothing behind me save that small, terrible tree!... The spiritual fight is as brutal as men in battle; but the vision of justice is for God's pleasure alone.

Yet this is the eve. Accept every wave of strength and true tenderness. And at dawn, armed with scorching patience, we shall enter the cities of splendour.

Why did I speak of a helping hand! My great advantage now is that I can laugh at all the old mendacities of love, I can prick with shame that bubble called The Couple—I have seen down there the hell of women—and now I shall be free to *possess truth in one soul and one body*.

STEPHANE MALLARMÉ

from *Poésies*

Salut

Rien, cette écume, vierge vers
A ne désigner que la coupe;
Telle loin se noie une troupe
De sirènes mainte à l'envers.

Nous naviguons, ô mes divers   5
Amis, moi déjà sur la poupe
Vous l'avant fastueux qui coupe
Le flot de foudres et d'hivers;

Une ivresse belle m'engage
Sans craindre même son tangage   10
De porter debout ce salut

Solitude, récif, étoile
A n'importe ce qui valut
Le blanc souci de notre toile.

Brise marine

La chair est triste, hélas! et j'ai lu tous les livres.
Fuir! là-bas fuir! Je sens que des oiseaux sont ivres
D'être parmi l'écume inconnue et les cieux!
Rien, ni les vieux jardins reflétés par les yeux,
Ne retiendra ce cœur qui dans la mer se trempe,   5
O nuits! ni la clarté déserte de ma lampe
Sur le vide papier que la blancheur défend,
Et ni la jeune femme allaitant son enfant.

TRANSLATED BY E. H. AND A. M. BLACKMORE

from *Poems*

Toast

Nothing, this foam, this virgin verse
designating the cup, no more;
so plunges far away a corps
of sirens, many in reverse.

We all, my various friends, we sail
with myself on the poop-deck now
while you as the majestic prow
cleave wintry seas of blast and gale;

spurred by a fine intoxication
and fearless even of its swerving
I stand and offer you this toast

solitude, star, or rocky coast
to things of any kind deserving
of our sail's white preoccupation.

Sea Breeze

The flesh is sad—and I've read every book.
O to escape—to get away! Birds look
as though they're drunk for unknown spray and skies.
No ancient gardens mirrored in the eyes,
nothing can hold this heart steeped in the sea—
not my lamp's desolate luminosity
nor the blank paper guarded by its white
nor the young wife feeding her child, O night!

Je partirai! Steamer balançant ta mâture,
Lève l'ancre pour une exotique nature!   10
Un Ennui, désolé par les cruels espoirs,
Croit encore à l'adieu suprême des mouchoirs!
Et, peut-être, les mâts, invitant les orages,
Sont-ils de ceux qu'un vent penche sur les naufrages
Perdus, sans mâts, sans mâts, ni fertiles îlots...   15
Mais, ô mon cœur, entends le chant des matelots!

L'Après-midi d'vn favne

Églogve

LE FAVNE

Ces nymphes, je les veux perpétuer.

                            Si clair,
Leur incarnat léger, qu'il voltige dans l'air
Assoupi de sommeils touffus.

                    Aimai-je un rêve?

Mon doute, amas de nuit ancienne, s'achève
En maint rameau subtil, qui, demeuré les vrais   5
Bois mêmes, prouve, hélas! que bien seul je m'offrais
Pour triomphe la faute idéale de roses.
Réfléchissons...

                ou si les femmes dont tu gloses
Figurent un souhait de tes sens fabuleux!
Faune, l'illusion s'échappe des yeux bleus   10
Et froids, comme une source en pleurs, de la plus chaste:
Mais, l'autre tout soupirs, dis-tu qu'elle contraste
Comme brise du jour chaude dans ta toison?
Que non! par l'immobile et lasse pâmoison
Suffoquant de chaleurs le matin frais s'il lutte,   15
Ne murmure point d'eau que ne verse ma flûte

I'm off! You steamer with your swaying helm,
raise anchor for some more exotic realm!
Ennui, crushed down by cruel hopes, still relies
on handkerchiefs' definitive goodbyes!
Is this the kind of squall-inviting mast
that storm-winds buckle above shipwrecks cast
away—no mast, no islets flourishing?...
Still, my soul, listen to the sailors sing!

A Favn in the Afternoon

Eclogve

THE FAVN *speaks:*

I'd love to make them linger on, those nymphs.

                      So fair,
their frail incarnate, that it flutters in the air
drowsy with tousled slumbers.

                         Did I love a dream?

My doubt, hoard of old darkness, ends in a whole stream
of subtle branches which, remaining as the true
forests, show that I've offered myself (quite alone, too)
the roses' ideal failing as something glorious.
Let me reflect...

              what if these women you discuss,
faun, represent desires of your own fabulous
senses! Illusion flows out of the chilly blue
eyes of the chaster one, like a fountain in tears:
the other, though, all sighs—do you think she appears
in contrast like a day's warm breeze across your fleece?
Not at all: through the lazy languishing release
stifling with heat the cool dawn's struggles, not a sound
of water but my flute's outpourings murmurs round

Au bosquet arrosé d'accords; et le seul vent
Hors des deux tuyaux prompt à s'exhaler avant
Qu'il disperse le son dans une pluie aride,
C'est, à l'horizon pas remué d'une ride,   20
Le visible et serein souffle artificiel
De l'inspiration, qui regagne le ciel.

O bords siciliens d'un calme marécage
Qu'à l'envi de soleils ma vanité saccage,
Tacites sous les fleurs d'étincelles, CONTEZ   25
» *Que je coupais ici les creux roseaux domptés*
» *Par le talent; quand, sur l'or glauque de lointaines*
» *Verdures dédiant leur vigne à des fontaines,*
» *Ondoie une blancheur animale au repos:*
» *Et qu'au prélude lent où naissent les pipeaux,*   30
» *Ce vol de cygnes, non! de naïades se sauve*
» *Ou plonge...* »

                    Inerte, tout brûle dans l'heure fauve
Sans marquer par quel art ensemble détala
Trop d'hymen souhaité de qui cherche le *la*:
Alors m'éveillerai-je à la ferveur première,   35
Droit et seul, sous un flot antique de lumière,
Lys! et l'un de vous tous pour l'ingénuité.

Autre que ce doux rien par leur lèvre ébruité,
Le baiser, qui tout bas des perfides assure,
Mon sein, vierge de preuve, atteste une morsure   40
Mystérieuse, due à quelque auguste dent;
Mais, bast! arcane tel élut pour confident
Le jonc vaste et jumeau dont sous l'azur on joue:
Qui, détournant à soi le trouble de la joue
Rêve, dans un solo long, que nous amusions   45
La beauté d'alentour par des confusions
Fausses entre elle-même et notre chant crédule;
Et de faire aussi haut que l'amour se module
Évanouir du songe ordinaire de dos
Ou de flanc pur suivis avec mes regards clos,   50
Une sonore, vaine et monotone ligne.

the thicket steeped in music; and the one stir of air
my dual pipes are swiftly shedding everywhere
and then dispersing in a sonorous arid sleet,
is, over the horizon that no ripples pleat,
the visible, serene and artificial sigh
of inspiration reascending to the sky.

O fringes of a placid mere in Sicily
thus plundered by my sun-rivalling vanity,
silent beneath the blooms of brilliant light, PROCLAIM
how I was cropping here the hollow reeds made tame
by talent, when, across the blue-green gold of things
far off—verdures devoting their vines to the springs—
came shimmering to rest a pallid animal glow;
and when the pipes were brought to birth, how at their slow
prelude this flight of swans—no! naiads—fled away
or dived. . . .

       All things burn in the fulvid time of day,
inert, failing to show by what art it dispersed,
that nuptial excess craved by someone seeking A
natural; and then I must waken to the first
passion, erect, alone, beneath an age-old light,
lilies! and one among you, a simple neophyte.

Other than that sweet nothing voiced by their lip, the kiss
giving assurance softly of the faithless, this
virgin-proof breast of mine bears witness to some bite
of a mysterious kind from sacred teeth; but wait!
that certain esoteric something chose the great
twin reed played under heaven as its secret friend;
diverting the cheek's disturbances for its own end,
it dreams, in a long solo, that we have seduced
the beauties round about us by a false confusion
of them with the naïve melody we've produced;
and dreams of, high as love itself can modulate,
evacuating from the commonplace illusion
of some pure loin or rear that my shut eyes create
a sonorous, monotonous and empty line.

Tâche donc, instrument des fuites, ô maligne
Syrinx, de refleurir aux lacs où tu m'attends!
Moi, de ma rumeur fier, je vais parler longtemps
Des déesses; et par d'idolâtres peintures,   55
A leur ombre enlever encore des ceintures:
Ainsi, quand des raisins j'ai sucé la clarté,
Pour bannir un regret par ma feinte écarté,
Rieur, j'élève au ciel d'été la grappe vide
Et, soufflant dans ses peaux lumineuses, avide   60
D'ivresse, jusqu'au soir je regarde au travers.

O nymphes, regonflons des SOUVENIRS divers.
» *Mon œil, trouant les joncs, dardait chaque encolure*
» *Immortelle, qui noie en l'onde sa brûlure*
» *Avec un cri de rage au ciel de la forêt;*   65
» *Et le splendide bain de cheveux disparaît*
» *Dans les clartés et les frissons, ô pierreries!*
» *J'accours; quand, à mes pieds, s'entrejoignent (meurtries*
» *De la langueur goûtée à ce mal d'être deux)*
» *Des dormeuses parmi leurs seuls bras hasardeux;*   70
» *Je les ravis, sans les désenlacer, et vole*
» *A ce massif, haï par l'ombrage frivole,*
» *De roses tarissant tout parfum au soleil,*
» *Où notre ébat au jour consumé soit pareil. »*
Je t'adore, courroux des vierges, ô délice   75
Farouche du sacré fardeau nu qui se glisse
Pour fuir ma lèvre en feu buvant, comme un éclair
Tressaille! la frayeur secrète de la chair:
Des pieds de l'inhumaine au cœur de la timide
Que délaisse à la fois une innocence, humide   80
De larmes folles ou de moins tristes vapeurs.
» *Mon crime, c'est d'avoir, gai de vaincre ces peurs*
» *Traîtresses, divisé la touffe échevelée*
» *De baisers que les dieux gardaient si bien mêlée;*
» *Car, à peine j'allais cacher un rire ardent*   85
» *Sous les replis heureux d'une seule (gardant*
» *Par un doigt simple, afin que sa candeur de plume*
» *Se teignît à l'émoi de sa sœur qui s'allume,*
» *La petite naïve et ne rougissant pas:)*
» *Que de mes bras, défaits par de vagues trépas,*   90

Try, then, to flower again, organ of flights, malign
syrinx, across the lake-flats where you wait for me!
Proud of these sounds of mine, I'll speak perpetually
of goddesses; I'll lift more of the drapery
up from their shadows with idolatrous displays:
so, when I've sucked the gleam of grape-flesh, to erase
this disappointment that my sleight has scattered, I
raise the void cluster, laughing, to the summer sky;
avid for drunkenness, I blow into its light-
filled skins, and stare through them until the fall of night.

Nymphs, let's expand again various MEMORIES.
My gaze delved through the reeds, darted on each of these
immortal throats plunging their heat into the flow
with cries of fury at the forest heavens; so
the glorious cascade of tresses slipped from view
in glitterings and shiverings—such jewelleries!
I sped there; at my feet lay linked (and wounded through
the languor tasted from this pain of being two)
a sleeping pair of nymphs in their lone careless braid
of limbs; I seized without unlacing them, and flew
here to this thicket hated by the frivolous shade
where roses dry up all their fragrance in the sun
and where our frolics may be squandered like the light.
I love these virgin angers, this untamed delight
of nude and sacred burdens slipping away to shun
my burning lips that drink in, as a lightning-sheet
quivers! the flesh's secret terror, from the feet
of the cruel girl to the heart of the timid one
simultaneously abandoned by an innocence, damp
with foolish tears or fluids of a less grim stamp.
My offence, in my joy at conquering these sly
terrors, was that I pried apart the tousled wry
kisses the gods had kept so deftly mingled: I
no sooner strove to hide this ecstasy of mine
within one girl's happy recesses (with a fine
fingerhold on the other one—naïve and slight,
not blushing in the least—so that her feathery white
might be tinged as her sister's passion caught alight),
than from my arms, untwined by some vague perishings,

» *Cette proie, à jamais ingrate se délivre*
» *Sans pitié du sanglot dont j'étais encore ivre.* »

Tant pis! vers le bonheur d'autres m'entraîneront
Par leur tresse nouée aux cornes de mon front:
Tu sais, ma passion, que, pourpre et déjà mûre,   95
Chaque grenade éclate et d'abeilles murmure;
Et notre sang, épris de qui le va saisir,
Coule pour tout l'essaim éternel du désir.
A l'heure où ce bois d'or et de cendres se teinte
Une fête s'exalte en la feuillée éteinte: 100
Etna! c'est parmi toi visité de Vénus
Sur ta lave posant ses talons ingénus,
Quand tonne un somme triste ou s'épuise la flamme.
Je tiens la reine!

                    O sûr châtiment...

                                        Non, mais l'âme
De paroles vacante et ce corps alourdi   105
Tard succombent au fier silence de midi:
Sans plus il faut dormir en l'oubli du blasphème,
Sur le sable altéré gisant et comme j'aime
Ouvrir ma bouche à l'astre efficace des vins!

Couple, adieu; je vais voir l'ombre que tu devins.   110

Sainte

A la fenêtre recélant
Le santal vieux qui se dédore
De sa viole étincelant
Jadis avec flûte ou mandore,

Est la Sainte pâle, étalant   5
Le livre vieux qui se déplie
Du Magnificat ruisselant
Jadis selon vêpre et complie:

this everlastingly ungrateful captive springs
free, careless of my still-intoxicated sighs.

Never mind! Other nymphs will draw me nonetheless,
their tresses tangled on my horns, to happiness:
how, purple, freshly ripe, the pomegranates rise
and burst and murmur with the bees, my passion knows;
our blood, allured by what may seize its fancy, flows
for the swarm of desires eternally released.
Among the dead leaves, at times when the forest glows
with gold and ashen tints, there rises up a feast:
Etna! across your very slopes, then, Venus goes,
and on your laval ground she rests her artless toes
when sad slumbers are sounding and the flame has ceased.
I've got the queen!

              The punishment is certain....

                                No,

but the soul void of words and heavy body slow-
ly fall before noon's haughty calm. No more ado;
must sleep now, must forget the blasphemy and blame,
spread on the thirsty sand; and as I love to do
open my mouth to the wines' potent star!

                           Both of you,
farewell; I'm going to see the shadow you became.

Saint

    At the window that veils her old
    sandalwood viol voiding gold
    which used to cast its glitter in
    the past with flute or mandolin

    is the pale Saint displaying that
    old volume the Magnificat
    unfolded, from which vespers or
    evensong used to stream before:

A ce vitrage d'ostensoir
Que frôle une harpe par l'Ange   10
Formée avec son vol du soir
Pour la délicate phalange

Du doigt que, sans le vieux santal
Ni le vieux livre, elle balance
Sur le plumage instrumental,   15
Musicienne du silence.

Plusieurs Sonnets

Quand l'ombre menaça de la fatale loi
Tel vieux Rêve, désir et mal de mes vertèbres,
Affligé de périr sous les plafonds funèbres
Il a ployé son aile indubitable en moi.

Luxe, ô salle d'ébène où, pour séduire un roi,   5
Se tordent dans leur mort des guirlandes célèbres,
Vous n'êtes qu'un orgueil menti par les ténèbres
Aux yeux du solitaire ébloui de sa foi.

Oui, je sais qu'au lointain de cette nuit, la Terre
Jette d'un grand éclat l'insolite mystère   10
Sous les siècles hideux qui l'obscurcissent moins.

L'espace à soi pareil qu'il s'accroisse ou se nie
Roule dans cet ennui des feux vils pour témoins
Que s'est d'un astre en fête allumé le génie.

Le vierge, le vivace et le bel aujourd'hui
Va-t-il nous déchirer avec un coup d'aile ivre
Ce lac dur oublié que hante sous le givre
Le transparent glacier des vols qui n'ont pas fui!

at this ostensory pane draped
by a harp that the Angel shaped
in his flight through the evening shade
for the delicate finger-blade

as she is poising to caress,
neither old wood nor old edition,
but instrumental featheriness—
being the silence's musician.

A Few Sonnets

When the shade threatened with the fatal decree
that old Dream, my bones' craving and their blight,
pained to die under the funereal height
it bowed its doubt-less plumage deep in me.

Splendour—ebony hall where, to allure
a king, illustrious wreaths writhe in their doom—
you are merely a pride lied by the gloom
to the faith-dazzled Solitary viewer.

Yes, Earth has cast into this night afar
the startling mystery of sheer dazzlingness
beneath dread aeons darkening it less.

Space, its own peer, whether it fail or grow
rolls in this tedium trivial fires to show
the genius kindled by a festive star.

This virginal long-living lovely day
will it tear from us with a wing's wild blow
the lost hard lake haunted beneath the snow
by clear ice-flights that never flew away!

Un cygne d'autrefois se souvient que c'est lui　　　　5
Magnifique mais qui sans espoir se délivre
Pour n'avoir pas chanté la région où vivre
Quand du stérile hiver a resplendi l'ennui.

Tout son col secouera cette blanche agonie
Par l'espace infligée à l'oiseau qui le nie,　　　　10
Mais non l'horreur du sol où le plumage est pris.

Fantôme qu'à ce lieu son pur éclat assigne,
Il s'immobilise au songe froid de mépris
Que vêt parmi l'exil inutile le Cygne.

Victorieusement fui le suicide beau
Tison de gloire, sang par écume, or, tempête!
O rire si là-bas une pourpre s'apprête
A ne tendre royal que mon absent tombeau.

Quoi! de tout cet éclat pas même le lambeau　　　　5
S'attarde, il est minuit, à l'ombre qui nous fête
Excepté qu'un trésor présomptueux de tête
Verse son caressé nonchaloir sans flambeau,

La tienne si toujours le délice! la tienne
Oui seule qui du ciel évanoui retienne　　　　10
Un peu de puéril triomphe en t'en coiffant

Avec clarté quand sur les coussins tu la poses
Comme un casque guerrier d'impératrice enfant
Dont pour te figurer il tomberait des roses.

A swan of old remembers it is he
superb but strives to break free woebegone
for having left unsung the territory
to live when sterile winter's tedium shone.

His neck will shake off this white throe that space
has forced the bird denying it to face,
but not the horror of earth that traps his wings.

Phantom imposed this place by his sheer gleam,
he lies immobile in scorn's frigid dream
worn by the Swan dismissed to futile things.

The fine suicide fled victoriously
blaze of fame, blood in foam, gold, storm and stress!
If, below, regal purple is to dress
only my absent tomb, what mockery!

What! out of all that brilliance not one shred
stays, in the dark that fêtes us (it's dead night)
except the arrogant treasure of a head
sheds its caressed nonchalance with no light,

yours yes a constant pleasure! yours alone
retaining from the heavens that have gone
a trace of childish triumph for your crown

of light when on the pillows you lay it prone
like some child-empress's war-morion
that in your likeness showers roses down.

Ses purs ongles très haut dédiant leur onyx,
L'Angoisse ce minuit, soutient, lampadophore
Maint rêve vespéral brûlé par le Phénix
Que ne recueille pas de cinéraire amphore

Sur les crédences, au salon vide: nul ptyx,   5
Aboli bibelot d'inanité sonore,
(Car le Maître est allé puiser des pleurs au Styx
Avec ce seul objet dont le Néant s'honore).

Mais proche la croisée au nord vacante, un or
Agonise selon peut-être le décor   10
Des licornes ruant du feu contre une nixe,

Elle, défunte nue en le miroir encor
Que dans l'oubli fermé par le cadre se fixe
De scintillations sitôt le septuor.

Le Tombeau d'Edgar Poe

Tel qu'en Lui-même enfin l'éternité le change,
Le Poëte suscite avec un glaive nu
Son siècle épouvanté de n'avoir pas connu
Que la mort triomphait dans cette voix étrange!

Eux, comme un vil sursaut d'hydre oyant jadis l'ange   5
Donner un sens plus pur aux mots de la tribu
Proclamèrent très haut le sortilège bu
Dans le flot sans honneur de quelque noir mélange.

Du sol et de la nue hostiles, ô grief!
Si notre idée avec ne sculpte un bas-relief   10
Dont la tombe de Poe éblouissante s'orne

With her pure nails offering their onyx high,
lampbearer Agony tonight sustains
many a vesperal fantasy burned by
the Phoenix, which no funerary urn contains

on the empty room's credences: no ptyx,
abolished bauble, sonorous inanity
(Master has gone to draw tears from the Styx
with that one thing, the Void's sole source of vanity).

Yet near the vacant northward casement dies
a gold possibly from the decorations
of unicorns lashing a nymph with flame;

dead, naked in the looking-glass she lies
though the oblivion bounded by that frame
now spans a fixed septet of scintillations.

The Tomb of Edgar Allan Poe

Changed to Himself at last by eternity,
with a bare sword the Poet has bestirred
his age terrified that it failed to see
how death was glorying in that strange word.

The spell was drunk, so they proclaimed aloud
(as vile freaks writhe when seraphim bestow
purer sense on the phrases of the crowd),
in some black brew's dishonourable flow.

If our idea can carve no bas-relief
from hostile clod and cloud, O struggling grief,
for the adornment of Poe's dazzling tomb,

Calme bloc ici-bas chu d'un désastre obscur
Que ce granit du moins montre à jamais sa borne
Aux noirs vols du Blasphème épars dans le futur.

Le Tombeau de Charles Baudelaire

Le temple enseveli divulgue par la bouche
Sépulcrale d'égout bavant boue et rubis
Abominablement quelque idole Anubis
Tout le museau flambé comme un aboi farouche

Ou que le gaz récent torde la mèche louche   5
Essuyeuse on le sait des opprobres subis
Il allume hagard un immortel pubis
Dont le vol selon le réverbère découche

Quel feuillage séché dans les cités sans soir
Votif pourra bénir comme elle se rasseoir   10
Contre le marbre vainement de Baudelaire

Au voile qui la ceint absente avec frissons
Celle son Ombre même un poison tutélaire
Toujours à respirer si nous en périssons.

Tombeau

Anniversaire—Janvier 1897

Le noir roc courroucé que la bise le roule
Ne s'arrêtera ni sous de pieuses mains
Tâtant sa ressemblance avec les maux humains
Comme pour en bénir quelque funeste moule.

Ici presque toujours si le ramier roucoule   5
Cet immatériel deuil opprime de maints
Nubiles plis l'astre mûri des lendemains
Dont un scintillement argentera la foule.

at least this block dropped by an occult doom,
this calm granite, may limit all the glum
Blasphemy-flights dispersed in days to come.

The Tomb of Charles Baudelaire

The buried shrine disgorges through its foul
sepulchral sewer-mouth slobbering sod
and ruby vilely some Anubis-god
its muzzle blazing like a savage howl

or when new gas wrings the wicks that erase
shiftily insults suffered (as we know)
it lights eternal loins with a wild glow
whose flight beds out according to its rays

What foliage dried in any nightless town
could consecrate as she can do and sit
against the marble of Baudelaire in vain,

departed from the veils that form her gown
with shimmers—she, his Shade, a guardian bane
to breathe forever though we die of it.

Tomb

Anniversary—January 1897

The black rock, cross (how the north wind has rolled
it on!) won't stop even by pious throngs
handling its parity with human wrongs
as if that consecrates some fatal mould.

Here almost always if the dove has cooed,
with nubile folds its immaterial sorrow
oppresses the ripe star of that tomorrow
whose glint will silver all the multitude.

Qui cherche, parcourant le solitaire bond
Tantôt extérieur de notre vagabond—
Verlaine? Il est caché parmi l'herbe, Verlaine

A ne surprendre que naïvement d'accord
La lèvre sans y boire ou tarir son haleine
Un peu profond ruisseau calomnié la mort.

Who, following our vagabond's withdrawn
leap (once external) still desires to see
Verlaine? Verlaine is hidden in the lawn

to catch no more than in plain harmony
before the lip drank there or spent its breath
a much-maligned and shallow trickle, death.

EXPLANATORY NOTES

Notes below are keyed to line numbers (shown in the margin).

ALPHONSE DE LAMARTINE

From *Poetic Meditations* (1820)

Isolation

Written 22–4 August 1818.

11 *chariot of the queen of night*: the moon.

38 *the true Sun*: God, the *verus sol* of the Roman breviary and 'the Sun of righteousness' of Malachi 4: 2, as distinct from the material sun of lines 29 ff. But this explanation makes definite what the poem deliberately keeps indefinite, a 'dim object' (l. 46) that 'never can be named on this world's shore' (l. 44).

The Valley

Written August–October 1819.

26 *Lethe*: in Greek mythology, a river in the underworld; those who drank its water forgot their past lives.

55 *Pythagoras*: the maxim 'Revere the echo in the storm', attributed to Pythagoras, has been very variously interpreted. In this poem, the echo is evidently that of the 'celestial harmony' (l. 56), the 'music of the spheres' which (Pythagoreans taught) emanated from the motions of the celestial bodies but was scarcely, if at all, perceptible to mortal ears.

59 *the mysterious star*: the moon.

The Lake

Written September 1817. In the manuscript the lake is identified as the Lac du Bourget at Aix-les-Bains, where Lamartine had vainly waited for Julie Charles to join him the previous month (see Introduction, p. xiii).

Autumn

Written October–December 1819.

From *Poetic and Religious Harmonies* (1830)

The West

Date of writing unknown, but evidently during the 1820s.

40 *all must blend!...*: the dots are Lamartine's concluding punctuation-marks, not indications of an omission or ellipsis.

The Infinite in the Skies
Written June 1828.

11 *Ether*: the tenuous fluid believed by nineteenth-century astronomers to exist in interstellar and interplanetary space.

65 *suns*: the stars.

67 *Symbols*: the letters and numerals assigned by astronomers to the stars of the constellations.

69 *convicting their vain alphabet*: demonstrating the inadequacy of the alphabet, since its symbols are too few to designate more than a small minority of the stars.

74 *Job*: Job 9: 9 and 38: 31 are commonly believed to refer to the constellation of Orion.

75–81 *The ship . . . and goat*: the constellations of Argo (now Carina, Vela, and Puppis), Bootes, Lyra, Cygnus, Pegasus, Libra, Coma Berenices, Aquila, Sagittarius, Aries, Taurus, and Capricornus.

97 *the crystal that brings worlds nearby*: the telescope.

103 *drifting gleams*: specks of dust illuminated in a shaft of sunlight.

111 *the gleams*: the Milky Way, which, in Greek legend, sprang from the breast of the goddess Hera when she was suckling the infant Herakles.

129 *his compass-burdened hand*: the astronomer's hand is burdened by the very compasses he uses to chart the orbits of the heavenly bodies.

From *Further Poetic Meditations* (1849)

The Lizard
Probably written in 1846. The incident is fictitious: there are no surviving bronze inscriptions in the Colosseum.

1 *the Colosseum*: the Flavian Amphitheatre in Rome, built mainly during the reigns of the emperors Vespasian and Titus as an arena for public games and gladiatorial contests.

4 *Tacitus*: the *Histories* and *Annals* of Tacitus, written at the beginning of the second century CE, are severely critical of the Roman emperors from Tiberius to Domitian.

15 *the Augustus*: the emperor; from the first century CE onwards, all Roman emperors adopted the title 'Augustus'.

VICTOR HUGO

From *Orientalia* (1829)

The Djinns

Written 28 August 1828. Hugo's own note to the *Orientalia* defines 'djinn' as a 'nocturnal spirit, genie'.

From *The Empire in the Pillory* (1853)

On 2 December 1851 Louis Napoleon (1808–73), the nephew of Napoleon I, seized power in a *coup d'état* that cost at least several hundred lives; he assumed the title of Emperor Napoleon III.

Hugo had more trouble finding a title for this book than for any of his others. His ultimate choice—*Les Châtiments*—has no real English counterpart; neither 'castigations' nor 'chastisements' carries the appropriate moral weight. We have therefore chosen to translate a title he had previously favoured: *L'Empire au pilori*.

That Night

Written 17 January 1853. The night in question is that of 1–2 December 1851, when the coup was carried out.

1 *the Élysée*: Louis Napoleon's official residence.

6 *Bill Sikes's trade*: in the original the name is that of the famous French thief and murderer Cartouche (executed in 1721).

10 *Bartholomew Massacres*: on Bartholomew's Day, 24 August 1572, a massacre of Protestants was carried out in Paris under the authority of Charles IX.

19 *the house of ill repute*: Hugo refers specifically to the maison Bancal, a brothel where a notorious murder had occurred in 1817.

20 *Maupas . . . Saint-Arnaud, Morny*: three of Napoleon III's closest associates in planning the *coup d'état*. Leroy de Saint-Arnaud (1798–1854) was minister of war at the time; Charlemagne-Émile de Maupas (1818–88) was prefect of police. (The word *grec* is applied to him here, not in the sense of 'Greek'—he had no Greek ancestry—but in the sense of 'cheat, trickster'.) Charles-Auguste-Louis-Joseph, ultimately Duc de Morny (1811–65), was Napoleon III's illegitimate half-brother.

31 *Reibell's and Sauboul's rowdies*: Reibell and Sauboul were army officers involved in the coup; the former was one of those responsible for the massacre on the night of 4 December 1851 (see the next poem).

32 *Byzantium*: Istanbul, capital of the 'barbaric' Ottoman Empire whose soldiers might more readily have been expected to be corrupted by money and drink.

33 *Korte, Dulac, and Espinasse*: prominent army officers involved in the coup.

43 *Brigandier-generals*: not a typographical error but a Hugolian distortion of 'brigadier-generals'.

45 *Monvoisin . . . Desrues*: notorious poisoners, executed in 1680 and 1777 respectively.

The Night of the Fourth: A Recollection

Written 2 December 1852. On the night of 4 December 1851, a couple of days after Napoleon III's *coup d'état*, his troops fired at random on bystanders in various Paris streets.

50 *his true name*: unlike his claim to be a Bonaparte (l. 34), which was doubted because of his mother's infidelities.

56 *Saint-Cloud*: one of Napoleon III's official residences.

Set Him Apart!

Written 14 November 1852. Hugo's Latin title associates his attitude with the ancient principle of 'setting apart' a notorious evildoer (as in the case of Cain).

12 *Pompey- or Caesar-style*: the Roman triumvir Pompey the Great was beheaded; his arch-rival Julius Caesar was stabbed to death.

21 *his ceremonial stole*: Napoleon III's imperial robe, a favourite target for Hugo's irony.

23 *The Boulevard Montmartre*: one of the places where the heaviest civilian casualties occurred on the night of 4 December 1851.

31 *the fratricide, the parricide*: in killing his fellow countrymen, Napoleon III is killing his brothers; this prepares for his identification with the world's first fratricide, Cain, at the end of the poem.

47 *a mark*: 'the Lord set a mark upon Cain, lest any finding him should kill him' after his murder of his brother Abel (Genesis 4: 15).

'Sound, sound forever...'

Written 19 March 1853. The account of Joshua leading the Israelites around the walls of Jericho follows Joshua 6: 1–20; the inhabitants' reactions are Hugo's inventions.

12 *Aaron*: the first high-priest of Israel; the priests carrying the ark are thus 'Aaron's race'.

From *Contemplations* (1856)

On 4 September 1843 Hugo's 19-year-old daughter Léopoldine and her husband were drowned in a boating accident at Villequier.

'Tomorrow, when the meadows grow...'

Written 4 October 1847. The poem describes a walk from Le Havre (where Hugo was then living) to Léopoldine's grave at Villequier.

4 *mountain-pass*: the ruggedness of the local terrain is heightened for the purposes of the poem.

At Villequier

Written 24 October 1846; ll. 105–12 were inserted eight or nine years later.

Shepherds and Flocks

Written 17 October 1854.

13 *like old Homer*: a new variation on the familiar saying 'even the good Homer nods' (from Horace, *Art of Poetry*, 259).

The Bridge

Written 13 October 1854.

At the Window in the Dark

Written 29 August 1854.

22 *Aldebaran*: first-magnitude star in the constellation of Taurus.

29 *Septentrion*: the seven principal stars of Ursa Major, the Great Bear.

32 *Hesperus*: the 'evening star', the planet Venus.

From *The Legend of the Ages* (1859–83)

This selection follows the text and numbering of the 1883 'definitive edition'; all the chosen poems were originally published in the First Series (1859).

Conscience

Written 29 January 1853. Hugo envisages Cain, at the time when he murdered his brother Abel, as already an old man surrounded by generations of descendants: Jabal, Zillah, Jubal, Enoch, Tubal-cain.

19 *Asshur*: Assyria.

47 *Enosh . . . Seth*: Cain's younger brother and nephew. As Cain did to his relative, so his descendants do to theirs; compare the description of Napoleon III as a 'fratricide' ('Set Him Apart!', l. 31).

Boaz Asleep

Written 1 May 1859.

11 *gleaning-woman*: such as Ruth herself (Ruth 2: 3–7, 15–16).

33 *Jacob*: whose dream of angels ascending and descending (Genesis 28: 12) suggests Boaz's dream here.

Judith: presumably added simply for the sonority.

40 *A king*: David the psalmist, great-grandson of Boaz and Ruth.

40 *a god*: Jesus Christ, descended from David.

61 *a Moabite*: therefore expected to be an enemy of Israel and a worshipper of false gods.

81 *Ur*: in Chaldaea.

Jerimadeth: either a characteristically Hugolian spelling of Jarmuth/ Jerimoth in Judah (contaminated by 'Judith'—the word that most recently came into his head when he needed a name for a rhyme), or else an invention for the rhyme (the spelling alone being modelled on that of 'Jerimoth'): a subtle distinction, but one that still causes heated debates and dogmatic assertions!

The Inquisition: Momotombo's Reasons

Written 6 February 1859. The epigraph is drawn from E. G. Squier, *Travels in Central America, Particularly in Nicaragua* (New York, 1853).

41 *Torquemada*: Tomás de Torquemada (1420–98), Spanish grand inquisitor, under whom thousands of executions for heresy were carried out.

43 *Holy Office*: tribunal of the Spanish Inquisition.

45 *Lima*: capital of Peru.

After the Battle

Written 18 June 1850. Hugo's father had fought in the Napoleonic army in Spain in 1809.

The Trumpet of Judgement

Written 15 May 1859; the final poem in the 'First Series' of the *Legend* (1859).

107 *larvae*: in Hugo, 'ghosts' (the word's Latin meaning), with a suggestion of 'embryos'.

163 *Epicurus*: Greek hedonistic philosopher of the third century BCE.

From *The Art of Being a Grandfather* (1877)

Hugo's son Charles died in 1871; the poet was legal guardian of Charles's two children, Georges (born 1868) and Jeanne (born 1869), from that time until their mother's remarriage in 1877.

Open Windows

Written 18 July, year unspecified (probably either 1870 or 1873). The setting is the island of Guernsey.

More About God (But With Some Reservations)

Written soon after 12 September 1875.

1 *Such a splendid place*: the zoo.

6 *Viennet*: Jean-Pons-Guillaume Viennet (1779–1868), a poet who clung determinedly to eighteenth-century tastes throughout the Romantic period.

23 *Réaumur*: René-Antoine Ferchault de Réaumur (1683–1757), an outstanding natural scientist.

34 *Gongorism*: stylistic extravagance of the kind associated with the Spanish Baroque poet Luis de Góngora (1561–1627).

40 *the Academy*: the Académie française, composed mainly of eminent literary figures. Lamartine and Hugo were members of it; Baudelaire and Verlaine sought membership but were not elected.

44 *Polonius's saws and Ockham's razors*: in the original French the ill-assorted weapon-wielders are Charles Batteux (1713–80), a classicizing literary critic, and Gaston, Marquis de Galliffet (1830–1903), a prominent army officer under Napoleon III.

59 *Planche*: Gustave Planche (1808–57), literary critic, one of the most savage opponents of French Romanticism.

70 *Nonotte . . . Baculard*: Claude-François Nonotte (1711–93) and François-Thomas-Marie de Baculard d'Arnaud (1718–1805), representative literary conservatives; the Café Procope was a favourite haunt of eighteenth- and nineteenth-century Parisian writers.

'Jeanne was holed up...'

Written 21 October 1876.

1 *Jeanne*: Hugo's granddaughter.

The Broken Vase

Written 4 April 1877.

9 *Mariette*: one of the household servants.

From *The Threshold of the Abyss* (1891)

Written February–June 1856 as the prologue to Hugo's long poem *Dieu* (*God*), though in his final notes on the subject (MSS 106/2[a] and 106/171[h]) he allowed that the two works could, if necessary, stand on their own. *God*, including the prologue, was eventually published posthumously by Hugo's literary executor Paul Meurice.

'I could see...'

This opening section was left untitled by Hugo. Paul Meurice named it after the 'Human Spirit' who appears in early drafts of the opening lines; however, Hugo ultimately decided to delete all mention of this 'Spirit' (see the note to ll. 1–38 below), so Meurice's title cannot be used for an edition of the section's final state.

1 *I could see . . .*: the opening line of the poem; it begins with the (unnamed) speaker already in mid-flight.

1–38 *I could see . . . the fleeing winter*: the initial draft of this passage was much longer (250 lines) and explicitly identified the 'very quiet voice' as that of 'the Human Spirit', the spirit of compromise and mediocrity opposed to all extremes. Hugo soon became dissatisfied with this, and abridged the passage to make it more mysterious and 'less specific' (MS 106/82[a]), cutting it down first to 172 lines, then to 38. His last known preference was for the 38-line form.

40–65 *I could see . . . temples of Shem's sons*: the speaker sees a bewilderingly diverse array of places with religious or superstitious associations, giving a sense of immense vistas that recede from the well-known through the half-known to the completely unknown. Thorough annotation would bring all the place-names, alike and equally, into full view, and would spoil the receding-vistas effect (on the rare occasions when Hugo wanted his readers to know the significance of an unfamiliar name—e.g. 'djinn' in the *Orientalia*—he supplied the information himself). In the following notes, brief identifying data will be supplied, so that anyone who wishes to pursue a particular name further may do so; but for most purposes a reader will do better to respond to the poem's half-lights and obscurities as they stand, ignoring editorial 'elucidations'.

45 *Hebron*: where God appeared to Abraham.

Medina, Mecca: sacred sites of Islam.

Thebes: a centre of ancient Egyptian religion.

47 *Jerome*: fourth-century theologian, who spent many years in a monastery at Bethlehem.

50 *Nineveh*: capital of Assyria.

Delphi: site of the oracle of Apollo.

Ephesus: centre of the cult of 'Artemis of the Ephesians'.

51 *Abdera*: home of the Greek philosophers Democritus and Protagoras.

Gregory: the Illuminator, reputed to have brought the message of Christ to Armenia.

55 *Aglaura's temple*: at Athens.

57 *Calvin's cave . . . Luther's chamber*: according to legend, John Calvin celebrated the Lord's Supper in a cave, and Martin Luther confronted the Devil in his chamber.

59 *Scylla*: transformed into a dog-like monster who snatched sailors from passing ships (*Odyssey*, xii. 73–100).

61 *Dodona*: site of sacred oaks in ancient Greece.

Horeb: Mount Sinai, where Moses received the law.

62 *Echmiadzin*: Armenian religious centre.

63 *cruach*: tumulus.

cromlech: circle of megaliths.

64 *Paestum*: ancient Roman resort, famous for its rose-gardens.

65 *Ham . . . Shem*: sons of Noah; respectively, ancestors of (mainly) North

African and Semitic peoples; to obtain a rhyme, the French has Seth (really a son of Adam) for Shem.

73 *Solomon*: used cedar from Lebanon to build the temple in Jerusalem.

74 *Teutates*: god worshipped in ancient Gaul, according to Lucan.

77 *Ombos*: sacred city of ancient Egypt.

85 *Minerva*: Greek goddess of wisdom; the epithet 'Apteros' ('wingless'), not elsewhere applied to her, no doubt alludes in this flight-filled poem to the limits of her wisdom.

89 *Apollonius*: of Tyana, Pythagorean philosopher of the first century CE.

91 *epopts*: initiates into the ancient Greek mysteries.

92 *eubages*: priests in ancient Gaul.

Circumcelliones: members of a fourth-century Donatist sect, said to have committed suicide in their desire for martyrdom.

97 *cavern*: the tomb of the Egyptian pharaoh Seti I, ascribed by the explorer Belzoni to King Psammetichus.

98 *Scotus Erigena*: ninth-century Scholastic philosopher.

99 *Rhipsima*: legendary fourth-century martyr.

Bruno: eleventh-century monk, founder of the Carthusian order.

Francis of Assisi: twelfth-century monk, founder of the Franciscan order.

102 *Cypselus*: seventh-century BCE ruler of Corinth, sometimes listed as one of the Seven Sages of ancient Greece.

106 *Mount Nebo*: from which Moses viewed the promised land of Canaan before his death.

110 *Ellora*: sacred caves in India.

Meru: in Indian legend, sacred mountain of precious stones.

115 *Sphaerus*: Stoic philosopher of the third century BCE.

119 *David, Ethan . . . Jeduthun*: authors of psalms in the Hebrew Scriptures.

120 *John*: author of the book of Revelation, which contains visions of the four cherubim.

121 *Dante*: Italian poet (1265–1321), who described the underworld ('Avernus') in his *Inferno*.

132 *Pythoness*: in the Classical world, a pagan soothsayer or priestess.

Canistro: in Macedonia.

133 *Syrinx-nooks*: the tombs of the pharaohs in the Valley of the Kings.

134 *satrap*: governor of a province of the Persian empire.

138 *Merlin*: presumably the sorcerer of Arthurian legend, not elsewhere associated with carbuncles.

139 *Job*: sufferer and questioner of the ways of God, central character of the book of Job.

Jerome: see note to l. 47.

140 *any daylight*: this line was originally followed by the passage that later became 'After the Voices', ll. 1–12.

173 *Aristophanes*: ancient Greek comic dramatist, often cited by Hugo as a typical exponent of scepticism.

176 *Diderot*: Denis Diderot (1713–84), French rationalist writer.

177 *Jeremiah*: ancient Hebrew prophet.

189 *Yet gradually the darkness*: the rhyme-scheme shows that there was meant to be at least one further line between ll. 188 and 189, but it was never written.

Another Voice ('Well, first of all...')

The opening section is followed immediately by a series of 'Voices' warning the narrator of the difficulties involved in his quest for God; Hugo drafted speeches for many such Voices, finally selecting twelve (one of which is now lost) for inclusion in the poem. The present Voice is the seventh of the series (numbered 'Voix VI' by Journet and Robert).

4 *Inside a triangle*: God has often been depicted as an eye within a triangle.

9 *Arius . . . Huss*: opponents of Catholic orthodoxy as affirmed at the Councils of Nicaea (325 CE) and Constance (1414–18) respectively.

13 *Galileo*: the astronomer Galileo Galilei (1564–1642), imprisoned by the Roman Catholic Church as a heretic for upholding the Copernican view of the universe.

14 *De Maistre*: Joseph de Maistre (1753–1821), extreme right-wing royalist and staunch advocate of Roman Catholicism.

34 *Bossuet*: Jacques Bénigne Bossuet (1627–1704), bishop and orator popular at the court of Louis XIV, where one of the royal mistresses was Madame de Montespan.

38 *Bridaine . . . Massillon*: representative eighteenth-century French preachers.

41–2 *giving up . . . Paris*: 'Paris is worth a Mass' was supposed to be Henri IV's explanation for his conversion to Roman Catholicism on becoming king of France in 1589.

44 *Sanchez*: Tomás Sanchez (1550–1610), Jesuit writer criticized by the Jansenist scientist and philosopher Blaise Pascal (1623–62).

47 *Notre-Dame and Quincampoix*: Parisian cathedral, and Parisian street where John Law's famous bank had been set up in 1716; thus, religious respectability and financial success.

50 *La Ramée*: Pierre La Ramée, Protestant philosopher killed in the Bartholomew's Day Massacre of 1572.

51 *Edicts of Toleration*: the Edict of Nantes, which gave French Protestants some religious freedom, was formally revoked in 1685.

82 *Colleoni*: Bartolomeo Colleoni (1401–75), Italian professional soldier noted especially for his deployment of field artillery.

100 *Gabar*: usually Zoroastrian, though Hugo extends the term to include other ancient religions of the Middle East.

102 *La Barre*: Jean-François Le Febvre, chevalier de La Barre (1747–66), executed for alleged sacrilege—an event vigorously denounced by Voltaire.

106 *a non-man*: castrati continued to be employed as singers in the Sistine Chapel at Rome throughout the nineteenth century.

115–16 *Locke . . . Grimm . . . Holbach*: John Locke (1632–1704), empiricist philosopher and believer in a God accessible to human reason; Friedrich Melchior, Baron Grimm (1723–1807), and Paul Heinrich Dietrich, Baron d'Holbach (1723–89), representative eighteenth-century sceptics.

130 *Amon*: a principal god in ancient Egypt.

Juggernaut: religious centre in India.

131 *Delphi*: site of the oracle of Apollo.

Suleimaniye: mosque at Constantinople.

140 *Brahma*: Hindu god.

151 *Diogenes*: Cynic philosopher of the fourth-century BCE, said to have conducted a fruitless search for 'an honest man'.

Another Voice ('You think yourself, perhaps...')

The tenth of the Voices (numbered 'Voix IX' by Journet and Robert).

8 *larva*: 'ghost' as well as 'embryo' (see the note on 'The Trumpet of Judgement', l. 107).

21 *Bridge of Saint-Cloud*: nets were hung in the River Seine at this point, to retrieve the bodies of those who had drowned themselves further upstream.

After the Voices

This section of the poem exists in a less finished form than any other, and would no doubt have been significantly revised if Hugo had prepared it for publication; but it is unlikely that drastic changes would have been made (Hugo made no major change to any part of *God* after 1856).

1–64 *I waited . . . and I died*: Hugo left several overlapping drafts of this narrative: ll. 1–12 on MS 106/126[c] (originally drafted as part of the poem's opening section, but later marked for excision and placement 'after the voices'); ll. 6–28 on 106/131[c]; ll. 19–64 in an 1856 notebook; and ll. 29–64 on 106/99[a]. Paul Meurice, the first editor of *God*, failed to note the overlaps on 106/131[c] and therefore mistakenly placed ll. 19–64 as a separate narrative at a different point in the poem.

13 *A third time*: the two earlier bursts of laughter were in the opening section of the poem ('I could see . . .', ll. 26 and 141). At one stage Hugo toyed with the idea of deleting 'I could see . . .', ll. 141–46 (so that the present line would have read 'A second time'); however, he later overruled this proposed deletion.

65–87 *In the mute alien . . . Night's hand*: after l. 64, MS 106/99[a] contains a marginal note: '(then the awakening) After death.' The only surviving draft of this awakening scene in Hugo's papers is 106/112[c], which is therefore placed at this point as ll. 65–87. The rhyme-scheme shows that there were meant to be one or more additional lines before l. 65 and after l. 87, but they were probably never written.

81 *larva*: 'ghost' as well as 'embryo' (see the note on 'The Trumpet of Judgement', l. 107).

88 *Spirit . . . I still know nothing*: the final line of verse on MS 106/99[a], after the awakening scene; apparently the climax—the punchline—of 'The Threshold of the Abyss'. (Immediately after it, 106/99[a] contains a marginal note summarizing the drift of the remaining sections of *God*: 'God is the infinite. He recedes endlessly—no transformation of life catches up with him—One merely goes forward in the light.' In those sections the narrator, continuing to ascend the heavens, encounters an infinite series of winged creatures, who proclaim an infinitely receding series of concepts of God.)

CHARLES BAUDELAIRE

From *The Flowers of Evil* (1857–61)

This selection follows the text and numbering of the second (1861) edition, but unless otherwise specified, all the chosen poems had already appeared in 1857. Dates of composition are noted wherever known.

To the Reader

The unnumbered preliminary poem of *The Flowers of Evil* in both editions. The theme is traditional ('Satan . . . deceiveth the whole world', Revelation 12: 9), though the treatment is strikingly new.

10 *Satan Thrice-Great*: Hermes the Egyptian, known as Trismegistus ('Thrice-Great'), was the legendary author of occult ('hermetic') literature. He was said to know the secrets of alchemy, but the real Satan's powers are alchemy in reverse: he turns gold into dross, and so 'lulls our captive soul'.

37 *Ennui*: more intense than the English 'boredom'; see the note on 'Spleen [I]', below.

38 *his water-pipe*: an Indian hookah, in vogue in mid-nineteenth-century Paris.

The Albatross

Probably written by 1842 (apart from ll. 9–12, inserted in 1859), but added to *The Flowers of Evil* only in the second edition (1861).

Head of Hair

Added to *The Flowers of Evil* for the second edition (1861).

Sed non satiata

Probably written by 1843. The title comes from Juvenal, *Satires*, vi. 130, where the Roman empress Messalina is described as coming home 'worn out with men but not satiated' after her sexual excesses.

3 *Faust*: legendary medieval magician who sold his soul to the Devil.

11 *the Styx*: in Greek mythology a river of the underworld, encircling the realm of the dead nine times; there is also a reminiscence of Ovid, *Amores*, III. vii. 26, where the speaker says that he supplied his mistress with 'nine bouts in one short night'.

12 *Megaera*: one of the Furies inhabiting the underworld (and therefore within the realm of Persephone); in French 'a Megaera' is a shrewish woman.

14 *Persephone*: queen of the underworld, where she lived during the colder half of each year; associated, because of her return to earth every spring, with the perennially renewed sexual fertility that this poem's speaker lacks.

A Carcass

Probably written by 1843.

The Harmony of Evening

37 *a monstrance*: in Roman Catholic usage, a vessel for displaying holy relics.

Autumn Song

Written 1859, added to *The Flowers of Evil* for the second edition (1861).

The Cracked Bell

Written by 1851; originally entitled 'Spleen'.

Spleen [I]

Written by 1851. By 'spleen' Baudelaire means a kind of intensified ennui—in James McGowan's words, 'a soul-deadening spiritual condition' that would 'drag man down towards the abyss'.

1 *Pluvius*: the Roman god of rain (Jupiter Pluvius), whose name was adopted in the French Revolutionary calendar (between 1792 and 1805) for the month from 21 January to 19 February.

Spleen [II]

13 *Bouchers*: François Boucher (1703–70), French rococo painter.

22 *An ancient sphinx*: the image is adapted from the statue of Memnon (Amenhotep III), which resonated with a 'singing' note at sunrise; but Baudelaire has made the statue more enigmatic (a sphinx) and the time of day gloomier (sunset).

Spleen [III]

15 *baths of blood*: the Romans believed that a bath of blood had rejuvenating properties.

19 *Lethe*: see note to Lamartine's 'The Valley', p. 295 above.

The Swan

Written 1859; added to *The Flowers of Evil* for the second edition (1861). The poem was dedicated to Hugo and carries a political subtext: the sympathetic treatment of Andromache, the expression of solidarity with 'captives, the defeated . . . many others more' (l. 52), and the statement that 'Paris may change, but in my melancholy mood | Nothing has budged' (ll. 29–30), all align the speaker with Napoleon III's opponents.

1 *Andromache*: after the fall of Troy Andromache, the widow of the Trojan warrior Hector, was assigned to the Greek leader Pyrrhus (Neoptolemus) and was taken by him into exile in Epirus; after having several children by her, Pyrrhus passed her on to his Trojan slave Helenus. Baudelaire is specifically recalling the account of this story in Virgil, *Aeneid*, iii. 294–505, where Andromache is shown presiding with Helenus over a new, lesser Troy in the land of her exile, and honouring the memory of Hector at an empty tomb.

4 *This fraudulent Simois*: the 'fictitious Simois' (Baudelaire characteristically intensifies the adjective) in the land of Andromache's exile was a stream named after the true River Simois of Troy (Virgil, *Aeneid*, iii. 302).

6 *the modern Carrousel*: the Carrousel in Paris, formerly an area of old lanes, underwent drastic clearance operations as part of Napoleon III's building programme from 1852 onwards; hence the workers' 'busy camp of huts' (l. 9) visible on the site.

26 *the man in Ovid's book*: 'man was made to hold his head | Erect in majesty and see the sky' (Ovid, *Metamorphoses*, i. 4–5, trans. A. B. Melville).

37–40 *Fallen Andromache . . . wife of Helenus*: see note to l. 1.

The Seven Old Men

Written 1859, with the title 'Parisian Ghosts'; added to *The Flowers of Evil* for the second edition (1861). Dedicated, like the previous poem, to Hugo.

The Blind

Added to *The Flowers of Evil* for the second edition (1861).

A Voyage to Cythera

Written some time between 1844 and 1852. The Greek island of Cythera (later known as Cerigo) was sacred in ancient times to the goddess of love, Aphrodite (or Venus). Baudelaire would have had in mind Watteau's famous *Embarkation for Cythera* (painted 1717) in the Louvre, which depicts a sinuous array of pairing lovers in a half-lit landscape; but his acknowledged inspiration was an 1844 tale by Gérard de Nerval, in which a modern visitor to the once-sacred island finds only three corpses hanging on a gallows.

41 *Dweller in Cythera*: the 'Hanged man' (l. 45).

43 *your infamous beliefs*: here, as elsewhere, Baudelaire takes an unambiguously negative view of the worship of Venus, in opposition to Nerval's suggestion that the island might have been cursed 'for having abandoned the good religion'.

Voyaging

Written 1859; added to *The Flowers of Evil* for the second edition (1861). Baudelaire wrote in a letter (20 February 1859) that the poem was 'enough to make Nature—and especially the lovers of progress—shudder'.

12 *Circe*: in *Odyssey*, x. 135 ff., a goddess whose enchantments turned men into swine.

33 *blessed isle*: Icaria in the Aegean Sea, where, in Greek legend, Icarus was buried after his failed attempt to fly.

38 *Eldorado*: the mythical 'city of gold' also mentioned in 'A Voyage to Cythera', l. 7; generally supposed to be somewhere in the Americas (cf. l. 43).

47 *Capua*: an ancient city near Naples, whose pleasures distracted Hannibal's army from proceeding towards Rome.

104 *my image*: Humanity, becoming 'Drunk on her genius', sees in God nothing more than a likeness of herself.

117 *the Wandering Jew*: in medieval legend, a man who mocked Jesus on his way to the crucifixion and was therefore condemned to roam the world till the day of judgement.

129 *eat the Lotus*: as l. 132 shows, Baudelaire is recalling Tennyson's 1832 poem 'The Lotos-Eaters'; those who eat the Lotos lose all interest in further 'roaming' and inhabit 'a land | In which it seemed always afternoon'.

134–5 *Pylades . . . Electra*: in Greek mythology Pylades, the devoted friend of the guilt-ridden murderer Orestes, was rewarded by being given Orestes' sister Electra in marriage.

PAUL VERLAINE

From *Saturnian Poems* (1867)

Verlaine's first volume; 'Autumn Song', its most famous poem, was probably written in 1864.

From *Fun and Games* (1869)

The French title *Fêtes galantes*, which has no precise English equivalent, is evocative of eighteenth-century aristocratic parties with a frivolous or mildly amorous atmosphere ('On the Grass' would be representative); the paintings of Watteau as seen, somewhat nostalgically and sentimentally, through the eyes of the nineteenth century.

On the Grass

The speakers are two couples—a stereotypically featherbrained marquis and a dancer (Camargo), a stereotypically crafty abbé and (at least when intoxicated!) a singer.

   4 *Camargo*: the historical Camargo (1710–70) was a dancer at the Paris Opera.

   10 *shepherdesses*: lovers, in the conventional language of eighteenth-century pastoral.

Weird as Puppets

The characters are taken from the Italian *commedia dell'arte*, very popular in eighteenth-century France.

   1 *Scaramouche and Pulcinella*: in the *commedia dell'arte* both are characteristically braggarts and intriguers.

   5 *Doctor*: usually named Balanzone Lombardi; pedantic and gullible.

   7 *His daughter*: the crafty soubrette Colombine, usually in love with Harlequin.

Colombine

The characters are again figures of the Italian *commedia dell'arte*, embroiled in a typical plot with the soubrette Colombine at its centre.

From *Songs Without Words* (1874)

'It's languor and ecstasy'

As with most of the *Songs Without Words*, the person addressed is deliberately left vague and is never identified. The epigraph comes from a 'forgotten arietta' by the librettist Charles-Simon Favart (1710–92): Verlaine has not lost his interest in the byways of the eighteenth century.

'Falling tears...'

The epigraph does not come from any of Rimbaud's surviving works: part of a lost poem, or a remark made casually in conversation?

'You see, we have to be forgiven...'

Again the person addressed is left too vague for identification: his wife Mathilde? his friend Rimbaud? The transposition of a male–female or male–male relationship into a female–female one is characteristic of Verlaine.

'The piano kissed...'

Pétrus Borel (1809–59) was one of Verlaine's favourite poets.

Brussels: Simple Frescos II

Dated 'The Jeune Richard Estaminet, August 1872' in *Romances sans paroles*.

  9 *the Royers-Collards*: the French statesman Pierre-Paul Royer-Collard (1763–1845) was seen by Verlaine as a quintessential enemy of poetry.

Malines

Dated 'August 1872' in *Romances sans paroles*. Malines, or Mechelen, is a town in Belgium.

  20 *Fénelon*: François de Salignac de la Mothe-Fénelon (1651–1715), refined author, lover of nature, and advocate of self-obliteration before the Divine Presence.

Green

Verlaine presumably intended his English title to carry some of its English connotations: greenery, innocence, inexperience.

Spleen

See the note on Baudelaire's 'Spleen [1]' (p. 307 above).

Streets I

Annotated 'Soho' in *Romances sans paroles*. In a letter of September 1872 Verlaine noted the popularity of public jig-dancing in nineteenth-century London.

Streets II

Annotated 'Paddington' (Regent's Canal) in *Romances sans paroles*.

Beams

Annotated 'Dover–Ostend, aboard the *Countess of Flanders*, 4 April 1873' in *Romances sans paroles*. One of Verlaine's most-debated pieces; critics have shown an amusing desire to 'identify' the girl (suggestions range from Christ to Rimbaud!), but surely her utter intangibility is an integral part of the poem's sense.

From *Wisdom* (1880)

'Beauty of women...'

Written September 1875—'after immense temptation', Verlaine later recalled.

'The humble life...'

Written 1875.

'Voice of Pride...'

Probably written in summer 1875.

  27 *the strong Word*: with an allusion to Christ, the Word of God.

'Hope like a wisp of straw...'

Written in prison, September 1873. The poem leaves both its setting and its characters indistinct and not precisely identifiable; as in the case of 'Beams', critics have frequently attempted to impose more specificity on it than Verlaine supplies.

'Peaceful eyes my only wealth'

Written in prison, August 1873. The historical Kaspar Hauser was a boy aged about 15, found under mysterious circumstances in Nuremburg in 1828, and (apparently) murdered under equally mysterious circumstances five years later; he was rumoured to be of noble, possibly royal, birth. Verlaine, however, is not writing history (or autobiography); as in *Fêtes galantes*, he is creating a fictitious scenario that raises some issues of interest to him.

'The sky above the roof...'

Written in prison, August–September 1873.

'The sadness, the languor...'

Date of writing uncertain.

'A cold wind...'

Written 1873, probably in September.

'Uneven rows...'

Written 1875 or 1877.

From ~~Once Upon a Time~~ (1884)

The Art of Poetry
Written April 1874 (or earlier?).

From *Love* (1888)

Parsifal

First published January 1886. *Parsifal* (1882) was the last music-drama of Richard Wagner (1813–83).

   1 *Parsifal*: the 'pure fool', who succeeds where his more sinful 'betters' have failed.

   the Maidens: the Flower-maidens, deployed against Parsifal as a sexual temptation in the central phase of the drama.

   5 *Woman*: Kundry, Parsifal's supreme temptress and the ambivalent tool of the forces opposed to Christ in the drama.

   9 *The lance*: the spear that had pierced Christ's side during the crucifixion.

   10 *the King*: Amfortas, king of the Grail Castle, wounded in the groin with

the spear after his seduction by Kundry; Parsifal retrieves the spear, heals Amfortas, and is himself made king.

11 *the holiest of Holy Treasures*: the Holy Grail, which in Wagner's drama is a vessel for the celebration of the Lord's Supper ('real Blood').

14 *those children's voices*: the ethereal boys' choir singing in the dome of the castle, during the Grail scenes of *Parsifal*.

ARTHUR RIMBAUD

Asleep in the Valley

Manuscript date October 1870; no doubt suggested by the Franco-Prussian War.

My Bohemia

Written by October 1870.

7 *at Great Bear Inn*: i.e. outdoors, under the stars.

Lice-Seekers

Date of composition uncertain; some time between September 1870 and early 1872.

Cheated Heart

Three drafts, dating from May, June, and August 1871, survive; the last is printed here. The poem's form (a triolet in eight-syllable lines) was conventionally used for light verse, and contrasts startlingly with its serious, indeed tormented, content, in which soldiers, sexuality, and tobacco are indistinctly glimpsed through a fog of wordplay.

Drunken Boat

Written late summer 1871, shortly before Rimbaud's meeting with Verlaine.

25 *bluities*: a Rimbaldian neologism for 'bluenesses'.

40 *phosphorsongs*: the luminous plankton of the open sea.

43 *Maryfeet*: in Roman Catholic tradition the Virgin Mary is said to have power to calm the seas.

50 *Leviathan*: the great aquatic creature of Job 41: 1–34; often used in the nineteenth century as a term for a huge ship.

58 *Dorados*: so-called dolphin fish (*Coryphaena*); no doubt with a reference also to the mythical land of gold, El Dorado.

71 *protection vessel*: Rimbaud alludes both to the ironclad vessels used during the American Civil War, and to the ships used by the medieval Hanseatic League to protect the Baltic Sea against pirates.

82 *Behemoths*: great aquatic creatures of Job 40: 15–24 (cf. the 'Leviathan' of l. 50).

100 *prison-ships*: old hulks used in the nineteenth century as prisons for criminals and (especially after the Paris Commune of 1871) political prisoners.

Vowels

Written late 1871 or early 1872. There have been many attempts to find logical connections between the letters and the qualities Rimbaud associates with them, but no such connections are embodied in the poem itself.

14 *Omega*: the last letter of the Greek alphabet; God is 'the Alpha and the Omega' (Revelation 1: 8), and the capitalization of 'Those Eyes' here suggests an allusion either to God or to a deified person (the poet himself, or someone else?).

Blackcurrant River

Manuscript date May 1872; the river is not precisely identifiable.

Lovely Morning Thought

Manuscript date May 1872.

6 *golden apple*: an allusion to the golden apples guarded by the Hesperides in Classical mythology.

14 *Babylon King's men*: workers are subjects of the King of Babylon (suggesting both Oriental opulence and tyrannic oppression); lovers are subjects of the Queen of Shepherds.

17 *Queen of Shepherds*: Venus as both evening star (beloved of shepherds) and Queen of Lovers ('shepherd' = 'lover', in eighteenth-century pastoral convention).

18 *eau-de-vie*: (a) brandy; (b) water of life.

20 *in the sea*: where Venus was born.

'O seasons, o châteaux...'

Date of composition uncertain (possibly August 1872); the poem is quoted in *A Season in Hell*. As in the case of 'Cheated Heart', several drafts survive; the latest known state (apart from that cited in the *Season*) is printed here.

7 *Gallic*: (a) pagan, pertaining to the pre-Christian world of ancient Gaul (this is the sense used elsewhere in *A Season in Hell*); (b) adjective derived from the Latin *gallus*, 'cock'.

From *Illuminations*

Dates of composition uncertain, perhaps 1872–5. The title carries not only its usual French sense—'enlightenments', 'flashes of inspiration'—but also (according to Verlaine) the English sense 'coloured illustrations'.

After the Flood

After the Flood (a conceptual flood, an 'idea' of a flood) comes a new world cluttered with the detritus of civilization: Madame ***'s grand piano, the Hotel Splendide, mass, first communions, bloodshed (from ancient Roman circuses, slaughterhouses, and the wife-murderer Bluebeard's home). 'Eucharis told me that it was Spring'—but Eucharis is a character in Fénelon's civilized Utopian tale *Telemachus* (1699), and the name also suggests the Catholic eucharist celebrated during 'mass and first communions': this proclamation of spring has come from civilization.

The speaker, finding the new world 'unbearable', calls for another Flood. Yet the rainbow denies that any such thing will come: it is a 'seal of God', like the rainbow sent in the time of Noah as a sign that the human race would never again be destroyed in this way (Genesis 9: 12–15).

Being Beauteous

The title is evidently Rimbaldian English for the *Être de Beauté* ('Being of Beauty') described in the text of the poem, a 'new and loving body' created in spite of the world's 'hisses of death'.

The last paragraph may possibly be a separate prose poem, which Rimbaud placed on the same page as 'Being Beauteous' simply because space was available there; whether by design or by accident, its anguished cries contrast strikingly with the exaltation that has preceded it.

Departure

Rimbaud himself, during these years, was constantly travelling (see the Chronology). The final punctuation-mark in the manuscript is possibly an exclamation-mark, possibly a question-mark.

Morning of Drunkenness

With this sketch of an 'unheard-of work' compare Rimbaud's letter of 15 July 1871, quoted in the Introduction. The 'assassins' at the end of the poem are evidently Oriental destroyers (the word 'assassinate' is used elsewhere in the *Illuminations* in that sense) and perhaps 'hashish-eaters' (cf. the poem's references to 'drunkenness').

City

A portrait of the supposedly modern 'metropolis', recognizably modelled on nineteenth-century London (which Rimbaud had visited with Verlaine during 1872–3); such a city, in Rimbaud's eyes, calls for 'new Erinyes' (in Greek mythology the Erinyes were the Furies who avenged crime and punished the guilty).

Promontory

A fantastic geographical synthesis of Europe (Epirus and the Peloponnese in Greece; Venice and Mount Etna in Italy; London with its Embankment and Scarborough with its Royal Hotel and Grand Hotel, in Britain), Asia (Japan and Arabia), Africa (Carthage), and America (Brooklyn).

Sales

The things offered for sale here are previously undiscovered, 'unsuspected' things, a point illustrated by the fact that 'the Jews have not sold' them ('the Jews' being stereotypically supposed to sell anything in existence). Compare the 'unheard-of' attainments in 'Morning of Drunkenness'.

From *A Season in Hell* (1873)

Dated 'April–August 1873' (the duration of the 'season' itself, or the date of composition?).

Night in Hell

The section was originally entitled 'False Conversion'. The speaker, who had declared in the previous section of *A Season in Hell* 'I have never been a Christian', now nevertheless finds himself 'the slave of my baptism' and suffers damnation for his sins ('my life was only sweet madness').

Morning

The speaker aspires to 'worship Christmas on earth', like the 'wise men' who followed a star across the desert to visit the newborn Christ; but the section is delicately poised between hope ('let us not curse life') and despair ('we are slaves').

Farewell

The final section of *A Season in Hell*; yet not a conclusion, but a mere step on the road ('onwards'). Art and its prospects of wisdom ('magus' refers back to the 'wise men' of the previous section) are sardonically rejected; instead, the speaker grimly determines to face life as a plain 'peasant'.

STEPHANE MALLARMÉ

From *Poems* (1899)

The collection was prepared and arranged by Mallarmé, though not published until the year after his death.

Toast

Written January 1893; recited by Mallarmé at a literary banquet the following month, and finally placed in italics at the head of his 1899 collection.

  1 *this foam*: in the glass held by the speaker as he delivers the toast.

  6 *with myself on the poop-deck now*: Mallarmé presents himself as lagging behind the younger and more adventurous writers in his audience.

 12 *solitude, star, or rocky coast*: the syntax is characteristically ambiguous and double-edged; the three things could be either literary goals ('things . . . deserving of our sail's white preoccupation') or dangers that might oppose the attainment of those goals.

Sea Breeze

Written May 1865.

13–15 *mast . . . no mast*: the awkward and self-contradictory phrasing reflects the chaos of the shipwreck.

A Favn in the Afternoon

Begun in 1865; after a long and complex gestation, first published in 1876. The faun of late Graeco-Roman mythology is both perennially lustful (especially in pursuit of nymphs) and a quintessential artist (since he plays the panpipe). Mallarmé's use of 'v' for 'u' in the title gives it the look of an ancient Latin inscription.

1 *those nymphs*: their identity is revealed gradually as the poem progresses. The nymphs were disturbed by the faun's flute-play (ll. 26–32); he caught two of them asleep and tried to make love to them, but they slipped away (ll. 63–92); the whole episode may have been merely his own fantasy (ll. 3–9).

2 *incarnate*: both 'flesh colour' and 'carnality'.

4 *My doubt . . . ends*: 'ends' is ambiguous; perhaps the doubt is dispelled, yet perhaps it is completed. The faun believes that he met the nymphs in these forests, and the forests are 'true' (l. 5), which may support the reality of the whole story—or else may show by contrast that the rest of the story was *not true*. What the faun took for nymphs, for instance, may have been merely 'roses' (l. 7).

7 *failing*: both 'guilt' and 'failure to exist'.

11–12 *the chaster one . . . the other*: here and elsewhere in the poem, one of the nymphs pursued by the faun seems to be more 'spiritual' (associated with whiteness, intangibility, and innocence), the other more 'carnal' (associated with darkness, passion, and cruelty).

15–17 *sound of water . . . stir of air*: i.e. the only sounds and breezes are those produced by the faun's own flute. Perhaps the 'chaster' nymph was an 'illusion' generated by the watery sound, and the 'other' by the breeze— in which case neither would have any existence outside his art.

21 *artificial*: both 'unnatural' and 'created by art'.

23 *mere in Sicily*: Sicilian swamps are a traditional home of fauns.

26–7 *made tame by talent*: the reeds are 'tamed' by the artisan's talent when they are shaped into a panpipe.

31 *naiads*: water-nymphs.

32 *fulvid*: both 'tawny' and 'wild'.

34 *nuptial excess*: 'excess', apparently, because of the faun's desire to possess both nymphs.

34–5 *A natural*: the note customarily played to tune orchestral instruments.

37 *lilies*: both a phallic symbol and a traditional emblem of chastity; the faun

is 'one among' the lilies, because the failure to consummate his passion has left him 'erect, alone' (l. 36).

38 *sweet nothing*: the kiss is 'nothing' (a) because it is not the consummation the faun seeks, and (b) because it may be imaginary.

44 *diverting . . . for its own end*: the panpipe transforms the artist's 'disturbances' into art.

45 *it dreams*: two different syntactic constructions hang from this one verb: the panpipe 'dreams . . . that we have seduced the beauties round about us' (ll. 45–7), and it 'dreams of . . . evacuating . . . a sonorous, monotonous and empty line' (ll. 48–51) from the 'commonplace illusion' of the faun's sexual fantasies.

52 *flights*: a triple allusion: (a) the flight of the nymph Syrinx, who was transformed into a reed to escape the pursuit of Pan; (b) the recent nymphs' flight from the speaker; (c) the flights of artistic fancy involved in playing the instrument.

53 *syrinx*: panpipe made from a series of hollow reeds cut to various lengths.

57 *the gleam*: both the glossy substance of the grapes, and the drunken illumination induced by them.

62 *expand*: the previous italicized narrative (ll. 26–32) was offered as a mere retelling ('proclaim . . .'); here an element of artistic elaboration becomes explicit.

64 *immortal throats*: the throats of the nymphs, as they cool themselves in the water.

69 *this pain of being two*: the nymphs, though 'linked', suffer because they are two separate creatures, as the faun himself suffers because he is separated from them.

70 *careless*: both 'heedless' and 'haphazard'.

72 *hated by the frivolous shade*: the thicket is in full sunlight, shunned by the 'frivolous' (unstable as well as unserious) shadows.

74 *squandered like the light*: their loveplay is to run parallel with the afternoon sunlight.

77–8 *as a lightning-sheet quivers*: the syntax is ambiguous; the quivering sheet of lightning is placed in apposition both to the faun's 'burning lips' and to the 'secret terror' of the nymphs' (and the faun's?) flesh.

90 *untwined by some vague perishings*: the faun, involved with the more 'carnal' nymph, is too weak to retain his hold on the more 'spiritual' one.

99–100 *at times when the forest glows with gold and ashen tints*: at evening (now approaching).

101 *Etna*: Sicilian volcano, where Venus went in the evening to visit her husband Vulcan.

103 *when sad slumbers are sounding*: Venus arrives, not during the eruption ('the flame'), but in the melancholy quiescence afterwards.

104 *the queen*: Venus, whom the faun sees as already in his possession.

110 *the shadow*: both 'the illusion' and 'the mystery' (with a reference back to l. 56, where the female genitals were seen as a realm of 'shadows').

Saint

Written 1865. Cecilia, the patron saint of music, is seen in an emphatically ancient ('old', 'in the past') stained-glass window.

2 *viol voiding gold*: either the gilt of the viol (an aptly antiquated musical instrument, and imagined rather than seen, since the window 'veils' it) is peeling with age, or the golden sunset (which used to illuminate it) is now fading.

6 *the Magnificat*: Mary's hymn 'My soul doth magnify the Lord . . .', as sung in the Roman Catholic liturgy.

7–8 *vespers or evensong*: religious rites of evening; in nineteenth-century Roman Catholic ritual the Magnificat was traditionally sung at vespers.

9 *this ostensory pane*: the illuminated window is compared to a monstrance or ostensory (a vessel for displaying holy relics).

10 *a harp*: the angel's flight makes his wing look like a harp, and from the viewer's perspective the saint's fingertips appear to be almost in contact with it.

13 *she*: the saint, not the angel (who is male).

A Few Sonnets

The casualness of the title ('Four Sonnets', or simply 'Sonnets', would have been more usual) contrasts slyly with the abstruseness of the poems themselves, which were written separately and not grouped together till the 1899 collected edition—where they stand at the centre, as the volume's 'holy of holies' (Yves-Alain Favre's term).

Because of the difficulty of these sonnets, we offer a continuous, though inevitably oversimplified, commentary on each.

'When the shade threatened with the fatal decree...'

Date of composition unknown; first published 1883.

The setting is a night sky ('shade', 'funereal height', 'ebony hall', 'gloom'), where 'trivial fires' are vanishing ('illustrious wreaths writhe in their doom') in the sight of the poet ('the faith-dazzled Solitary').

Some commentators regard the 'trivial fires' as the doomed glimmers of sunset, and the 'festive star' of l. 14 as the sun whose light has kindled the poet's genius. On this interpretation, the apparent 'splendour' of sunset is deceptive (ll. 5–7) because the earth's rotation has 'cast' the 'sheer dazzling-ness' of the sun below the horizon and into the 'night' (ll. 9–10). Nevertheless, as the sun submits to its fate, its flight is absorbed into the poet's thought ('it bowed its doubt-less plumage deep in me'); therefore, the 'dread aeons' darken it less than would otherwise be the case, and the 'trivial fires' of sunset 'show' (not only illuminate, but also act as a foil to) a continuing light—the light of the poet's kindled imagination.

Compare the progression of thought in the other sunset-poem of this group ('The fine suicide fled victoriously...'), where we are told: 'Out of all that brilliance not one shred stays . . . except the arrogant treasure of a head.'

Other commentators take the 'illustrious wreaths' of l. 6 as the stars, which are doomed ultimately to run out of energy. The 'sheer dazzlingness' of l. 10 would then be the poet's genius sent out through the darkness from the earth, and the 'festive star' of l. 14 would be not the sun, but the earth on which the poet lives.

Nevertheless, the basic drift of the poem is the same on either reading. Material things are 'trivial', never escaping from their own nature even when they seem to increase or decrease ('fail or grow', l. 12), and ultimately passing away; yet the immaterial things kindled by them may endure. 'The light that triumphs in this sonnet is both essential and internal, spiritual' (Rosemary Lloyd, *Mallarmé: Poésies* (London, 1984), 44).

'This virginal long-living lovely day...'

Date of composition unknown; first published 1885. The slow movement of the sequence. The other three sonnets are night-pieces, beginning with sunset, darkness, annihilation, yet struggling through to hint at something triumph- ant and enduring. This one is a day-piece in contrary motion: it begins with what is 'long-living' and 'lovely', yet ends with what is 'dismissed to futile things'.

Whiteness is everywhere, in this poem: the white swan is trapped in a white universe. And once we go beyond the opening line, the whiteness is presented almost entirely in negative terms: 'hard', 'sterile', 'frigid', 'white throe'.

The poem is full of attempts to escape—yet all such attempts are either doubtful ('will it tear . . .') or instantly and decisively opposed ('flights that never flew away', 'strives to break free woebegone', 'will shake off this white throe . . . but not the horror of earth'). No significant escape ever occurs; from the glacial realm of this poem, no 'territory to live' can be reached.

The swan is a familiar symbol of the poet. Nothing here limits the symbol to one particular poet or type of poet; there is nothing to suggest, for instance, that the sonnet is a lament for Mallarmé's own individual artistic sterility, or a criticism of the sterility of certain inferior verse-writers. On the contrary, the poem operates in general rather than specific terms; if anything, it moves away from the individual ('a swan of old') to the universal ('the Swan').

'The fine suicide fled victoriously...'

Written 1885. The scherzo of the sequence: the night- and sunset-themes of the first and fourth sonnets are taken up, but in a more playful, light-hearted mode; here, the 'triumph' remains at a relatively 'childish' level.

The characters are general, archetypal figures: the speaker is 'poet' (in the 1887 draft) and also sun (he sees the regal purple of sunset as being laid out for his own tomb); the listener is the stereotypic 'caressed' female, both child and empress, with the stereotypic associations of blonde hair as Mallarmé defined them in 1862: 'gold, light, richness, reverie, nimbus'.

The sun has set, and the scene now abounds with hard-won military and imperial glory ('blaze of fame, blood in foam', 'regal purple', 'triumph'). But if 'regal purple' is being lavished on the speaker's tomb, it is being lavished to no purpose, since the speaker's tomb is 'absent'; funeral rites are a little premature. The glorious spectacle passes, 'the heavens . . . have gone', yet one trace of them is retained: the gold ('treasure') of the listener's otherwise-unlit hair. In its limited ('childish') way, the hair has the imperial arrogance and triumph of a war-helmet ('morion'); when the glory of sky and war and empire has passed, part of it lingers ('stays', remains 'constant') in the admittedly childish head of the listener.

The 'roses' of the last line are an image ('likeness') of the listener herself, pictured as showering down beneath her helmet of hair.

'With her pure nails offering their onyx high...'

First published 1887, but a letter of 18 July 1868 has an earlier draft with some significant variants, particularly in the opening quatrain:

> Approving Night brightly begins to burn
> her onyx nails at pure lampbearing Crime
> of Dusk abolished by the vesper-time
> Phoenix whose ashes have no funerary urn . . . .

In the same letter Mallarmé describes the scene as follows: 'A window open at night, with both shutters fastened back; a room with nobody in it, despite the impression of stability given by the fastened shutters; and hung at the rear—in a night composed of absence and enquiry, with no furniture except the plausible outline of indistinct console-tables—a warlike mirror-frame in its death-agony, containing the stellar and incomprehensible reflection of the Great Bear, which alone links this world-forsaken dwelling-place to the heavens.'

Thus the sonnet is another night-piece. The Phoenix, the mythical bird repeatedly dying and being reborn from its ashes, has burned its 'vesperal' (both evening and ritual) fantasies and gone down to the underworld, to the River Styx. The gold decorations in the room—a scene of struggle between a naked water-nymph and unicorns (which could be overcome only by virginity)—are themselves dying or dead. Not even a funerary urn remains in the room to contain the ashes (compare the absence of the sun-poet's tomb in the preceding poem); and this is a still greater loss, because a funerary urn, 'bauble' and 'inanity' though it is, would at least be 'sonorous' (both hollow and—like a poem—resonant) and would therefore be the one thing in which the Void could take any pride. But alas! the urn is a mere 'ptyx', a McGuffin, something with no meaning and no existence (Mallarmé claimed to have chosen the word purely for the rhyme; its previous uses—with the sense 'fold, crease' in ancient Greek, and as the name of a faun in Victor Hugo—seem only peripherally relevant to the line of thought here).

The 'credences' of l. 5 are 'console-tables' (1868 draft and letter), but with an additional suggestion of 'beliefs' (compare the 'doubt-less plumage' and 'faith-dazzled Solitary' of 'When the shade threatened...').

Yet the mirror in the room reflects something 'incomprehensible' beyond itself, something which 'links' it 'to the heavens' (see Mallarmé's letter) and which 'sustains' the now-absent poet's burned and seemingly annihilated fantasies. Night (in the 1868 draft) or Agony (in the final draft) is lighting up her onyx nails (the stars) after the 'Crime of Dusk' (1868 draft) has occurred; and seven of those stars—the seven principal stars of the Great Bear—are reflected in the empty room's mirror, as a 'fixed septet of scintillations'.

The Tomb of Edgar Allan Poe

In 1875 a monument to Poe was erected in Baltimore; this poem, written to commemorate the event, was published in *E. A. Poe: A Memorial Volume* (Baltimore, 1877). On that occasion Mallarmé prepared a primitive English rendering with annotations for the guidance of his American translators; many of its explanations are cited below.

1 *Changed to Himself at last*: it is only after death that the poet's true identity emerges. 'In death the words take on their absolute value' (Mallarmé's English comment), so that the 'sword' is bared.

2, 4 *a bare sword . . . that strange word*: both phrases are descriptions of Poe's writings (in his English rendering Mallarmé substituted 'hymn' for 'sword').

6 *as vile freaks writhe*: in his draft translation Mallarmé himself rendered *sursaut* as 'writhing'. The freak is a hydra—a many-headed monster, a traditional symbol for the populace.

seraphim: the particular seraph under consideration is Poe himself (Mallarmé's explanation).

8 *in some . . . dishonourable flow*: 'in plain prose: [they] charged him with always being drunk' (Mallarmé's English explanation).

10 *hostile clod and cloud*: the heavenly ('cloud') and the earthly ('clod') are irreconcilable antagonists.

struggling grief: the French is *grief*, but Mallarmé rendered it 'struggle' in his English version. 'Actually, the poetic effect is of [both] that *and* grief at the poet's tragic life and death' (R. G. Cohn, *Toward the Poems of Mallarmé* (Berkeley, 1965), 155); therefore the present translation combines both.

12 *dropped by an occult doom*: the granite block is depicted as having fallen as a result of some obscure catastrophe.

14 *Blasphemy-flights*: 'blasphemy means against poets, such as the charge of Poe being drunk' (Mallarmé's English explanation).

dispersed: a characteristic ambiguity: will the 'Blasphemy-flights' be eradicated or spread more widely? In either case, the Baltimore memorial ('this block . . . this calm granite') may help to 'limit' them.

The Tomb of Charles Baudelaire

Written 1893.

1–3 *The buried shrine disgorges . . . some Anubis-god*: Baudelaire's poetry is compared to an underground temple containing an image of the jackal-headed Egyptian god Anubis.

sod and ruby: the constituents of Baudelaire's writings.

5–7 *new gas . . . lights eternal loins*: whereas older forms of literature, like the older and dimmer forms of street-lighting, used to conceal the 'eternal loins' of the prostitute, Baudelaire's poetry, like the recently invented gaslight, exposes them.

gas wrings the wicks that erase shiftily insults suffered: two main readings are possible: (a) the gaslight, as it flickers ('wrings the wicks . . . shiftily'), dispels the shameful activities that are 'suffered' (painfully endured, yet tolerated) in city streets; or (b) the gaslight does away with ('wrings') the older wick-bearing lamps which used to 'erase' such activities 'shiftily' by hiding them from view.

8 *whose flight beds out according to its rays*: the prostitute's fugitive street-walking ('flight') takes place by gaslight and in an alien or outlawed situation (it 'beds out').

9–10 *What foliage . . . could consecrate as she can do*: the prostitute is a more appropriate ornament for Baudelaire's tomb than any conventional tribute of laurel leaves.

any nightless town: modern towns have become 'nightless' since the invention of gaslight.

12–13 *the veils that form her gown with shimmers*: the flickering gaslight—and the work of Baudelaire.

she, his Shade, a guardian bane: the prostitute is now seen as Baudelaire's very ghost or spirit, both poisonous ('bane') and edifying ('guardian'). 'Departed' in l. 12 thus refers both to the prostitute's departure from the gaslight and Baudelaire's departure (through death) from his work.

Tomb ('The black rock, cross...')

Written, as the subtitle indicates, for the first anniversary of Verlaine's death.

1 *The black rock*: probably Verlaine's work, now beyond the reach of 'pious throngs'.

3 *handling its parity with human wrongs*: the 'pious throngs' think that, by detecting some resemblance between Verlaine's activities and 'human

wrongs', they may be able to assign him to some comfortable pigeonhole. Cf. the thought in ll. 5–8 of 'The Tomb of Edgar Allan Poe'.

5 *the dove*: a conventional symbol of conventional mourning.

7 *the ripe star of that tomorrow*: Verlaine's future glory, already 'ripe' and hence ready to shed the folds of conventional mourning which are currently obscuring it. The folds are 'nubile' (l. 6), and thus are ready to be discarded like a bride's garments.

9–10 *our vagabond's withdrawn leap*: Verlaine's 'withdrawn' (both isolated and isolating) departure from life.

11–14 *Verlaine is hidden . . . to catch . . . death*: he has departed purely to experience death, which he accepts with childlike simplicity ('in plain harmony') even before he has tasted it.

INDEX OF TITLES AND FIRST LINES

Titles and first lines of French poems are in *italics*; titles and first lines of English translations are in roman type.

A black, E white, I red, U green, O blue: vowels 251
A Carcass 157
A cold wind hurls itself at 231
A Favn in the Afternoon 277
A Few Sonnets 285
A gully of green, a laughing river 239
A jig! Let's dance! 219
A la fenêtre pendant la nuit 72
A la fenêtre recélant 282
A noir, E blanc, I rouge, U vert, O bleu: voyelles 250
A quatre heures du matin, l'été 252
A river in the street! 221
A Season in Hell 265
A summer night – a night whose wide-spread wings 21
A vendre ce que les Juifs n'ont pas vendu 264
A Villequier 56
A Voyage to Cythera 181
Adieu 270
After the Battle 93
After the Flood 255
After the Voices 139
Against the snow a tall Being of Beauty 257
Ainsi, toujours poussés vers de nouveaux rivages 10
Amour 236
And so I went, hands thrust in torn pockets 239
And, as a boiling vessel cools once more 17
Andromache, I think of you—this meagre stream 173
Andromaque, je pense à vous! Ce petit fleuve 172
Another Voice ['Well, first of all...'] 127
Another Voice ['You think yourself, perhaps...'] 137
Après la bataille 92
Après le Déluge 254
Après les voix 138
Art poétique 234
As earthquakes happened far too frequently 89
As soon as the idea of the Flood had subsided 255
Asleep in the Valley 239
Assez vu. La vision s 'est rencontrée à tous les airs 258
At the Window in the Dark 73
At the window that veils her old 283
At Villequier 57

Au Lecteur   146
Aube   260
Aussitôt que l'idée du Déluge se fût rassise   254
Autumn   15
Autumn Song ['Now will we plunge...']   163
Autumn Song ['The long sobs...']   197
Autumn this soon! But why hanker   271
Avec ses vêtements ondoyants et nacrés   154
Beams   220
Beams   221
Beauté des femmes, leur faiblesse, et ces mains pâles   222
Beauty of women, their weakness, those pale hands   223
Being Beauteous   256
Being Beauteous   257
Bientôt nous plongerons dans les froides ténèbres   162
Bizarre déité, brune comme les nuits   154
Blackcurrant River   251
Boaz Asleep   83
Bonne pensée du matin   252
Booz endormi   82
Booz s'était couché de fatigue accablé   82
Brise marine   274
Brussels: Simple Frescos I   213
Brussels: Simple Frescos II   215
Bruxelles: simples fresques I   212
Bruxeiles: simples fresques II   214
C'est l'extase langoureuse   206
C'est un trou de verdure où chante une rivière   238
C'est une nuit d'été; nuit dont les vastes ailes   20
Calm in the half-light   203
Calmes dans le demi-jour   202
Ces nymphes, je les veux perpétuer   276
Cette nuit-là   44
Changed to Himself at last by eternity   289
Chanson d'automne   196
Chant d'automne   162
Cheated Heart   243
City   261
City of swarming, city full of dreams   177
Colloque sentimental   204
Colombine   200
Colombine   201
Comme je descendais des Fleuves impassibles   242
Conscience   79
Consider them, my soul, they are a fright!   179
Contemplations   57
Contemple-les, mon âme; ils sont vraiment affreux!   178
Correspondances   150
Correspondences   151

Dans l'interminable   210
Dans le vieux parc solitaire et glacé   204
Dansons la gigue!   218
Dark was before my eyes. There lay the abyss   71
Dawn   261
De la musique avant toute chose   234
Demain, dès l'aube, à l'heure où blanchit la campagne   56
Départ   258
Departure   259
Devant une neige un Etre de Beauté de haute taille   256
Did I not once have a pleasant childhood   269
Drunken Boat   243
Elle voulut aller sur les flots de la mer   220
En sourdine   202
Encore Dieu, mais avec des restrictions   106
Endless sameness   211
Enough seen. The vision has been met in every air   259
Et d'abord, de quel Dieu veux-tu parler? Précise   126
Et je voyais au loin sur ma tête un point noir   114
Et la mer s'apaisait, comme une urne écumante   16
Et, sombre, j'attendis; puis je continuai   138
Exchange of Feelings   205
Falling tears in my heart   209
Fantoches   200
Farewell   271
Fenêtres ouvertes   104
Fêtes galantes   198
Folly and error, stinginess and sin   147
For sale what the Jews have not sold   265
Four a.m. in summertime   253
Fourmillante cité, cité pleine de rêves   176
Fun and Games   199
Further Poetic Meditations   33
Golden dawn and trembling dusk find our brig   263
Green   216
Green   217
Green-tinged pink tones fade   213
Harmonie du soir   158
Harmonies poétiques et religieuses   16
Head of Hair   151
Heavens! all China's on the ground, in pieces!   113
High heels fought a battle with long skirts   199
Hope like a wisp of straw shines in the stable   227
How bittersweet it is on winter nights   165
I'd love to make them linger on, those nymphs   277
I am an ephemeral and none too discontented citizen   261
I can hear voices. Through my eyelids, light   105
I could see, far above my head, a black speck   115
I followed deadpan rivers down and down   243

I have embraced the summer dawn   261
I have swallowed a mighty gulp of poison   265
I might as well be king of rainy lands   169
I saw among the clouds a monstrous trumpet   95
I waited, heavy-hearted; then went on   139
Il est amer et doux, pendant les nuits d'hiver   164
Il faut, voyez-vous, nous pardonner les choses   208
Il pleure dans mon cœur   208
Illuminations   255
In the old park frozen and alone   205
Invitation to the Voyage   161
Isolation   3
It's languor and ecstasy   207
J'ai avalé une fameuse gorgée de poison   264
J'ai embrassé l'aube d'été   260
J'ai plus de souvenirs que si j'avais mille ans   168
J'avais devant les yeux les ténèbres. L'abîme   70
J'entends des voix. Lueurs à travers ma paupière   104
Jadis et naguère   234
Je m'en allais, les poings dans mes poches crevées   238
Je suis comme le roi d'un pays pluvieux   168
Je suis un éphémère et point trop mécontent citoyen   260
Je suis venu, calme orphelin   228
Je vis dans la nuée un clairon monstrueux   94
Jeanne était au pain sec dans le cabinet noir   110
Jeanne was holed up (pitch darkness, bread and water)   111
L'abbé divague—Et toi, marquis   198
L'Albatros   148
L'allée est sans fin   214
L'Après-midi d'un faune   276
L'Art d'être grand-père   104
L'aube d'or et la soirée frissonnante trouvent notre brick   262
L'Automne   14
L'automne déjà!—Mais pourquoi regretter   270
L'échelonnement des haies   232
L'enfant avait reçu deux balles dans la tête   46
L'espoir luit comme un brin de paille dans l'étable   226
L'Infini dans les cieux   20
L'Inquisition   88
L'Invitation au voyage   160
L'Isolement   2
L'Occident   16
La bise se rue à travers   230
La chair est triste, hélas! et j'ai lu tous les livres   274
La Chevelure   150
La Cloche fêlée   164
La Conscience   78
La fuite est verdâtre et rose   212
La Légende des siècles   78

La Nature est un temple où de vivants piliers	150
La Rivière de Cassis	250
La Rivière de Cassis roule ignorée	250
La sottise, l'erreur, le péché, la lésine	146
La tristesse, la langueur du corps humain	230
La Trompette du jugement	94
La vie humble aux travaux ennuyeux et faciles	222
Le Bateau ivre	242
Le ciel est, par-dessus le toit	228
Le Cœur volé	242
Le Cygne	172
Le Dormeur du val	238
Le Lac	10
Le Lézard	32
Le noir roc courroucé que la bise le roule	290
Le piano que baise une main frêle	210
Le Pont	70
Le Pot cassé	112
Le Seuil du gouffre	114
Le temple enseveli divulgue par la bouche	290
Le Tombeau d'Edgar Poe	288
Le Tombeau de Charles Baudelaire	290
Le Vallon	6
Le vallon où je vais tous les jours est charmant	68
Le vierge, le vivace et le bel aujourd'hui	284
Le Voyage	184
Léandre le sot	200
Les Aveugles	178
Les chars d'argent et de cuivre	262
Les Châtiments	44
Les Chercheuses de poux	240
Les Contemplations	56
Les Djinns	36
Les étoiles, points d'or, percent les branches noires	72
Les Fleurs du mal	146
Les hauts talons luttaient avec les longues jupes	198
Les Illuminations	254
Les Ingénus	198
Les Orientales	36
Les Raisons du Momotombo	88
Les roses étaient toutes rouges	216
Les sanglots longs	196
Les Sept Vieillards	176
Let's hear the music first and foremost	235
Lice-Seekers	241
Lorsque avec ses enfants vêtus de peaux de bêtes	78
Love	237
Lovely Morning Thought	253
Ma Bohème (Fantaisie)	238

Maintenant que Paris, ses pavés et ses marbres	56
Malines	214
Malines	215
Marine	262
Matin	268
Matinée d'ivresse	258
Méditations poétiques	2
Méditations poétiques inédites	32
Momotombo's Reasons	89
Mon cœur; comme un oiseau, voltigeait tout joyeux	180
Mon cœur, lassé de tout, même de l'espérance	6
Mon enfant, ma sœur	160
Mon père, ce héros au sourire si doux	92
Mon triste cœur bave à la poupe	242
More About God (But With Some Reservations)	107
More memories than if I'd lived a thousand years!	169
Morning	269
Morning of Drunkenness	259
Murs, ville	36
Muted Tones	203
My Bohemia	239
My father—that kind smiling hero—went	93
My heart was like a bird that fluttered joyously	181
My sister, my child	161
N'eus-je pas une fois une jeunesse aimable	268
Nature is a temple, where the living	151
Night in Hell	265
No, Liberty! People, he must not die!	51
Non, liberté! non, peuple, il ne faut pas qu'il meure!	50
Nothing, this foam, this virgin verse	275
Now it is nearly time when, quivering on its stem	159
Now that the city with its masonries	57
Now will we plunge into the frigid dark	163
Nuit de l'enfer	264
O ciel! toute la Chine est par terre en morceaux!	112
O fleece, billowing even down the neck!	151
O la rivière dans la rue!	220
O mon Bien! o mon Beau! Fanfare atroce	258
O saisons, ô chateaux	254
O seasons, o châteaux	255
O toison, moutonnant jusque sur l'encolure!	150
Often, when bored, the sailors of the crew	149
Oh my Good, my Beauty! Atrocious fanfare	259
On the Grass	199
On the mountain, in the old oak's domain	3
On the poop-deck my sad heart drips	243
Once Upon a Time	235
Once, in the Colosseum—that	33
Open Windows	105

Orientalia 37
Over in the fields the wind provokes 215
Overcome by fatigue, there Boaz lay 83
Parsifal 236
Parsifal 237
Parsifal a vaincu les Filles, leur gentil 236
Parsifal has conquered the Maidens, their sweet 237
Pasteurs et troupeaux 68
Peaceful eyes my only wealth 229
Plusieurs Sonnets 284
Pluviôse, irrité contre la ville entière 166
Pluvius, this whole city on his nerves 167
Poèmes saturniens 196
Poems 275
Poésies 274
Poetic and Religious Harmonies 17
Poetic Meditations 3
Port, walls 37
Pour l'enfant, amoureux de cartes et d'estampes 184
Promontoire 262
Promontory 263
Quand l'ombre menaça de la fatale loi 284
Quand le ciel bas et lourd pèse comme un couvercle 170
Quand le front de l'enfant, plein de rouges tourmentes 240
Quel beau lieu! Là le cèdre avec l'orme chuchote 106
Rappelez-vous l'objet que nous vîmes, mon âme 156
Remember, my love, the object we saw 157
Rien, cette écume, vierge vers 274
Romances sans paroles 206
Sacer esto 50
Sagesse 222
Saint 283
Sainte 282
Sales 265
Salut 274
Salut! bois couronnés d'un reste de verdure! 14
Saturnian Poems 197
Scaramouche and Pulcinella 201
Scaramouche et Pulcinella 200
Sea Breeze 275
Seascape 263
Sed non satiata 154
Sed non satiata 155
Ses purs ongles très haut dédiant leur onyx 288
Set Him Apart! 51
She wanted to tread the surge of the sea 221
Shepherds and Flocks 69
Silver chariots, and copper 263
Singular goddess, brown as night, and wild 155

So, driven to new shores incessantly   11
Solde   264
Songs Without Words   207
Sonnez, sonnez toujours, clairons de la pensée   54
Sound, sound forever, trumpet-calls of thought!   55
Souvenir de la nuit du 4   46
Souvent sur la montagne, à l'ombre du vieux chêne   2
Souvent, pour s'amuser, les hommes d'équipage   148
Spleen   216
Spleen   217
Spleen [I]   166
Spleen [I]   167
Spleen [II]   168
Spleen [II]   169
Spleen [III]   168
Spleen [III]   169
Spleen [IV]   170
Spleen [IV]   171
Streets I   218
Streets I   219
Streets II   220
Streets II   221
Stupid Leander   201
Such a splendid place! The cedar and elm are whispering   107
Sur l'herbe   198
Take this fruit, these flowers, these branches and leaves   217
Te figures-tu donc être, par aventure   136
Tel qu'en Lui-même enfin l'éternité le change   288
That Night   45
The abbé rambles—Marquis, I think you'll find   199
The Albatross   149
The Art of Being a Grandfather   105
The Art of Poetry   235
The black rock, cross (how the north wind has rolled   291
The Blind   179
The Bridge   71
The Broken Vase   113
The buried shrine disgorges through its foul   291
The child had got two bullets in the head   47
The Cracked Bell   165
The Djinns   37
The Empire in the Pillory   45
The fine suicide fled victoriously   287
The flesh is sad—and I've read every book   275
The Flowers of Evil   147
The Harmony of Evening   159
The humble life of dull and easy work   223
The Infinite in the Skies   21
The Inquisition   89

The Lake   11
The Legend of the Ages   79
The Lizard   33
The long sobs of   197
The Night of the Fourth: A Recollection   47
The path goes on and on   215
The piano kissed by a slender hand   211
The roses were bright red   217
The sadness, the languor of the human body   231
The Seven Old Men   177
The sky above the roof's   229
The stars, gold specks, are piercing the dark leaves   73
The Swan   173
The Threshold of the Abyss   115
The Tomb of Charles Baudelaire   291
The Tomb of Edgar Allan Poe   289
The Trumpet of Judgement   95
The Valley   7
The way her silky garments undulate   155
The West   17
The wide-eyed child in love with maps and plans   185
This vale—my daily haunt—is a delight   69
This virginal long-living lovely day   285
Three friends were with him at the Élysée   45
Tired of all things—with even hope put by   7
To the Reader   147
Toast   275
Tomb ['The black rock, cross...']   291
Tombeau /« Le noir roc courroucé... »/   290
Tomorrow, when the meadows grow   57
Trois amis l'entouraient. C'était à l'Élysée   44
Trouvant les tremblements de terre trop fréquents   88
Un jour, seul dans le Colisée   32
Un Voyage à Cythère   180
Une Autre Voix /« Et d'abord, de quel Dieu... »/   126
Une Autre Voix /« Te figures-tu donc... »/   136
Une Charogne   156
Une Saison en enfer   264
Uneven rows of hedges   233
Unsuspected Blackcurrant river rolls   251
Vers les prés le vent cherche noise   214
Victorieusement fui le suicide beau   286
Ville   260
Voice of Pride: shout of blaring trumpets   225
Voici des fruits, des fleurs, des feuilles et des branches   216
Voici venir les temps où vibrant sur sa tige   158
Voix de l'Orgueil: un cri puissant comme d'un cor   224
Vowels   251
Voyaging   185

Voyelles   250
Weird as Puppets   201
Welcome, woods crowned with sparse remains of green   15
Well, first of all, just which God do you mean?   127
When low and heavy sky weighs like a lid   171
When the boy's head, full of red torment   241
When the shade threatened with the fatal decree   285
When, with his children clad in animal-skins   79
Wisdom   223
With her pure nails offering their onyx high   289
Without Guile   199
You see, we have to be forgiven things   209
You think yourself, perhaps, more than a speck   137

The Oxford World's Classics Website

www.worldsclassics.co.uk

- Information about new titles
- Explore the full range of Oxford World's Classics
- Links to other literary sites and the main OUP webpage
- Imaginative competitions, with bookish prizes
- Peruse *Compass*, the Oxford World's Classics magazine
- Articles by editors
- Extracts from Introductions
- A forum for discussion and feedback on the series
- Special information for teachers and lecturers

www.worldsclassics.co.uk

American Literature

British and Irish Literature

Children's Literature

Classics and Ancient Literature

Colonial Literature

Eastern Literature

European Literature

History

Medieval Literature

Oxford English Drama

Poetry

Philosophy

Politics

Religion

The Oxford Shakespeare

A complete list of Oxford Paperbacks, including Oxford World's Classics, OPUS, Past Masters, Oxford Authors, Oxford Shakespeare, Oxford Drama, and Oxford Paperback Reference, is available in the UK from the Academic Division Publicity Department, Oxford University Press, Great Clarendon Street, Oxford OX2 6DP.

In the USA, complete lists are available from the Paperbacks Marketing Manager, Oxford University Press, 198 Madison Avenue, New York, NY 10016.

Oxford Paperbacks are available from all good bookshops. In case of difficulty, customers in the UK can order direct from Oxford University Press Bookshop, Freepost, 116 High Street, Oxford OX1 4BR, enclosing full payment. Please add 10 per cent of published price for postage and packing.